THE

NAZIFICATION

OF

RUSSIA

SEMYON REZNIK

The Nazification of Russia

Antisemitism in the Post-Soviet Era

Challenge Publications
Washington DC

Copyright © 1996, by Semyon Reznik

All rights reserved. No part of this book may be reproduced in any form or by any electronic or mechanical means without written permission except by a reviewer who may quote brief passages in a review.

Jacket and cover design by Greg Kapelyan

Library of Congress Catalog Number: 96-83319

Reznik, Semyon, E. 1938-
The Nazification of Russia:
Anti-Semites in the post-Soviet Era.

Bibliography: p.
Includes index.

1. Reznik, Semyon—Ultranationalism and anti-Semitism—Russia (Soviet Union)—History—Politics. 2. Communism and ultranationalism—History—Politics. 3. Russian fascism and government policy—Politics. I. Title

ISBN 0-9651360-9-4 /hardcover
ISBN 0-9651360-8-6 /softcover

Printed in the United State of America

Challenge Publications, Washington DC

At 1993 [parliamentary] elections, Vladimir Zhirinovsky discovered weak spots in our society the very presence of which we had never suspected. And one of them is the lack of immunity against fascism.

Boris Yeltsin
President of Russia

Discrimination, racial and ethnic prejudice, xenophobia and anti-Semitism had spread around the country to such an extent that they influence the country's social life... These extremist organizations and their ideas penetrate Russia's trade unions, businesses, the armed forces, and law enforcement agencies and spread quickly among migrants, workers, and students... Xenophobia and anti-Semitism in Russia are not just a reality but a growing reality.

Sergei Sirotkin
Deputy chair of President Yeltsin's
Human Rights Commission.
Testimony at a House international
subcommittee hearing.
Washington DC, February 1996.

CONTENTS

ACKNOWLEDGEMENTS   5

Introduction. VLADIMIR ZHIRINOVSKY'S "UNEXPECTED" VICTORY   7

PART ONE: FROM RED TO BROWN

Chapter 1. UNPREDICTABLE PAST   17
Chapter 2. SOVIET SCIENCE—ZIONOLOGY: VLADIMIR BEGUN   35
Chapter 3. ZIONOLOGIST ALEXANDER ROMANENKO   49
Chapter 4. THE YEMELIANOV CASE   61

PART TWO: FREEDOM TO HATE

Chapter 5. METASTASIS OF NAZISM IN THE ERA OF GLASNOST   85
Chapter 6. DMITRY VASILIEV AND IGOR SYCHEV   107
Chapter 7. "RUSSOPHOBIA"   129

Chapter 8. INVASION WITHOUT ARMS 143
Chapter 9. BLOOD LIBEL 161

PART THREE: AT THE HIGHEST LEVEL

Chapter 10. NAZIFICATION UNDER GORBACHEV 179
Chapter 11. NAZIFICATION UNDER YELTSIN 203
Chapter 12. ZHIRONOVSKY AGAIN 229

INSTEAD OF CONCLUSION 247

REFERENCE NOTES 251
INDEX 263

ACKNOWLEDGMENTS

This book is based on *The Red and the Brown* (1991), my Russian account that has been translated into English by Vera Krylova with a contribution by Gregory Katzenelinboigen and my son Dmitry Reznik. While updating and adapting the manuscript to a non-Russian audience, I had to restructure and rewrite the entire manuscript. It was an extremely difficult task for a person with a predominantly Russian background and could be accomplished only with the assistance and guidance of my "Americanized" son Dmitry. In the final stage, a valuable contribution was made by Maureen Martin, a talented and highly professional editor.

I felt great moral support and received concrete aid from many people and organizations who informed me of different events and facts and supplied me with bibliographic directions, newspaper clippings, tape-recordings, and unpublished materials. Of special value was the assistance I got from the Union of Councils for Soviet Jews (UCSJ) with its national president Pammel Cohen and its national director Micah Naftalin; the Southern California Council for Soviet Jews (affiliated member of the UCSJ) with its chairman Si Frumkin; the Russian Anti-Fascist Center in Moscow with its chairman Yevgeny Proshechkin; as well as from Lyudmila Alexeeva (Washington DC, Moscow); Lyudmila Chernaya (Moscow); Mikhail Chlenov (Moscow); Yuri Druzhnikov (Davis, CA); Nathan Eidelman (Moscow); Bill Freeman (Washington DC); Agnes Gereben (Budapest); Stephen Grant (Washington DC); Sergei Ivanov (Moscow); Nina Katerli (St. Petersburg); Aron Katzenelinboigen (Philadelphia); Sergei Lezov (Moscow); Vladimir Matlin (Washington DC); Mikhailo Mikhailov (Washington DC); Vladimir Mushinsky (Moscow); Vladimir Pribylovsky (Moscow); Vladimir Porudominsky (Moscow, Koln); Vadim Shcheglov (Boston); Larisa Silnitsky (Washington DC); Vadim Sokolov (Moscow); Galina Starovoitova (Moscow); Leonid Stonov (Moscow, Chicago); Ilya Suslov (Washington DC.); Vladimir Tsesis (Chicago), Roald Zalechonok (Israel); my wife, Rimma, who was my first reader, critic, and editor, and many others.

Publication of the book has become possible thanks to the support of the sponsors listed on a separate page.

I express here my whole-hearted gratitude to all those who helped me—both mentioned here or not.

SPONSORS

UNION OF COUNCILS FOR SOVIET JEWS
(Washington DC)

CHAMAH (New York)

Vladimir TSESIS, Md. (Chicago)

INTRODUCTION

ZHIRINOVSKY'S "UNEXPECTED" VICTORY

1.

Soon after the October 1917 Bolshevik takeover in Russia, an American journalist, John Reed, a first-hand witness of the events in St. Petersburg, published a book entitled *Ten Days that Shocked the World.*

The book displayed the Russian drama in detail and was successful. But the world was not shocked. The Western public and policy makers, preoccupied with World War I, looked at the Russian revolution mostly in the context of the war. Would Russia continue to fight against Germany or not? Other considerations were secondary.

Nobody at that time could imagine that the war would end soon, while bolshevism would become a major factor of global development through most of the century. Nobody could imagine that the Bolsheviks would create one of the most cruel tyrannies that ever existed and that, with the hard labor of millions of slaves, they would build a mighty industry and a powerful modern army; that they would help Nazi Germany start World War II; and that after Hitler's defeat, they would start the Cold War and terrorize the entire world with the threat of nuclear annihilation. In short, in spite of early warning, the West overlooked one of the most important events of the 20th century.

The historical significance of the December 1993 parliamentary elections in Russia was not comparable with the October revolution. Nevertheless, these elections have shocked the world. They were the first free elections in Russia after 75 years of Communist domination and the crumbling of the Soviet empire. The West was confident that the followers of democratic reforms would prevail. For us, even the worst form of democracy is hundreds of times more attractive than totalitarianism. Thus, who could dream more about democracy if not the Russians, who have suffered so much under the iron heel of dictatorship? Why, after all, did they reject Communist rule a few years ago, if not for the sake of democracy? Why did they prevent the coup against newly born freedom in August 1991, when the party hard-liners detained Soviet President Mikhail Gorbachev and moved tanks into Moscow streets? And why did they allow Russian President Boris Yeltsin to dissolve the Supreme Soviet of the Russian Federation dominated by hard-liners in September 1993 and crush their resistance two weeks later?

It seemed only natural to expect that, after all her terrible experience, Russia would vote for democracy, civil rights, and free market economy. Western policy makers, as well as scholars, widely shared these views—as did the reporters and analysts of key Western papers and news agencies. Those few "eccentrics" who tried to voice another opinion found no forum among the leading publications and other media services.

Vice-president Al Gore timed his visit to Moscow so that he could personally congratulate the victorious democrats on the election day and join their festivities. But the celebration was stolen by the so-called Liberal-Democratic Party, which is essentially a Nazi faction. Its vicious leader, Vladimir Zhirinovsky, a short, short-haired man with the short thick neck of a professional wrestler and harsh sparkling eyes, is ready to solve any domestic or international problem with force, including nuclear warheads.

2.

The Russian Fuehrer immediately captured front-page headlines throughout the world. Leading papers quoted his maniacal statements.

- "Zhirinovsky says that he will bury radioactive waste along the Lithuanian border and set up fans to blow the radiation into the 'betrayer' republic."
- "He is ready to start a new war in Afghanistan and to use Uzbeks and Tajiks as cannon fodder."
- "Zhirinovsky insists that Russia should have a common border with Germany; that means he wants to eliminate an independent Poland."
- "He will stop reducing the size of the army and conversion of the military industry."

- "Zhirinovsky said that if Germany interfered in his affairs, he would nuke her—and do the same with Japan."
- "Zhirinovsky demands the United States return Alaska and compensate Russia for all natural resources extracted from Alaska's soil."
- "Zhirinovsky wants Bulgaria to become the 16th Soviet republic and Yugoslav republic of Macedonia—a part of Bulgaria."
- " Zhirinovsky believes that Rumania is an artificial entity founded by the descendants of Italian Gypsies."
- "Zhirinovsky said that he would replace dark-haired TV announcers with blond, blue-eyed ones so the audience could enjoy looking at their kind, Russian faces."
- "Zhirinovsky said that both his parents were Russian and he will not tolerate any doubts about that."
- "He stated that he is not an anti-Semite, but that Jews are guilty of all Russian troubles, that Jews themselves provoke anti-Semitism."
- "He suggested that all Jews should be deported to an island like Madagascar and live there in total isolation from the rest of the world, that it would be the best solution to the Jewish problem."
- "He openly declared that he may kill one hundred thousand Russians to secure peace for the other 300 million."
- "According to him, only the Russian army could solve the conflict in Bosnia and that he is ready to deploy five divisions there."
- "He'll order the shooting of all suspects on the spot to reduce the crime rate."
- "Zhirinovsky offers his help to White America to get rid of Blacks and Hispanics."
- "Zhirinovsky believes that some of Hitler's ideas were not so bad."

3.

The new Fuehrer's rhetoric speaks for itself. And if we take into account that the Russian Communist Party combined with individual communists, received even more seats in the parliament than the Zhirinovsky's Liberal-Democratic Party, the new reality turns into a nightmare.

Traditionally, communists (who call themselves *the Red*) are left-wing extremists while Nazi-like ultra-nationalists (often called *the Brown*, a reference to the color of Hitler's storm troops' uniforms)—right-wing extremists. That is not the case now in Russia. The *Red* and the *Brown* have practically no serious ideological differences. The newly organized Russian Communist Party is, in fact, a National-Communist faction. Party-head Gennady Zyuganov was among the founders of the National Salvation Front, a united organization of "patriots," whose goal is to restore the totalitarian empire under the banner of Russian ultra-nationalism.

The *Red* and the *Brown* together won more than half of the seats in the new Russian parliament.

In the meantime, the West believed that Russia was transforming into a civilized society with respect for human rights, freedom, and other values of Western democracy.

What caused this fundamental miscalculation?

4.

First, modern Russian nationalism is not in favor among Western scholars. Of the hundreds of books on Russia published in this country in the last two decades, only a few have focused on it. Although the current rise of Russian ultra-nationalism started as early as the late 1960s, it went unnoticed for a long time.

Professor John Dunlop was one of the first to conduct an extensive research of nationalist sentiments in Soviet society during the Brezhnev era. But his first book on this topic was not published until 1983. [1]

Surprisingly, Dunlop viewed Russian nationalism as a positive trend which deserved our support. He used simple reasoning: Since the nationalist ideology lies beyond the framework of orthodox communist doctrines, we should welcome the Russian nationalists. Professor Dunlop and like-minded scholars developed a theory of two-wing opposition against Communist rule in Soviet society: The left-liberal and the right-conservative. They overlooked or neglected a fundamental fact—that the Communist leadership deliberately encouraged Russian nationalism, chauvinism, and anti-Semitism.

Decades earlier, Winston Churchill, one of the greatest statesmen of this century, had to admit his helplessness in understanding what was going on behind the Kremlin scenes. He noted with dark humor that Moscow's Byzantine tricks reminded him of a "bulldogs' closed fight under the rug."

The Kremlin strictly controlled and carefully dosed information "leaked" from Russia to the West, feeding the sovietologists leftovers from the Kremlin table. They had to make conclusions based only on fragments of unreliable information, so fundamental mistakes were unavoidable.

That time is over now. The iron curtain has gone. Russian society is as open today, and the bulldogs are fighting in an open field. Everyone with eyes can see, and everyone with ears can hear.

But after the last Soviet president, Mikhail Gorbachev, started his policy of *glasnost* (which means openness) and *perestroika* (reconstruction) the West became too enthusiastic about these changes. The destruction of the Berlin Wall and the end of the Cold War turned our enthusiasm into euphoria. Some scholars, eager to announce the "end of history," could not accept that the real situation was not rosy. Meanwhile, Russia and the other former Soviet republics, their nuclear arsenals still intact, were entering a new historical phase typical of a defeated country. One need not be a prophet to predict that high social tensions, political instability, an extremely high level of corruption, impoverishment of the majority of the population, and the rise of aggressive nationalism would characterize this phase. This means that we in the West still have a long way to go before we turn our victory in the Cold War into guaranteed security and peace for our children and grandchildren.

Alexander Yanov, in his book *The Russian Idea and the Year 2000*,[2] expressed serious concerns about the rise of Russian nationalism, but it was mostly ignored by mainstream scholars.

Professor Walter Laqueur wrote the latest—and the best—book on Russian ultra-nationalism.[3] He collected and analyzed a great deal of material. He studied the roots of Russian nationalism and demonstrated how the ideas of the great Russian thinkers of the 19th century—the Slavophiles*—deteriorated into a proto-Nazi ("Black Hundred") movement.

When approaching modern time, however, Laqueur begins to retreat from his own methodology. He knows, for example, that there were several different Black Hundred organizations in Russia at the beginning of this century. They had slightly different tactics—their leaders often quarreled and fought with each other—but their differences meant almost nothing in comparison with their similarities. All these organizations were "patriotic," anti-Semitic, and violent; all collaborated with the secret police, and the Czarist government secretly funded them. Their goal was to preserve and strengthen the decrepit Czarist regime. Their main method was to spread hatred against liberals, Jews, and other minorities and to organize violent mass actions under the slogan "Kill kikes, save Russia."

---

* At the beginning and in the second half of the 19th century, the Slavophiles developed a theory of a "special" Russian spirituality and moral outlook which Fyodor Dostoyevskycalled "the Russian idea."

It seems logical to look at today's heirs of the Black Hundred groups in the same way as at their forerunners—by concentrating on their common philosophy, basic values, goals, and tactics. Walter Laqueur, however, concentrates mostly on their differences.

"To retrace all the splits and mergers that occurred on the extreme right would be nearly impossible,"[4] admits the author, but he makes extraordinary efforts to meet the challenge. He seems not to have missed a single name or a single, even the smallest, group. But, while forcing his way through the jungle, he failed to see the forest for the trees. He portrayed the broad mighty movement rooted deeply in the history, mentality, and culture of the Russian "soil" as scum on the surface of a busy turbulent flow directed to the bright future of flourishing democracy.

As a result, even Dr. Laqueur did not expect the victory of Vladimir Zhirinovsky in the 1993 parliamentary elections. "Zhirinovsky won twice [as many votes] as I expected," he said in an interview to the Russian newspaper *Izvestia*.[5]

Meanwhile, a telephone poll conducted in Moscow in October 1992 showed that almost 18 percent of Muscovites strongly believed that the Russian people had become victims of the so-called Jewish-Masonic conspiracy.[*] Another 25 percent considered this "explanation" of their hardships a serious possibility. Thus, more than a year before the elections, there was a clear indication that the Black Hundreders had indoctrinated 43 percent of Muscovites. Those 43 percent blamed not only the Jews, but the West as well for all Russia's problems. They see nothing good in democracy and free market economy, feel nostalgic for the Communist past, and dream of restoring the mighty totalitarian empire.[6]

We have to keep in mind that Moscow's population is the most educated and westernized in the country; the provinces are much more conservative. Thus, it is safe to assume that more than half of Russian adults are prejudiced against Jews, the West, and democracy. This assumption corresponds to the percentage of votes cast for the *Red* and the *Brown*. Thus, a significant part of

---

[*] The "theory" of the Jewish-Masonic (or Zionist-Masonic) conspiracy is based on a belief that the Jews and Masons have formed a super-secret organization with the intention of conquering the entire world. At the beginning of this century, this "theory" served as an important tool of Russian government and ultra-nationalistic propaganda to compromise the democratic and revolutionary movement as just a part of the Jewish plot against Russia. Later, the theory became central to the ideology of the German Nazis. In the USSR, the idea of the Jewish-Masonic plot was revived under Brezhnev, and now it is an integral part of Russian popular consciousness. We will speak more about this "theory" later in the book.

the Russian society is contaminated not just with anti-Semitism, but with Nazism.

Anti-Semitism, and other prejudices may exist in any society, serving as a fertile soil for nazism, which begins to grow when some individuals or groups start to *exploit* these prejudices for political gains. This is exactly what Adolf Hitler successfully attempted in Germany. His Russian predecessors, the Black-Hundreders, did the same in the Russian Empire, but were defeated by more skillful demagogues, the Bolsheviks. Now, Russian ultra-nationalists believe that their time has come again.

5.

However, numbers do not tell the whole story. There are a lot of things in life that could be understood only if personally endured from the inside—not just observed from the outside.

Each chapter of this book describes one remarkable event or a few leading characters. I have chosen them because they were typical and because I was personally involved with them in a greater or smaller degree. This allowed me to present them in a manner that may capture not only the reader's mind, but imagination as well.

It does not mean, however, that this book is just my personal life story. It is far from that. Over the last 20 years, I have accumulated thousands of documents on the Russian Nazi movement, and I widely use and analyze this collection. But it is not an academic study addressed only to scholars. This book is written for a wide Western audience. It is an attempt to break through cultural barriers and to offer insights which mostly remain inaccessible to outside observers.

In describing dozens of different characters, I have tried to demonstrate that the seeds of the Red-Brown propaganda are falling into fertilized soil and are forming poisonous shoots. The inclination peculiar to the Russian mentality to blame the West, Tartars, Germans, Jews, "Caucasians," and everyone but themselves for all their misfortunes has created a spiritual environment in which modern fascist organizations are flourishing.

I would like to guide my reader through the Nazi kitchen, to introduce to him some of its cooks, and to show how they, in their gurgling coppers, are extracting the *Brown* poison from the foul pluck of *Red* ideology. If after the reader is through with the book, he has a sense of having been there, I will regard my goal achieved.

PART ONE

FROM RED TO BROWN

CHAPTER 1

UNPREDICTABLE PAST

Miracle

Those days are forever imprinted in my mind. I still lived in Moscow and worked for a big book-publishing company. I was the editor of an extremely popular series of biographies, *The Lives of Remarkable People*. I shared a small office with two other editors; the office of our editor-in-chief, Sergei Semanov, lay behind a thin wall. We, his subordinates, heard his hasty steps from one corner to another and back. We only exchanged glances, silently nodding or whispering to each other as if there were a dying person in the next room.

For several days on end, Semanov had been keeping to his office, not showing himself and not allowing anyone in except to sign proofs or look over an urgent paper.

When necessity arose, we had to knock on his door with great perseverance, but he was in no hurry to respond. We would knock five or six times. Then the steps in his office would die away and we could hear a cautious turn of the key. An eye with a guarded and restless look would appear in a narrow opening in the doorway. The compressed strip of his face seen through the barest of cracks would be red with tension. And when he appeared at last, he would look like a helpless beast that had fallen into a trap. His situation was desperate.

The *Lives of Remarkable People* series played a significant role in the cultural and intellectual life of the Soviet Union, which, by that country's traditions, also made it an important ideological and political landmark. In 1933, Maxim Gorky[*] founded the series. He wanted to bring the characters of outstanding reformers and innovators of the past to a wide audience and to tell the stories of their great contributions to science, technology, philosophy, literature, fine arts, and political thinking. It went without saying that this would help the readers become adherents to the ideals of Communism, deemed to be the highest achievement of human thought and spirit.

Gorky issued a number of books, which made the series very popular. But after World War II, when the ideological control reached its peak, the series fell on hard times. They could publish no more than five books a year, all of them invariably boring, dry, and overburdened with quotations from Marx, Engels, Lenin, and Stalin. It was the only way to demonstrate the "correct" Marxist-Leninist approach to history. Even limited editions of those books did not sell well. Only the prestige of the series' founder, Maxim Gorky, prevented the shutdown of the publication.

The situation began to change in 1956, after the 20th Congress of the Communist Party, when party-leader Nikita Khrushchev gave his famous address denouncing Stalin's "mistakes." That was the start of a renewal in all areas of social life, including literature and history.

Officially, the Communist Party remained "the ruling force of Soviet society." Writers were only allowed to help the party educate the masses in the spirit of Communist ideology. However, standards of "ideological correctness" became somewhat ambiguous. A number of past instructive documents could now be viewed as obsolete and ignored as "Stalin's errors." The actual decisions were pretty much up to the individual officials and determined by their personal courage.

One of the party liberals ready to play fast and loose with official doctrines was young historian and bibliophile Yuri Korotkov. At that time, he became the editor-in-chief of the *Lives of Remarkable People* series. Trying to make the series more attractive to the public, he began offering contracts to gifted writers and giving them the freedom to describe the lives, activities, and personalities of great individuals more realistically than was previously allowed. The weak-

---

[*] Maxim Gorky (Alexei Maximovich Peshkov, 1868-1936), a famous author with an international reputation, was regarded in the Soviet Union as an extremely valuable treasure. A close friend of both Lenin and Stalin, he used his talents and influence to reveal to the entire world "the advantages of socialism" and to instill into the Soviet readers a commitment to the Communist ideology. He was proclaimed the first of the true "proletarian" writers and a founder of "Socialist realism." But sometimes he failed to be in line with the image he had to bear, and allegedly Stalin's secret police assassinated (poisoned) him.

ening of censorship also helped him, as did a more liberal access to the archives.

The party bureaucrats, still in control of literature, were much more preoccupied with modern-day themes. Many ideas blocked by the censors in publications dealing with contemporary life had a fairly easy time getting through in biographies of people who lived a hundred or two hundred years ago. Both potential authors and readers picked up on the new trend. The best writers, historians, and scholars realized that the biographical genre promised them more creative freedom than any other; thus, they started to approach the editors with their proposals. The number of annual publications quickly grew, along with the number of copies printed. By 1963, when I became one of the staff editors, we did not have to worry about selling our books. The demand grew much faster than the circulation: There was always a shortage of paper for good books. A few years later, the books of the series—issued in the hundreds of thousands—would sell out in a couple hours.

The Lives of Remarkable People series had become one of the most popular and prestigious national book publications, but the party leadership started having second thoughts about it. Preparing a celebration of the 50th anniversary of the Bolshevik revolution in November 1967, the Communist Party Central Committee issued a secret instruction to the mass media and publishing industry. It demanded to play up positive achievements of the Soviet system and avoid criticism of past mistakes and errors. From that point on, the censors struck out almost any sentence mentioning the purges or other Stalin "excesses."

This turn in the policy effected me quite personally when I finished my own first book—a biography of a great Soviet biologist Nikolai Vavilov (1887-1943). He spent the last years of his life battling "voodoo scientists" who rejected the revolutionary advances in biology as contradicting the philosophy of Karl Marx. These "ideologically correct" obscurants branded all those who disagreed with them as "bourgeois" scientists. Stalin supported Vavilov's arrest in 1940, and later the scientist died in prison.

My manuscript told the truth about Vavilov's fate as well as about the struggle in the Soviet biology. The editor cut out a hundred pages prior to the publication. The censor, surprisingly, approved it only with minor additional cuts. In spite of that, however, the Communist Party Central Committee found the book "ideologically harmful" and held up its distribution of one hundred thousand copies already printed. They remained in a sealed room in a warehouse for nearly a year. Only the involvement of many prominent scientists saved them from the shredder.

Sensing that their time had finally come, the hard-line Stalinists went on the offensive against liberal publications. In a couple of years, their attacks resulted in the firing of the entire editorial board of *Novy Mir*, the most liberal literary journal, headed by Alexander Tvardovsky. Some other liberal editors lost their jobs as well, and Yuri Korotkov was among the victims.

Sergei Semanov, who replaced Korotkov, immediately became an influential figure in the worlds of both scholars and writers and, naturally, in the publishing arena.

Semanov often wrote for the journal *Molodaya Gvardia* (Young Guard). His main theme was the Communist Party struggle against the Trotskyists in the 1920s and 1930s. According to the official textbooks of the history of the Communist Party, Leon Trotsky and his followers held to a "bourgeois" ideology and wanted to restore capitalism in Russia. Semanov developed a slightly different concept, claiming that the Trotskyists sought to destroy Russia's traditions and deprive the nation of its roots. He extolled the wisdom of the party (i.e., of Stalin, though he did not mention him directly) that defeated Trotskyism. The party managed to secure the Russian national heritage against the encroachments of the "cosmopolitans without kith or kin" (as the Jews were called during Stalin's anti-Semitic campaigns). Semanov eulogized Russia's military might, its victories in World War II and many other wars centuries ago. He believed in a special historical path for Russia. According to him, Russia had no use for innovations and progress. Rapprochement with the West had but a corrupting influence. A tough authoritarian regime grown deep into national roots was the only guarantee for her prosperity and protection from both internal and external enemies.

These ideas sharply contradicted the basic Communist doctrine of "class struggle" and "proletarian internationalism," but that did not mean that they were new or unknown. Quite the contrary. Their roots were in the Russian past. They could be traced to the 15th century, when Moscow's Grand Duke had liberated the country from the Mongol-Tartar yoke and started to re-build the independent Russian state.

Just at that time, the Turks destroyed the Byzantine empire from which Russia had borrowed her Greek-Orthodox Christianity that had had a tremendous impact on Russian culture. For centuries, the Russians viewed themselves as the humble pupils of their Byzantine mentors, and suddenly, Russia became the only bearer of the "true" religion. Under these circumstances, the Russian spiritual elite came to believe that God had assigned a special mission to Russia—to maintain the Orthodox tradition in its original purity and to protect them from the hostile world of darkness and depravity. According to this ideology, this mission was initially assigned to Rome, but the Romans failed and God turned His back on them. He transferred the mission to Byzantium. The capital of Byzantine empire, Constantinople, became the Second Rome. But Byzantine did not meet the challenge either and was destroyed. The Russians, however, had enough courage and strength to fulfill the honorable task to God's full satisfaction. "Moscow is the Third Rome, and the Fourth one will never be!" the Russian-Orthodox monk Filofey stated at the beginning of the 16th century.

In practice, this ideology required strong resistance against everything untraditional. It cultivated suspicion and fear of everything non-Russian as a potential source of evil ideas, false values, seductive and harmful innovations. Thus, xenophobia and super-conservatism became an important part of the Russian cultural tradition.

This trend of thought was not always dominant, but it was always there. It contributed a lot to the general backwardness of the Russian historical development. Even such reformers as Peter the Great (1698-1725) could not keep up with Western Europe because of strong conservative resistance.

In the 19th century, educated intellectuals—the Slavophiles—believed in the spiritual superiority of the "Russian" idea over all others. They stood for the restoration of "unspoiled" Russia as she had been before the reign of Peter the Great. They claimed that his "westernizing" innovations only derailed Russia from her traditional path.

Sergei Uvarov, minister of education in the administration of Nicholas I (1825-1855), developed a bureaucratic modification of these ideas. He offered a formula, "Orthodoxy, Autocracy, The People," that meant a strong authoritarian regime, obedience, and the preservation of the traditional way of life.

In the beginning of the 20th century, when the revolutionary movement became powerful, these ideas deteriorated into the Black Hundred movement. Its main goal was to preserve the outdated Czarist regime by scapegoating the Jews and other minorities.

Bolsheviks considered the ideas of the Slavophiles and, especially, the Black Hundreders as the most reactionary part of the Russian national heritage. But at the time when Semanov started to glorify these ideas in a slightly modified form, they had already been in the mainstream of the monthly *Molodaya Gvardia* as well as *Ogonyok* (The Light), *Moskva* (Moscow), and *Nash Sovremennik* (Our Contemporary). Similar ideas were increasingly penetrating leading dailies and weeklies, so it was obvious that the party leadership supported them.

Thus, the full two-page publication that appeared in a weekly *Literaturnaya Gazeta* (Literary Gazette) on November 15, 1972, came as a shock.[1] The article condemned several "young critics" for disregarding the Marxist approach toward history and regarding pre-Revolutionary Russia as a flourishing harmonious society. The name of Sergei Semanov was among several mentioned.

The article was special in a number of aspects. First, its tone was of an instructive, not debating, character. Second, next to the author's name, Alexander Yakovlev, stood the rank of doctor of history. Combined with the tone, it added to the article the weight of an academic authority. But most importantly, the author was an acting chief of the Propaganda Department of the Communist Party Central Committee.

Usually such high party officials did not interfere directly with literary polemics. They had enough means to act effectively behind the scenes. The use of such heavy artillery could have had only one meaning: The party demonstrated to the public that it would not tolerate the ideology advocated by the "young critics."

Yakovlev's article aroused conflicting emotions in me. Any peremptory shout from above meant further pressure on literature. It implied tougher censorship, a heightened alertness among our petty bosses and everyone whose job was "to hold and not let go." From this point of view, the article was an ill omen. But the target of the shout provided a reason for brighter prospects.

The article by Alexander Yakovlev signaled a dramatic change at the top. No one doubted that Semanov would be fired, least of all, Semanov himself. A few days later he was summoned to the party Central Committee. He called his comrades in misfortune—those also mentioned in the article—only to learn that all of them had been summoned for the same day and hour. No doubt, they were invited for an "execution." I remember how haunted Semanov looked when he left for the Central Committee. At the time, I felt sorry for him. Only a miracle could save him.

And a miracle did happen.

The Central Committee explained to the "young critics" that comrade Yakovlev was an important scholar and they should not disregard his reasoning. At the same time, the Committee let them know that the article did not mean that the party had any political grudge against them. Dr. Yakovlev had merely expressed his personal opinion.

What had been going on in the corridors of power while Semanov had been dashing around his tiny office? What mechanisms had been set in motion? How could it have happened that Alexander Yakovlev, who had grown up among the party functionaries, could publish such an article without approval from the top? Or, perhaps, protectors of a higher rank had suddenly betrayed him?

It all remained a mystery, but the message conveyed to the "young critics" was clear. The party did not denounce their national-Stalinist line. Shortly afterwards came further, more tangible proof: Alexander Yakovlev (who 15 years later became the architect of the policy of *glasnost)* was removed from the Central Committee and sent to Canada as an ambassador. Thus did Soviet leaders treat those who fell into disgrace.

In literary circles everyone understood the meaning of Yakovlev's dismissal. If there still were a hope that the fanning of national-Stalinist sentiments was limited to the initiative of a number of authors and editors who, whatever influential protectors they might have had, were not omnipotent, it vanished. I understood that my days as an editor of the *Lives of Remarkable People* series were numbered. And rather soon, Sergei Semanov told me (in a friendly tone, I should admit) that I had to choose. My new book—a biography of a great Russian biologist Ilya Mechnikov, already typeset, censored, and prepared for reproduction and binding—could not be released while I remained on the staff.

The choice was obvious: I had to resign "voluntarily."

Communism and Anti-Semitism

I believed that I was knowledgeable about anti-Semitism in my country. I had grown up in one of the poorest crime-ridden Moscow neighborhood, with many drunkards wandering the streets ready for any quarrel or fight. During such confrontations, they slung many vulgar words at each other, but "You are a kike" or "You are a Jew" expressed the highest level of scorn and anger. It was an insult of far greater import than "fool" or "thief" or "coward" and was not necessarily related to ethnic background. Children on the streets copied the adults, and I was a pariah among them since everybody in my neighborhood knew that I really was a Jew, the only one among the neighborhood children.

It was especially painful for me because I honestly could not understand the difference between other boys my age and me. We played together in the yard, studied the same subjects at school, read the same books, saw the same movies, and listened to the same radio and TV broadcasts. I did not speak Yiddish or Hebrew, did not know Jewish history or traditions. My parents knew more but insulated me from my heritage because they did not want me to be different. They had suffered as Jews and tried to shield me from the rancor of prejudice. Most Soviet Jews preferred not to remember their ancestry; and the best way they could please each other was to say, "You look absolutely not Jewish!" I knew that to be Jewish was bad, very bad, and that I would carry this brand my entire life.

Later, when I found myself in more sophisticated surroundings, anti-Semitism did not touch me in such a direct way. Educated people from my social milieu had no negative feelings toward Jews—or at least had not shown them. But administrative anti-Semitism was prevalent. Jews faced many more obstacles when applying to a university, looking for work, seeking a promotion or a scholarly degree, or attempting to have their articles or books published, than Russians or people from other groups.

All this discrimination, however, was not as overt as it had been in Czarist Russia with her anti-Jewish legislation. Soviet officials acted according to indirect instructions, which left room for different interpretations. When, in 1962, a vacancy appeared on the editorial staff of the *Life of Remarkable People* series, Yuri Korotkov interviewed many applicants and chose one, Alexander Levin, who had the bad luck to be Jewish. The series came under the administrative jurisdiction of the *Molodaya Gvardia* book-publishing house (which should not be confused with the monthly journal *Molodaya Gvardia* mentioned above). The director of the publishing house, Yuri Melentyev, looked through Levin's application and refused to hire him on the ground that Levin had received a reprimand five years before for tardiness. Korotkov, who was on close terms with Melentyev, was furious at this hypocrisy. He told his staffers, "If he told me honestly that he did not want a Jew, I would take it into account. But he does not want this particular Jew because of his reprimand. Fine, I will find another one—without a reprimand."

I was his second choice, and I was hired.

To understand the reasons for the "diffidence" of such bosses as Yuri Melentyev, one should look deeper into the roots of the Communist ideology and its concept of "proletarian internationalism."

The Communist era began in 1848, when two young German philosophers—Karl Marx and Friedrich Engels—published *The Communist Party Manifesto*. The authors believed that they had found a scientific method of building a just and prosperous society in which everyone would be happy.

With capitalism developing rapidly in Europe, the owners of new factories, mines, railroads, and other enterprises generated big profits while the employees had to work long hours in horrible conditions for wages that barely kept them from dying of starvation. The authors of *The Manifesto* blamed private property for social injustice, postulating that the interests of employers and employees were irreconcilable and that a compromise between them was impossible. The authors predicted an imminent social uprising which would eliminate private property and class society. The workers would expropriate private property and own everything collectively. Their work for the benefit of the society would be joyful and highly productive, and everyone would get his fair share. Marx and Engels theorized that the main vices of people—selfishness, envy, money-grubbing—were engraved in human beings by the unjust society, not by nature, and would disappear along with private ownership. Wars, violence, crime, deception, prejudices, and intolerance would disappear as well. They called this future society of equal and happy people (heaven on earth) *communism*.

Marx and Engels believed that to be successful, the revolution should occur in most capitalist countries simultaneously. To insure the end, the workers needed a strong international organization to coordinate their struggle. "The proletarians have no fatherland. They have nothing to lose but their own chains, and they can acquire the whole world....Workers of the world, unite!" *The Communist Manifesto* stated.

Proletarian internationalism became one of the highest priorities in the workers' movement. Even the proletarian hymn written four decades later in France became known as *The International*. The anthem spurred revolutionary action through intensely emotional imagery:

> Stand up, you, branded with damnation,
> the whole world of hungry slaves!
> Our minds are boiling with indignation,
> and we are ready to fight to death.

In October 1917, the most extreme Marxist group in Russia, the Bolsheviks (who later renamed themselves Communists), took power and declared the beginning of the world proletarian revolution. They confiscated all private property, arrested or forced to flee abroad landowners and capitalists, and persecuted all other political parties and groups, including more moderate socialist parties.

In 1919, they created the *Communist International,* which incorporated communist parties formed by that time in many countries from the most extreme Marxist groups. The goal was to spread the proletarian revolution to as many countries as possible. However, it soon became clear that to achieve this goal is much more difficult than to declare it. Although in Russia the Bolsheviks won the Civil War and consolidated their power, the Communist Parties of other countries failed. They had to admit that the majority of workers did not follow their lead and that the rest of the world would remain "capitalist" in the foreseeable future.

Thus, the ideas of internationalism did not work in the world arena. But they became extremely valuable inside the newborn Soviet country with her more than one hundred nationalities and ethnic groups. In December 1922, the Bolsheviks created the Union of Soviet Socialist Republics (USSR) as a voluntary confederation of independent states ruled by elected Soviets (Councils). Each of the republics, in theory, had an explicit right to get out at any time. Smaller nations and ethnic groups received the status of autonomous republics, autonomous regions, or national districts, mostly depending on population size. They did not have the option to leave the Union, but received a large degree of self-rule.

However, all this was just decoration. The true power belonged to the Communist Party. The party established strict totalitarian control over all aspects of life in all republics, regions, and districts—down to each family and individual. The Bolsheviks started to create "a new human being" devoted to communism and without "bourgeois" instincts. They closed most churches, mosques, and synagogues since old religions were irreconcilable with Communist doctrine. Traditional ways of life became illegal.

At the same time, the Communist leaders tried to convince the public that the Soviet Union was the only country in the world where the working people were free from exploitation and all nationalities enjoyed full equality. The concept of proletarian internationalism instilled a new mission: To keep the Union together regardless of cultural differences between the ethnic groups. The "brotherhood of the people" required curbing Russian chauvinism on the one hand and fighting the "bourgeois" nationalism of minorities on the other.

Jews present the best example of how this policy was implemented.

Fighting against the "bourgeois prejudices" among the Jews, the Bolsheviks closed synagogues and religious schools *(heders* and *yeshivas)* and ridiculed or persecuted those who continued to observe Sabbath and other Jewish laws and traditions. Rabbis were arrested and sent to labor camps. Zionists were severely persecuted; the idea of a Jewish state in Palestine was viewed as "bourgeois nationalism" since the national interests in that idea had a priority over class interests. Even Hebrew became illegal as the language of a religion.

At the same time, the Bolsheviks actively fought against any attempts to consider Jews second-class citizens and to discriminate against them. The press condemned manifestations of anti-Semitism; the courts sentenced the most severe offenders to prison terms. Bolshevik propagandists traveled around the country proving that anti-Semitism was a "bourgeois" prejudice cultivated by the enemies of communism.

This policy proved effective. It did not eliminate street anti-Semitism; but young Jews made up a significant fraction of students at the leading universities, and five to ten years later they played a prominent role in industry, science, medicine, education, the arts, and literature. They broke with their religion and Jewish traditions relatively easily, sincerely believing that their heritage served the capitalist system.

Similar processes took place among other minorities as well.

In the mid-1930s, this policy started to change. In 1939 and 1940, after signing a secret treaty with Hitler to divide Europe between Germany and the USSR, the Soviets invaded and annexed part of Poland, Lithuania, Latvia, Estonia, and Bessarabia. They also started an unsuccessful war with Finland. These actions signified a return to the imperialist policy of Czarist Russia. But Moscow commissars sent with the army were not in a hurry to establish their administration. They relied on local communists to get rid of the "bourgeois" governments, to arrest and kill "capitalists," to organize "elections" into the newly born Supreme Soviets of the republics, and in their name to declare "voluntary" merges with the Soviet Union. All this decorum was the only way to legitimize the annexation in the eyes of the Soviet people. The concept of the proletarian internationalism was so deeply implanted in the society that the authorities had to demonstrate their devotion to it at least in words.

During and after the war with Germany, Stalin's policy took an even more cynical turn. In August 1941, two months after Hitler attacked the Soviet Union, Stalin deported ethnic Germans—the descendants of German colonists invited by Catherine the Great in the 18th century to settle unpopulated lands in the Volga River region. They created their own autonomous republic after the Revolution. Without warning, special security units surrounded villages and towns and forced the entire German population—including the aged, children, and women—into railroad freight cars. Sealed in those cars, up to half of them died without food and medical care during the many-month journey to Kazakhstan and Siberia. Those who survived worked like slaves for many years. Other ethnic groups, accused of collaboration with the Nazis—Crimean Tartars, Chechens, Ingushes, Balkars, Turks-Mesketints, and Kalmyks—suffered a similar fate during the final months of World War II.

Soon after the war, Stalin singled out the Russian people as "the first among equals." All Russian military victories for a thousand years—both real or imagined—became a matter of special glorification. Russian generals became the bravest and the wisest military figures in the world, and even some Russian Czars became "the most progressive rulers of their times." This policy gave birth to a cult of everything Russian—literature, music, science, and technology. Hundreds of books determinedly proved that the Russian empire was a progressive state which all minorities joined voluntarily, not as a result of conquests; that Russians made all the great discoveries and inventions first and then foreigners stole them. As a schoolboy, I learned from my textbooks that the Russian genius Ivan Polzunov invented the steam-engine much earlier than James Watt; that Alexander Mozhaisky, not the Wright brothers, designed the first airplane; that Alexander Popov invented radio, not Gulielmo Marconi; and Alexander Lodygin constructed the first light bulb many years before Thomas Edison. The list had no end.

Simultaneously, Stalin started a campaign against the "cosmopolitans without kith or kin." In English and in other languages, including Russian, the words "cosmopolitanism" and "internationalism" are synonyms. But Stalin made them antonyms with an exclusively negative context for "cosmopolitanism" and positive connotation for "internationalism." According to the Soviet propaganda, cosmopolitans were traitors and enemies of socialism and their home nation who kneeled before everything foreign. Most of those accused of cosmopolitanism were Jews. Many of them barely remembered anything about their roots. They were fired from their jobs, expelled from the Communist Party and from prestigious organizations such as the Writers' Union; many were arrested and sentenced to labor camps. The Yiddish culture, in spite of its "socialist content," was destroyed; leading Jewish writers and artists were executed.

This campaign culminated in the "Doctors' Plot." The secret police arrested a group of leading Soviet doctors who treated the highest Soviet officials (most of the doctors were Jewish) and accused them of plotting to kill Stalin and his closest associates. Under torture, the accused "confessed" their guilt. According to Stalin's scenario, they would appear in an open trial and confirm their "crimes." Then they would be hanged in Red Square and all Jews would be deported to Siberia. Stalin's death in March 1953 interfered with this plan. The doctors were released, and the campaign against cosmopolitans gradually died without any explanation to the public.

When the new Communist Party leader Nikita Khrushchev officially denounced Stalin's "mistakes" and declared a return to "Lenin's norms of party life," it meant, among other things, the return to "proletarian internationalism." But since all "returns" were done halfheartedly, only the most direct and cynical forms of Russian ultra-nationalism and anti-Semitism were disallowed. The Jews remained undesirable, although nobody openly admitted that.

Thus, I knew that I could be attacked in the street by drunkards if they realized that I was a Jew. Some officials hated me just because I was Jewish. To achieve something as a writer and a journalist, I had to work ten times harder than my Russian colleagues. Although unwritten, the rules of the game were obvious and I had no choice but to adjust accordingly.

But I did not imagine then that some powerful forces in my country were ready to go even further than Stalin—as far as Hitler and Goebbels. Under the umbrella of official internationalism and the brotherhood of the peoples, they started to develop a set of ideas about the incompatibility of Russians and Jews which automatically made every single Jew an enemy of the Russian people.

Rewriting history

This new phase of Russian anti-Semitism began soon after the Soviet Army cracked down the Prague Spring in Czechoslovakia in August 1968.

In January of that year, after student protest demonstrations in Prague, Antonin Novotny, the head of the Czechoslovak Communist Party and the Kremlin's watchdog, had to resign. The new party leadership, headed by Alexander Dubchck, started democratic reforms aimed at building "socialism with a human face." Many people in the USSR, especially Moscow intellectuals, met that experiment with hope and wanted to have it repeated in their own country. This unexpected development created panic in the Kremlin. Brezhnev's ideologists had no illusions. They understood that Soviet socialism can not be humanized. As soon as you start this process, you have to go further and further. You have to allow basic freedoms—respect human rights, tolerate an independent press, private enterprise, and private ownership. All this means replacing socialism with capitalism.

After all attempts to persuade the Czechoslovakian leaders to stop their seductive reforms failed, Soviets invaded the "brotherly" country. Soviet generals carried out the military operation perfectly. Just forty minutes after it started, they arrested Alexander Dubchek and his entourage. But after that victory, the people in the Soviet Union lost their last hopes for a gradual liberalization of their own society. They suddenly understood that socialism was just another name for despotism and the "bright future of communism" preached by Soviet ideologists was just a myth.

Thus, the society lost its perspective. The system could prop itself up by tanks, but it could not justify itself anymore. The Soviet Union found itself in a deadlock that neither Stalin's purges nor Khrushchev's unexpected moves could have brought about.

At that time, Andrei Sakharov presented a way out of the impasse in his famous *Memorandum*—convergence with the West, *glasnost*, expanding human rights and freedoms, and eventual democratization of the society. But this humanizing line had been pursued by the Czechoslovakian leaders during the Prague Spring. Kremlin had already rejected it, thus it was absolutely unacceptable to the Soviet leadership. Another way out of the impasse was a slow drive to Russian chauvinism, i.e., fascism.

After the forced resignation of Nikita Khrushchev in 1964, Brezhnev became the head of the Communist Party but was regarded as a transitional figure. He expended much time and effort to acquire a reliable majority in the ruling Politburo. Very much concerned about boosting his authority, he introduced the "confidence in the staff" policy, bribing party bureaucrats with an ever-growing number of privileges and granting them security in their positions. He acted in sharp contrast to Khrushchev's "voluntarism," when no high-ranking official could be sure that he would not be fired tomorrow. Brezhnev tolerated idleness, white-wash, bribe-taking, and embezzlement of public property. His subordinates could get away with anything, if their personal loyalty to the General Secretary remained unquestioned. His style passed down the whole chain of command. Soon the majority of big and petty bosses both in the center and in the provinces came to look upon themselves as fully uncontrolled princes. Their unwritten law placed personal devotion to the boss above any other quality.

This situation satisfied Brezhnev. He was reluctant to make any changes. But those who actually wielded power in his regime, knew that the status-quo could not be preserved without a new perspective.

The movement for free emigration, human rights, and intellectual freedom was on the rise. Repressive measures against dissidents were merciless. The most active of them were arrested and sentenced to long prison terms. Others ended up in psychiatric hospitals. Many were fired from their jobs, searched and harassed by the KGB. But there was not the slightest possibility of persecuting people on a Stalin-like scale. The hordes of fanatical "knights of the revolution" of the Lenin and Stalin eras needed to maintain mass reparation were replaced by cynics in the new generation. They did not believe in anything. The Marxist-Leninist ideas, "the bright future of Communism" were ridiculed in hundreds of jokes, and the authorities were quite aware of that. The lack of a righteous goal can deprive the most hardened butchers of zest. Alternative ideas were necessary, and it was only logical to use old Russian ultranationalism for this purpose. After all, Stalin had already tested this ideology in practice and proved that it could work.

Thus, little by little, they were lowering the *Red* Banner from the flagstaff and raising the *Brown*.

The *Lives of Remarkable People* series headed by Sergei Semanov exemplified this new approach. Here are just a few examples of how it worked.

For instance, Yuri Loshchits wrote a biography of Ivan Goncharov, a great Russian novelist of the 19th century.[2] (Loshchits, by the way, joined the series editorial staff after I had to resign, and it was not an accident. His views corresponded perfectly with the new policy.)

Ivan Goncharov's most famous novel *Oblomov* had made him one of the greatest Russian authors and won him world recognition. It is a study of indolence unprecedented in world literature: Its main character, Ilya Oblomov, lies almost motionless on a sofa throughout the 700-page story. Oblomov, a typical Russian *pomeshchik* (land and serf owner), was brought up to have his every wish and whim immediately fulfilled by numerous servants—his serfs. Eventually, this leaves him completely devoid of any desires or aspirations, his willpower fully atrophied.

The novel appeared two years before the abolition of serfdom in 1861, and the public saw it as a death sentence for the passing historic epoch. A radical literary critic, Nikolai Dobrolyubov, put into circulation a new word *oblomovshchina* (Oblomov-like lifestyle), and it became a common definition for a peculiarity of the Russian national character resulting from centuries of the inert and sluggish reality of serfdom.

In his biography of Ivan Goncharov, Yuri Loshchits decided to glorify *oblomovshchina* and the life of the serf village as "uniquely Russian" phenomena. He viewed agronomy booklets, railways, and any other innovations as odious and suspect. This foreign bane, the author claimed, was deliberately injected into the healthy body of the Russian society in order to destroy the nation's values, traditions, and originality. The author denounced the last century's entire liberal movement as a devilish enterprise and a plot against Russia masterminded from "foreign Masonic centers."

Much in the same manner, Mikhail Lobanov in his biography of the greatest Russian 19th century playwright, Alexander Ostrovsky,[3] puts forth a "new" concept of his tragedy *The Storm*. The message of the play, a protest against the old ways, parallels Goncharov's novel. The scene is set not in the landlords' but the merchants' milieu with its savage and merciless customs. One of the central woman characters, Kabanikha, stands a watchful guard over the patriarchal ways of the old Russian merchantry. She terrorizes her daughter-in-law Katerina, who starts resisting Kabanikha's despotism. Eventually Katerina comes out in open protest but fails to change things and commits suicide.

Commenting on the play, the above-mentioned critic, Nikolai Dobrolyubov, called Katerina "a ray of light in the kingdom of darkness." This became the traditional interpretation of all critics and scholars, not to mention play producers.

However, the playwright's biographer describes Kabanikha as a positive character keeping up the long-standing traditions of the Russian merchants while rebellious Katerina is the citadel of sin and depravity. It is even more remarkable that Lobanov presents this point of view not as his own, but attributes it to Ostrovsky.

Then Lobanov shifts fire from fictional characters to real historical figures and cracks down on the 19th century Russian feminist movement that produced many outstanding women. Some of them became key symbols of Russian culture. However, in Lobanov's opinion, and allegedly in Ostrovsky's, too, this movement was imported from abroad and, thus, was nothing but an anti-Russian "George-Sandism."

A biography of Vasily Bazhenov, a Russian architect of the 18th century, by Vadim Pigalev is no less graphic an example of the same distorted attitude. Pigalev deals, to a large extent, with the "unmasking" of Freemasonry as an anti-Russian invasion secretly orchestrated from abroad.[4]

Such a radical reinterpretation was applied not only to Russian literature and art, but to Russian political and military history as well. Perhaps, the most characteristic in this respect was the biography of Russian World War I General Alexei Brusilov, written by Sergei Semanov, the editor-in-chief of the series, himself.[5]

General Brusilov was famous for "Brusilov's break-through" in 1916, the only successful military operation of the Russian army during World War I. Later, he participated in the plot of the high military command which arrested Czar Nicholas II and forced him to sign an abdication. His next heroic deed, described in all Soviet history textbooks, was his active support of the Bolsheviks in 1918.

During World War I, ungifted Russian generals, losing one battle after another, constantly needed scapegoats. They accused the Jews of espionage and deported entire communities by the thousands from the zones of military activities. General Brusilov energetically participated in these operations. A famous bacteriologist, Daniil Zabolotny, who once had said in Brusilov's presence that he needed monkeys for his experiments, wrote in his memoirs:

"The general asked seriously, 'And what about kikes? I have kikes here, spies, I will hang them anyway. So take the kikes.' Without waiting for my response, he sent an officer to figure out how many spies they had waiting to be hanged. I started to explain to His Excellency that people could not be used in my experiments, but he did not understand me and pressed his point, goggling his eyes:

'People are smarter than monkeys. If you inject poison into a human being, he can tell you about his feelings while a monkey cannot.'

The officer came back and reported that there were no Jews among people arrested under suspicion of spying, only Gypsies and Rumanians. 'Can you use Gypsies? No? It's a pity,' [the general said]."[6]

Surely, this description is missing from Semanov's book. He portrayed Brusilov as a noble man, a great Russian patriot. However, the most significant parts of the book were not devoted to Brusilov's personality or his military activities, but to the general political background.

Vladimir Lenin characterized World War I as imperialistic and anti-proletarian and put forward a slogan: "To turn the imperialistic war into the civil war." Thus, the Bolsheviks agitated Russian soldiers not to shoot at their German class brothers, but instead, to make a short shrift of their own commanders and turn their bayonets against the emperor's palace. According to the official Soviet interpretation, the rank-and-file followed the Bolsheviks' lead, thanks to which the 1917 February and October revolutions took place in close succession.

Semanov's approach to these events was radically different. According to him, World War I was just and patriotic for the Russian people. Soldiers fought for their national heritage and dignity against the German aggression. Russia was a mighty industrial and military power. She could have easily won the war if not for the destructive activities of special secret forces which wanted to crush the Czar's regime from the inside. These secret forces understood that if Russia won the war, they would never achieve their goal. Thus, they did everything to prevent the victory. They sabotaged weapon and ammunition supplies to the front, disorganized the economy and transportation, and even provided the enemy with secret military information. Those inside enemies of Russia did not care about people's sufferings and the blood unnecessarily spilled. Their own selfish purposes were of a higher priority to them. One could expect that the author had the Bolsheviks in mind and be astonished by the fact that the censorship could approve such an "anti-Soviet" book for publication. But the author targeted his denunciations against Masons, whose very existence in Russia at that time is hardly a proven historical fact. According to Sergei Semanov, the Masons secretly ruled all "bourgeois" political parties which led Russia to defeat, overthrew the Czar, and took over power in February of 1917. Bolsheviks, in this interpretation, saved Russia by overthrowing Masons in October of that same year.

Semanov did not invent this new conception of World War I, however. He borrowed it from a book *August 1, 1914* by Nikolai Yakovlev,[7] which had come out in a mass edition a few years before and won a Lenin Komsomol (Young Communist League) Prize "for the patriotic upbringing of youth." Semanov quoted Yakovlev's most biting statements against the treasonous tactics of the "bourgeoisie run by Masons" and enriched the concept by adding that Masons, in their turn, were ruled by Zionists, who channeled their espionage information to the German military headquarters through "their stable connections with Germany."[8]

The new line of the *Life of Remarkable People* series was typical for all genres of literature as well as for journalism and humanities: Prose and poetry, historical novels and utopias, literary criticism and historical research, theater, movies, art, and other fields of culture.

In a totalitarian country, the party censorship, determined to nip in the bud the slightest digressions from the officially adopted line, controls the entire mass media. Thus, the reevaluation of all Russian historical concepts by individual scholars and writers was approved by the regime. A bitter joke started to circulate among Moscow intellectuals:

"Russia is a country with an unpredictable past."

CHAPTER 2

SOVIET SCIENCE—ZIONOLOGY: VLADIMIR BEGUN

Consequences of the Six-Day War

In June 1967, Israel badly beat the Arab allies of the USSR in the Six-Day War. The Soviet leadership, which granted the Arabs unlimited political and military support, shared the shame of that catastrophic defeat. Soviet advisers had trained Arab soldiers; Soviet generals had prepared the strategic blueprint for the war, and Arabs forces fought with Soviet arms. Although the Soviet officials never admitted their direct military involvement in the Middle East conflict, their one-sided position was too obvious.

Angry Soviet leaders broke diplomatic relations with Israel, and then—under pressure from Moscow—all the Warsaw Pact countries but Rumania followed suit. The Soviet press denounced the "Zionist aggression." But these malicious assaults against Israel did not wash with the public. The stereotypical image of the Jew as a small, helpless, and defenseless coward who could be insulted and beaten and would make no attempt to fight back no longer held sway. People saw the intense anti-Zionist propaganda as nothing more than helpless verbal revenge for the military defeat. The public reacted only with funny jokes, underscoring the Russian adage "Don't wave your fists after the fight."

However, as time went on, the campaign against Zionism did not show any signs of decline. Anti-Zionist books appeared in rapid succession. And after the 1973 Yom Kippur War, when Arabs were defeated again (but not as shamefully as in 1967), the flow of this literature turned into a deep, mighty river.

For years, I did not pay attention to those publications. Although this campaign might have contributed to anti-Semitic sentiments in the Soviet Union, I was sure that the main purpose was to harm Israel, and if so, all the attempts were senseless. Despite Soviet authorities claim that the Middle East was "in the close proximity to the Soviet border," these verbal attacks could hardly seriously damage Israel.

But when I started to examine some works on Zionism, I was shocked to discover few comments about the Jewish state. The target of these works was not Israel. I began to question with new insight the reasoning behind this campaign. "If the purpose is not to attack Israel and demonstrate solidarity with the Arabs," I asked myself, "then what is all this about?"

In search of answers, I decided to conduct a serious analysis of one of the "anti-Zionist" books, *The Invasion Without Arms* by Vladimir Begun.[1] My choice was not accidental. The book had enjoyed wide and favorable coverage in the press, and both the 1978 and 1979 editions had sold out in minutes. In spite of a quarter of a million copies in circulation, I could procure a copy for myself only on the black market—in exchange for a valuable bibliographical rarity.

The Terrible One

Vladimir Begun repeatedly declared in his book that his purpose was to expose Zionism. Such declarations leave little hope for objective treatment. However, the reader might reasonably expect that the author would at least be familiar with Zionist literature. Thus, while I could overlook the aggressive tone and the biased opinions in the book, I was unprepared for the author's nearly complete ignorance. He did not discuss the history of Zionism, the ideological and social pre-conditions of its origin, and its different trends. Begun relied almost *in toto* on a few works printed at the beginning of the 20th century. And he made almost all references to Russian publications—an indication that the author had no command of any foreign language.

Begun selected and interpreted quotations to create a specific impression. For example, he quoted and commented on the article *Nietzsche's Teaching and Judaism* by Ahad Ha-Am[*] (Asher Gintsberg), a Jewish writer and advocate of "spiritual Zionism" of the late 19th and early 20th centuries.

---

[*] *Ahad Ha-Am* (Hebrew) means "One of the people."

To understand why Begun chose this particular article, we should know that the works of German philosopher Friedrich Nietzsche (1844-1890) were never published in the USSR, but all textbooks portrayed him as a reactionary, anti-humanist thinker who had justified violence and built an ideological platform for nazism.

Ahad Ha-Am's works have not been published in Russia for many decades as well, and 99 percent of Begun's potential readers had never heard his name. Introducing him as an outstanding representative of Zionist thinking, Begun claimed that Ahad Ha-Am supported the essence of Nietzsche's teaching about a "superman," who, focused on achieving his goals, "steps over the dead bodies of the weak or even crushes them with his feet." According to Begun, Ahad Ha-Am complemented the idea of a "superman" by his own teaching of a Jewish "super-nation." This super-nation, like a superman, has a moral right and even obligation "to pursue its goal stamping upon other people's dead bodies and act regardless of everything and everybody to secure the dominance of 'the Chosen People' over the 'pagans.' Such a 'scholar' as Ahad Ha-Am," Begun explains to his readers, "reeks a mile off of a double-dyed fascism." (V. Begun, p. 43).

"Could it really be so?" I asked myself, and after many unsuccessful attempts, I was lucky to find the quoted article in a very rare two-volume 1919 edition of Ahad Ha-Am's *Selected Works*. Then it was not difficult to figure out that the author had addressed certain Jewish "followers of Nietzsche" whom he *opposed*. He asserted that if these followers had a correct understanding of Nietzsche, "they would find that the teaching of the ruler of their minds really comprises two different aspects, one being common to all mankind and the other being exclusively Aryan."[2] Ahad Ha-Am believed that the aspect common to all mankind in Nietzsche's teaching was the *idea* of a superman, an "elevation of a human type presented by a select breed of men and women over the general level of the herd." The "merely Aryan" aspect, according to Ahad Ha-Am, was Nietzsche's *ideal* of the superman *(die Blonde Bestia)*—"strong, handsome, ruling over everything, and acting of his own free will." Instead of the Aryan cult of physical strength and force, Ahad Ha-Am introduced the Judaic ideal of spiritual force, the ideal of a *righteous man*. The Jewish thinker accepted Nietzsche's thesis that a superman is allowed everything only on a certain condition. The superman himself should not allow anything immoral, baneful for other people, as from that moment he would stop being a *righteous man* and, consequently, a superman.[3]

In no way did Ahad Ha-Am call upon the Chosen People "to seek supremacy acting regardless of everything and everybody." Begun simply turned the ideas of the "exposed" author upside down, knowing that it was almost impossible to find the work he quoted. In any case, censored Soviet press would hardly publish an objection.

Begun devoted another "exposure" to Hayyim Nahman Bialik, one of the greatest Hebrew poets of this century. The poem *The Scroll of Fire* is one of his most significant works. It was brilliantly translated into Russian by Vladimir Zhabotinsky and never published after the revolution.[4] The main character of the poem, The Clear-Eyed Youth, feels drawn to the love of God and a woman. He goes through complicated spiritual trials, curses God and comes back to him, and thus acquires an oracular gift and becomes a preacher like the ancient Judaic prophets.

The poem reflects an agonizing search for "truth" and God by the poet himself. In particular, it reflects Bialik's negative attitude toward the Russian revolutionary movement. The poet viewed the revolution as a cause of "the possessed," of the "devil." Like all ideologists of Zionism, he believed that the participation of the Jewish youth in the Russian revolutionary movement was a tragic mistake. Zionists urged the Jews to accomplish their national task: The creation of their own state in Palestine. They viewed any active involvement in the political life of the countries of their Diaspora as an inadmissible waste of effort.

Begun ignored this concept of Bialik's poem, quoting only the "Song of the Terrible One" (the devil), which he took out of the context. The Terrible One sings about the "black fire" of the revolution that burns everything. He tries to seduce the Jewish youth to active participation. Begun claims that the song expressed the author's attempt to rouse his fellowers against the gentiles when in the context of the poem, the "Song" represented precisely what the poet emotionally and philosophically denied. Thus, here we see the same "methodology": Ideas of the quoted author are turned upside-down.

But the most striking feature of Begun's book lay in the total lack of any other quotations or references to Zionist writings or documents.

Declaring that "connection with Judaism" is "the most basic peculiarity of Zionism," Begun shifted his fire to a topic with which he felt more comfortable, if not more familiar.

"The Zionists are guided by the Judaic morality relying on the rule 'I may do to others what they must not do to me'," the book says (p. 48). Yet the author could hardly be ignorant of the famous wording of Rabbi Hillel, who lived nearly two thousand years ago. When asked by his student to articulate the essence of Judaism "while standing on one foot," he answered, *"Never do to others what you would not like to be done to you."*

To support his accusations against Judaism, Begun borrows from the Old Testament, though clearly he never held the Bible in his hands: His own text evidenced that. Quoting Solomon's parables, for example, he cited the numbers of the verses, but not the chapters from which he took them. He apparently had no idea that biblical books are divided into chapters.

Thus, Begun made use of second- or third-hand biblical quotations, not to mention Talmudic passages. He never revealed his true sources, but I did not find it difficult to identify them. They were the writings of the Black-Hundreds' ideologist Alexei Shmakov, whom Russian proto-Nazis had considered the highest authority on Judaism.

"The biblical instruction that supposedly all peoples, according to God's will, are to become slaves of the Jews," V. Begun wrote (p. 36) just paraphrasing Shmakov: "The Talmud tries to impress it on its followers that the Jews are the only rulers of the world."[5]

Here are two other quotations to compare:

V. Begun: "'The Holy Writ' elaborates to the minute detail the double morality regulating the attitude of an Israelite toward another Jew, on the one hand, and toward a goyim (a non-Jew), on the other. In the first case it proclaims certain humanistic principles (do not steal, do not kill, *etc.*), In the second case it is absolutely immoral and inhumane." (p. 34).	A. Shmakov: "The Talmudic laws for the inner life of Jewish communities come as the admonitions of an infinitely proud and loving mother. As to the attitude of the Jews toward non-Jews, the Talmud's prescriptions arise from the principle that non-Jews are beast-like pagans who challenged the 'divine' power of the Jews and the Jews must treat them with adequate strictness."[6]

Thus, Vladimir Begun only repeated in his book the interpretation of the Judaic morality which Black Hundred "scholars" had widely exploited at the beginning of this century to justify discrimination and violence against the Jews.[*]

There was a big irony in these borrowings.

---

[*] One can see a difference here as well. In Czarist Russia, with Orthodox Christianity as the official state religion, Shmakov could "denounce" the Talmud, but not the Bible (The Holy Writ'), as sacred both for the Jews and Christians. In Soviet atheistic Russia, Begun applied these "denunciations" to the Bible.

Bolsheviks considered the ideas of Alexei Shmakov and other Black Hundred ideologists especially harmful, and they took particular precautions to protect the public from them. Their works were not available even in the largest libraries. Those few copies which had not been destroyed after the revolution were stored in special divisions. Only some scholars who could prove that they needed this literature for their professional work could get permission to read it in special reading rooms. At the same time, however, officials authorized the circulation of a quarter of million copies of a book which promoted the same ideas!

"Popular Anger"

"The First International Anti-Semitic Congress opened on September 17, 1882, in one of the spacious pubs at Johannisstrasse," a Russian participant at this historic gathering reported from Germany. "Nearly all outstanding figures of Europe's anti-Semitic movement attended the Congress, with a North American representative also contributing. It was Mr. Smith, an American resident of Canada. ... Practically all major trends of current anti-Semitism were represented at the Congress, which accounts for the sharp polemics that took place there. The polemics were never conducted here along the lines we, the Russians, are used to because of a lame word uttered by someone or personal grudges. Instead, it was all about the essence of various social, moral, political, economic, and ideological problems that are coming to the fore in the anti-Semitic struggle."[7]

I adduce here this long quotation to demonstrate how those old times were naive and unsophisticated. After Hitler and the Holocaust, comparable language does not readily occur in the press. It cost six million Jewish lives to have the word "anti-Semitism" regarded as an obscenity. Today, few individuals openly acknowledge their anti-Semitic sentiments. That is why in analyzing Begun's book, I was in no hurry to call it anti-Semitic.

Some people are too quick to accuse. They fail to realize that a critical view of Zionism, Israeli policies, an individual Jew, or the Jewish national character at large is not the equivalent of an anti-Semitic stance. I believe that critics may even do the Jews a favor, for an unprejudiced word of truth is more valuable than a hypocritical adulation.

Anti-Semitism does not stem from any real criticism. It stems from a lie. It does not matter what is at issue: Zionism, Judaism, the state of Israel or some particular Jewish rascal.

All Begun's "exposures" were ill-meaning lies borrowed from his pre-Revolutionary predecessors, who never tried to conceal their anti-Semitism.

Meanwhile, Begun conveyed his own interpretation of anti-Semitism in the chapter titled *The Tears That Should Not Be Trusted*. Referring to such events as the Jewish pogroms in Czarist Russia, he suggested in every case to figure out first *"which* Jews were subjected to persecution—rich or beggary, money-lenders and merchants or semi-literate artisans and rags sellers?" (p. 63)

Using Marxist ideology, as he understood it, Begun explained that "if popular anger had swept Jewish money-lenders, pot-house keepers, factory owners, merchants, and other exploiters, the reason was not in ethnic but in class antagonism." And what if the "popular anger" swept the poor? Begun offered a "Marxist" interpretation for that as well. Jewish pogroms "were directed by the ruling class—by the bourgeoisie, landlords, and the police," so it was a class struggle again. (p. 63).

As a result, Begun completely eliminated anti-Semitism from Russian and world history. According to him, prejudice against the Jews never existed. Jews are artificially inventing stories about discrimination and harassment to win sympathy. They "are spreading ingenious old-wives tales about their sufferings" that "now and again provide for the desired effect on people inexperienced in politics" (p. 63).

During the years of the Civil War in Russia (1918-1921), Jewish pogroms reached incredible proportions. "The total number of those killed in pogroms can in no way be estimated at less than 200 thousand people," wrote Sergei Gusev-Orenburgsky, a Russian Orthodox priest who personally witnessed many pogroms and later conducted an extensive research in this subject.[8] Estimates of other scholars are close to his figures, which means that out of the two million Jews residing in Russia at that time, every tenth was killed, not to mention the injured, crippled, and orphaned. This was nothing short of genocide, though not as well-organized as the sweeping exterminations of the Third Reich. As we know from the previous chapter, when the Civil War came to an end, Bolshevik authorities—preoccupied with their "internationalist" ideas—tried to combat anti-Semitism as a counter-revolutionary and "bourgeois" ideology. Begun in his book, adopted by the Communist censorship, denounced that policy. According to him, since the Jews "had acquired the widest access to science ... to all fields of social life as well as to state management" in 1920s, anti-Semitism ceased to exist. "Nevertheless, the campaign against the non-existent anti-Semitism was very much in evidence in the press of that time. Books, booklets, and articles were being written against outlawed and actually non-existent anti-Semitism, while really existing Zionism was being spoken of rarely and in a most obscure manner" (p. 68).

Having turned himself to the contemporary situation, Begun warned his readers that "Zionists had concentrated their efforts on corrupting socialism from within" (p. 56), "Zionists seek to sow on the sly poisonous seed and decay" (p. 57), "Zionist agents always count on a coup from above, ... their primary purpose is to deliver a blow to the Marxist-Leninist ideology, to paralyze the work of ideological institutions, to take over leading posts in the party and government, the institutions of culture, etc." (p. 103).

Zionists "corrupting socialism from within" by no means could be the foreign Jews who could come to the Soviet Union as tourists, journalists, or diplomats. It would be impossible for them to "take over the leading posts." Thus, Begun pointed his finger to the Soviet Jews, "denouncing" them as henchmen of enemy centers seeking to overthrow the Soviet regime and establish a rule of their own. He also looked into the forthcoming future, predicting: "We shall make no mistake if we look for and find the presence of Zionists behind any imperialistic institution when it is out to launch its regular anti-Communist or anti-Soviet attack" (p. 134).

Thus, the author postulated in advance the presence of "Zionists" in every future activity that might be interpreted as aimed against the Soviet Union or socialism. Should there be no Jew in sight, Begun had at his service "two thousand Masonic lodges in 42 countries."

In 1985, Mikhail Gorbachev became General Secretary of the Communist Party and started the policy of *glasnost* and *perestroika*, which mean *openness* and *economic reforms*. His initial goal was to make socialism more efficient. But, as could be predicted, the process went out of control and resulted in the total collapse of both socialism and the Soviet empire.[*] That gave right-wing Russian nationalists a reason to interpret Gorbachev's *perestroika* as a "coup from above" master-minded by Masons and Zionists. Thus, Vladimir Begun turned out to be a prophet. The truth, however, is that he had borrowed this "prophecy" from unnamed predecessors as well. I have culled fragments from two documents as proof. One of them is an appeal of French "patriots" to their Russian colleagues in the first decade of this century:

---

[*] We will discuss these events in further chapters.

Zionology: Vladimir Begun

"Revolutionaries are controlled by Free-Masons and Jews." "Free-Masons and Jews never changed their methods. They would like to make use in Russia of the means that were such a success in France in the late 18th century.* Since the Russians, fortunately, have preserved in their country the fatherly rule of their Czars, we adjure them to make every sacrifice to protect it from the Jewish lust for power and Freemasonry intrigues." "Only under the Czar's orb will the Russian people be able to protect their Christian faith and Russian land from foreign claims!" "Down with Free-Masons, down with the Jews! Long live Russia! Long Live the Czar!"** [9]

Another fragment is from a work by the untiring Alexei Shmakov:

"Judaic policy comprises a chess game of the kahal with governments and nations. Freemasonry is the principal tool of the Jews in this respect, it also supervises their spies. ... Freemasonry's primary task is to destroy thrones and altars. With this purpose in mind, the Masons along with the Jews are seeking to penetrate into state police and higher government bodies."[10]

These are only two examples out of thousands, which are easy to find in pre-Revolutionary Black Hundred publications. To Begun's credit, he skillfully manipulated their ideas and language. If Shmakov and other Black-Hundreders tried to "protect" the *thrones and altars* from the revolution masterminded by the Jews and Masons, then Begun protected the *Revolutionary Communist regime* from the counter-revolution masterminded by Zionists and Masons.

Attempts to oppose

Begun's book would hardly be mentioned, much less studied, if it had been just an isolated publication. But it was a mainstream work, widely lauded as the greatest achievement of Soviet "Zionology." Dozens of reviews echoed his ideas in major periodicals. One of them, written by M. Avakov, Professor and Doctor of Law, appeared in *Chelovek i Zakon* (Man and Law) monthly magazine.[11] It attracted my special attention, partly because it was a popular publication with a circulation of more than a million copies and partly because Sergei Semanov, my former boss, was the editor-in-chief. (He had gotten this

---

* Feference to the Great French Revolution

** Three decades later, spiritual heirs of those French "patriots" betrayed their country to Hitler.

big promotion* soon after I had to quit my job for the *Lives of Remarkable People* series.)

Upon completion of my 35-page analysis of both the Begun book and Avakov's review, I pondered where to get it published. I had already tried to critique some other anti-Semitic and chauvinistic works, sending my articles to the most liberal publications, like *Novy Mir* or *Literaturnaya Gazeta,* and knew that applying to them would be useless. After considering different publications, an unexpected idea came to my mind. I decided to mail this article to *Kommunist* (The Communist), the principal journal of the Communist Party Central Committee. After all, who should defend the principles of internationalism and brotherhood between nationalities, if not the official Party publication?

A month later I was invited to the editorial office to meet Vyacheslav Kuzmenko, the head of the journal's bibliographic division. A gray-haired man with intelligent blue eyes looking through eyeglasses spoke with noticeable sadness in his voice. He expressed sympathy to my article, but admitted that it would hardly be possible to publish it. I answered that it was necessary to start doing something against growing nazism.

"The so-called exposure of Zionism has nothing to do with real Zionism," I argued. "The purpose of all these works is to provoke hatred against Soviet Jews."

"It may be so," Kuzmenko said, neither agreeing nor objecting, "but it is pointless to submit your article as it is to the editorial board. It would be rejected anyway. I wish we could support it with some authoritative review..."

I was astonished at what he said. I had presumed that my whole venture was absolutely hopeless. All my friends were of the same opinion. They were perplexed that I spent my time and effort on such quixotic escapades, and I myself had no rational explanation of these activities. I felt that I just had to express myself. And here was a party official who took it all in earnest and really wanted to help.

After the encouraging talk with Kuzmenko, I called Bonifaty Kedrov, a member of the Academy of Sciences who had the reputation of a liberal philosopher, but was at the same time very influential. I had had several contacts with him before on different occasions. About ten years earlier he had been one of the scientists who had helped to rescue my anti-Stalinist book about Nikolai Vavilov from being shredded.

---

* In the Soviet publishing industry hierarchy, the position of an editor-in-chief of a major magazine was two or three steps higher than the position of an editor-in-chief of a book series.

But, at this time, hardly had I explained what was at issue when he changed the subject and started speaking of upcoming conferences and reports, implying that he would not be involved.

After several other similar attempts, I called Kuzmenko to bring him up to date.

"All right, I'll think myself what can be done," he answered.

Another month passed before he invited me again to his editorial office. He looked somber. "I forwarded your article to the Institute of Marxism-Leninism," he said. "Here is their reply. You may read it."

The reply was authored by M. Kulichenko, head of the section on the theory of nationalities and ethnic relations. Kulichenko noted that his section had given a go-ahead to Begun's book, which obviously meant that he would do everything to have my article buried.[12]

Kulichenko mentioned with annoyance that he had to respond to many letters of protest. But all letters, articles, or complaints were destined to lie hidden forever in a maze of offices and departments, and that was the fate of my article.

In the Light of Glasnost

Not until May 1987, nine years after the publication of Begun's book and two years after the initiation of *glasnost*, did critical articles on Russian chauvinism and anti-Semitism begin to appear in the Soviet press. It was not an accident that at precisely that time Alexander Yakovlev was promoted to a full Politburo member. The Central Committee had forced him from its ranks in 1972 for criticizing the chauvinists, and he had subsequently spent the next 10 years as ambassador to Canada. Yuri Andropov, who had become General Secretary after Brezhnev, summoned Yakovlev back to Moscow but kept him away from the party apparatus. Only after Gorbachev took office, did Yakovlev return to his former position in the Central Committee, and then he quickly scaled the party ranks to become the architect of *glasnost*.

The attacks in the liberal press were directed against the *Pamyat* society, the first anti-Semitic and chauvinistic organization which called itself a "historical-patriotic society." But hard-line party authorities, the KGB, and most local officials patronized *Pamyat*, thus the society continued to carry on its activities with its former zeal.

In June 1987, *Sovetskaya Kultura* (The Soviet Culture) newspaper published an article citing Vladimir Begun and two other well-known *zionologists*, Yevgeny Yevseev and Alexander Romanenko, as *Pamyat* lecturers. All three regarded this accusation as an insult. They denied their involvement with *Pamyat* and took the newspaper to court.

During the trial, Vladimir Begun stated that since the notice in *Sovetskaya Kultura* he had become a victim of physical and moral terror. He could hardly fight off the hooligans trying to force their way into his apartment at night and repeatedly had to appeal to his local police station for assistance. He claimed that all this harassment was the result of the newspaper "libel." In response, the editorial board submitted a document from Begun's local police department showing that he had never lodged any complaint,[13] adding one more unsavory detail to Begun's profile.

Experts testified at the hearing that Begun's works borrowed from Hitler's *Mein Kampf*, a choice that the author found laughable.

I believe, it is likely that Begun had never seen *Mein Kampf*, just as he had never seen the Bible. The coincidence has an easy explanation. Alexei Shmakov, from whom Begun extensively borrowed his ideas and partly his language, used the same German sources as Hitler and other Nazi ideologists. Some of them were directly influenced by their Russian predecessors. Indeed, Alfred Rosenberg, who had a great influence on Fuehrer in the early stages of the National-Socialist movement, had emigrated from Russia where he had been educated by the Black Hundred.

The court's decision was ambivalent. On the one hand, it threw out Begun's suit. But, on the other hand, it tried to play down public influence of Begun's activities, concluding that "not a single expert-historian had written a positive review on his works."[14] It simply was not true. Vladimir Begun had built his entire academic career "exposing" Zionism. He successfully defended his thesis, received a Ph. degree in philosophy, and obtained a position as a senior scholar at the Institute of Philosophy and Law of the Belorussian Academy of Sciences. His books were printed and reprinted in mass editions, enjoyed wide publicity and backing from many officials and influential scholars, including those from the Marxism-Leninism Institute of the Communist Party Central Committee, as we have seen.

Ignoring these facts, the court did not want to face the reality. It pretended that such people as Vladimir Begun were lonely lunatics, thus the illness of anti-Semitism and Nazism was their personal problem—not the problem of society at large. Thus, while Vladimir Begun suffered a significant setback, he turned out the winner—if not in the short, then in the long run.

The first sign of his victory appeared very soon, on the pages of *Nash Sovremennik*, a national monthly journal, a front-runner among ultra-nationalistic periodicals. It printed an angry letter by a covey of scholars from

Zionology: Vladimir Begun

Minsk, Begun's home city. They denounced the court ruling as "Zionist" and insisted that their colleague Vladimir Begun was a highly competent scholar and a true Marxist.

New offensive of Nazi forces began. Vladimir Begun could not lead them very long. Two years later, he died "keeping watch." However, his cause did not die with him. There were more than enough people around to pick up his Brown banner and carry it farther. It was brightly lit in an obituary notice, written by his comrade-in-arms Alexander Romanenko.

"On June 19, 1989, Vladimir Begun, a research-scholar and uncompromising critic of Zionism, died of a heart attack. In fact, he was killed by the most dangerous Zionist weapon... a special tool of terror. The assassins escape all formal, bureaucratic, and legal responsibilities for their deed.... This dedicated Communist, infinitely loyal to the cause of the Great October,* to Leninism, to our Soviet motherland, was accused by these foul slanderers of 'notorious anti-Semitism.' The murderers accuse of 'anti-Semitism' anyone who is fighting against the most dangerous variety of fascism, i.e., Zionism. The murderers badly hurt the Soviet patriot Vladimir Begun by the poison of libel. They acted and continue to act according to the scenario of the counter-revolutionary forces. They seek to overthrow Soviet power and restore a bourgeois society (i.e., Zionist domination), for a bourgeois society today is nothing else but the omnipresent fascist rule of Zion! Let the memory of Vladimir Begun, the all-nation hero of anti-fascist, anti-Zionist resistance, live forever among the people. Let us hold rallies, gatherings to commemorate the hero of the anti-fascist, anti-Zionist resistance. Thousands must replace the killed fighter. Motherland is in danger!
        A. Romanenko,
        a participant of the Great Patriotic war,
        warrior-internationalist."[15]

The next chapter is about the author of this obituary.

---

* The October Revolution.

CHAPTER 3

ZIONOLOGIST ALEXANDER ROMANENKO

Zionology: Preliminary results

Alexander Romanenko's book *On the Class Essence of Zionism* published in 1986, had a runoff of 50 thousand copies, a modest distribution for a work of this kind.[1] Many other books had a much wider circulation and a greater impact on the society.[2] A group of Leningrad *refuseniks*[*] estimated that 230 books "exposing" the Zionist-Masonic conspiracy against Russia and the entire world were published in the Soviet Union between 1969 and 1985. Their total circulation was 9.4 million copies.[3] In addition, according to Moscow's ethnographers, between 1981 and 1986 alone the Soviet press carried 48.5 thousand different articles inciting hatred against the Jews.[4]

This "patriotic" propaganda emphasized Russian national values and traditions, subtly encouraging chauvinism and its inherent xenophobia to everything foreign, western, or simply different. Anti-Zionism provided a direct and aggressive foundation for the ideological offensive.

Two reasons induced me to single out Romanenko's book for our examination. First, it came at a time when Gorbachev's policy of *glasnost* and *perestroika* was in full swing, but the Communist Party had not yet lost its control over the press. Thus, the book was in line with the new government policy, promoted as a liberal *new thinking*. In addition, it was *a Historiographic Sur-*

---

[*]*Refusenik* is a literal translation of the Russian word *otkaznik*, created from *otkaz*—*refuse*. The sobriquet referred to those Jews who applied for emigration, but their appeals were refused.

vey of Literature, as the subtitle outlined. Thus, the volume was an observation of works on Zionism written in the Soviet Union.

The book contains four chapters of unequaled content and size. The first chapter deals with the pre-Revolutionary period. It might have been informative had the author studied the works of Zionist thinkers and their opponents of that time. But Romanenko did not. The 35-page chapter devotes a quarter of its space to works by Marx and Engels, in whose time there was no Zionism as such. The remaining three quarters of the chapter review Lenin's polemics against *Bund* (the Jewish Social-Democratic Party).

All textbooks of the History of the Communist Party of the USSR analyzed these polemics, in which Vladimir Lenin outlined the main principles of "the party of a new type" he intended to build. Lenin believed that the revolutionary party should be centralized, hierarchical, and bound with strict party discipline. All party units should work as military detachments. All decisions of the party leadership should be obligatory for all its members. If someone disagrees with a certain decision or is not quick to fulfill it, he should be immediately expelled from the party ranks. Less extreme leaders of Russian social-democracy wanted to build a party on a more democratic base, but Lenin and his supporters (the Bolsheviks) attacked them zealously.

Jewish socialists united in *Bund* wanted to join the Russian Social-Democratic Party but to preserve their autonomy within its ranks. They argued that Jewish workers in such an anti-Semitic country as Czarist Russia had their specific interests, which *Bund* should represent.

Since any kind of autonomy within the party was not compatible with Lenin's vision, he sharply denounced Bund's "bourgeois nationalism and opportunism." This is an interesting subject to study, but has nothing to do with Zionism.

In the second chapter of Romanenko's book, the author presents a survey of Soviet literature on Zionism from October 1917, to the mid-1930s—in just seven pages. Much of this brief compendium focuses on a critique of the article *Jews* in the first edition of the *Big Soviet Encyclopedia*. The author himself calls attention to the chapter's brevity with the observation that during the period under consideration "literature about Zionism was scanty in this country."

Equally scanty was, should we take the author's word for it, the literature about Zionism in the period between the mid-1930s and the late 1960s. The survey in the book's third chapter also takes up only seven pages, with a considerable portion devoted to an article on the 17th century developments in the Ukraine. This examination of the relationship between the Ukrainians and the Jews under Polish domination has nothing to do with Zionism either. Meanwhile, the period under consideration in the chapter does include Stalin's notorious campaign against "cosmopolitans without kith or kin." The crusade gave birth to thousands of publications in Soviet newspapers and magazines at least partly related to Zionism. But this vast array of literature remained beyond the historiographer's vision, and for good reason. Stalin's anti-Zionist and anti-Cosmopolitan campaign was compromised as an anti-Semitic slur. Thus, Romanenko had to condemn this campaign or to expose himself as a dedicated Stalinist and anti-Semite. He preferred to pretend that all this literature had never existed.

The picture changes drastically, however, in chapter four (the *Reactionary Essence of Zionism from the Late 1960s up to Now*). This chapter takes up nearly 200 pages. The author is literally bogged down in the overabundance of material. At his disposal were hundreds of major and minor works ranging from bulky volumes to skimpy lengthy prestigious "academic" collected works to a variety of periodicals including purely academic journals like *Voprosy Istorii* (Questions of History) and mass journals like *Chelovek i Zakon* (Man and Law), as well as such peculiar publications as *Agitator Armii i Flota* (Agitator of the Army and the Navy) and *Kommunist Vooruzhennykh Sil* (Communist of the Armed Forces), that provided material for the political education of Soviet servicemen.[5]

The quantitative explosion of anti-Zionist publications since the late 1960s speaks volumes, exceeded only by the obvious qualitative gains of Soviet "Zionology." Soviet "scholars" promulgated that everything the Zionists wrote or said about the aims, methods, and membership of their movement was a well-thought-out lie covering absolutely different aims and actions. This radical contention inevitably spanned a number of conclusions that evolved without benefit of due process into basic tenets.

Goals of Zionism. Usually Zionists proclaim that their goal is to create and strengthen the Jewish state on the historical motherland of the Jews. However, Zionologists "ascertained" that the creation of a Jewish state is only an intermediate link, a means for achieving a far more important goal—establishing the world supremacy of the Jewish "bourgeoisie" and the subjugation and enslaving of all non-Jews.

Origin of Zionism. Zionists assert that Zionism emerged in the milieu of the Jewish intelligentsia in the late 19th century as a response to anti-Semitism. Zionologists came to the opposite conclusion, that the drive of the Jews for world supremacy—i.e., Zionism—had emerged in the ancient time, when Jewish tribes had conquered Palestine.

Network of world Zionist organizations. Zionists have created an extensive network of religious, philanthropic, women's, youth, and other organizations. They are regarded as independent of one another. According to Zionologists, however, all this is camouflage. In reality, the Soviet authors claim, all these organizations work under a single control and are well-knit by secret discipline. Their activities are masterminded from a single center through secret channels.

Zionism and Judaism. Zionologists pay special attention to the Jewish religion, which, according to them, serves as the ideological basis for Zionism. Marxism regards all religions as "reactionary" because they preach humility and resignation to one's fate. By promising happiness in the next world, they paralyze the drive for happiness on Earth and distract the laboring masses from the struggle for their rights. That is how Soviet experts on "scientific atheism" traditionally described all religions, including Judaism. However, in keeping with the discoveries of Zionologists, Judaism's poison stems from other roots. The Jewish ethic, they say, does not demand obedience and resignation to one's fate at all. It requires all Jews to support each other in their drive to domination over all other nations. On the contrary, Zionologists maintain, aggressiveness and hatred for all non-Jews permeate the Jewish outlook. Judaism, they say, attests that non-Jews are working cattle to serve the Jews.

Zionism and Free-Masonry. In order to deceive the non-Jewish world with greater success, the theory says, Zionists prefer to act whenever possible not through Jews but through obedient representatives of these very peoples whom they intend to enslave. Free-Masonry serves this purpose. Some Jewish organizations, such as B'nai-B'rith (the Sons of the Testament), are simultaneously Masonic lodges. They control other Masonic lodges that are non-Jewish. Because of the strict secrecy and discipline that oblige the lower-ranking brothers to blindly obey the orders of the higher-ranking ones, Masons themselves often do not suspect that they work against their own peoples for the benefit of Zionist enslavers.

Enslavement of Western countries. Soviet scholars contend that Zionists have already enslaved the entire Western world, especially the United States, although most Americans are completely unaware of that. As proof, they cite that Zionists dominate all important spheres of Western life. Soviet authors suggest that Zionist control from 40 to 80 percent of Western capital. Valery Yemelianov insisted that this figure was as high as 95 percent. A parallel thesis concentrates 95 percent of Western mass media in the hands of Zionists. Zionists decisively influence the policy-making of the United States and other Western countries. The outcome of presidential and parliamentary elections depends on Zionists. Their henchmen fill key posts.

Zionism in socialist countries. Following the Zionologists' line of thought, since Zionism already established its control over the West, its next target logically extends to socialist countries. Pursuing their sophisticated tactics, Zionists joined Communist parties and, secretly assisting each another, they pushed their cadres to the highest positions in the bodies of central and local governments, in the mass media, in science, culture, and most other important spheres of life. At the first opportunity they carry out a coup and tear a state away from the socialist community. Soviet authors ascribe Zionist intrigue to the anti-Soviet and anti-Socialist events in Hungary and Poland in 1956, in Czechoslovakia in 1968, and in Poland again in 1980-81. According to this theory, the dramatic changes in Eastern Europe and the dismantling of the USSR constituted nothing less than a successful Zionist plot.

Zionism and Russian revolution. Zionologists developed their own vision of the Russian revolution. In pre-Revolutionary Russia, they claim, Zionists and Masons wormed their way into the leadership of all "bourgeois" and "petty bourgeois" parties* and acted in keeping with a single plan. Differences between the parties were a sham, merely camouflage. They acted jointly against Russia and her traditional way of life. They overthrew the Czar's regime, took control, and shaped the Provisional Government. Fortunately for Russia, Lenin saw through this perfidious plan. The Bolsheviks arrested the Provisional Government and thus saved Russia from enslavement by the Zionists. Yet, after the October revolution, the Zionists continued their struggle against Russia. For this purpose, they penetrated the Communist Party leadership to undermine its unity and ruin the Soviet regime. The crushing of the Trotskyites and all other opposition groups disrupted these crafty designs.

Zionism and anti-Semitism. Although Zionists frequently accuse their opponents of anti-Semitism, the notion of anti-Semitism is not scientific. What Zionists describe as anti-Semitism is the class struggle. When the working people smashed up rich Jews, it was the struggle of the exploited against the exploiters; when the Black Hundreds staged pogroms of poor Jews, it was the struggle of the exploiters against the exploited.

Class approach. Zionologists occasionally point out that Zionists are enemies of all working people, including working Jews. However, they immediately emphasize that the Jewish working class has always been very small,

---

* According to Marxism-Leninism, any political party represents interests of a certain social class. Since they claimed that only the Bolsheviks represented the working class, they called all other parties, including the social-democratic, bourgeois or petty-bourgeois.

accounting for an insignificant percentage. Even this percentage was closely connected with the Jewish bourgeoisie and served as an obedient tool in its hands.

Scale

I will not insist that I have exhausted all major "discoveries" of Zionology, but those mentioned will suffice to show that the numerous books and articles revived the myth of the Judo-Masonic plot persistently cultivated before the revolution by the Russian Black Hundreds and carried further by Hitler's propaganda. Thus, it becomes understandable why Romanenko, as well as Begun and other Zionologists, hush up their pre-Revolutionary predecessors' works officially outlawed in the Soviet Union. By sidestepping these sources, Romanenko impoverishes his work, especially its first chapter.

However, the last chapter of his book, while overflowing with material, does not even mention many significant works, for instance, the many books and articles of Lev Korneev, one of the most active Zionologists.

After Leningrad scholar Ivan Martynov had read and analyzed some of them, he mailed a letter to the *Highest Certifying Commission*. This special body reviews all dissertations and gives the final approval to confer the scientific degree of Candidate or Doctor of Science[*]. Martynov denounced Korneev's works as anti-Semitic falsifications and demanded they revoke Lev Korneev's scientific degree. After the Commission ignored his demand, Martynov renounced his own Candidate of Science standing. He did not deem it possible, he wrote to the Commission, to hold the same academic degree as a falsifier and anti-Semite. Persecution by the KGB eventually forced Ivan Martynov (who was not Jewish) to emigrate to Israel, while Lev Korneev continued to promote Soviet Zionology.

Since Romanenko never mentions any of Korneev's works as well as many others, his book does not give an adequate picture of the scale of the anti-Semitic propaganda launched in the Soviet Union in Brezhnev's period. Now, this epoch is described as "stagnation." However, there was no stagnation in the field of "dismasking" Zionism!

---

[*] The degree of Candidate of Science is the approximate equivalent of the Ph D. in the United States, although it is much more difficult to get because of numerous formalities. The degree of Doctor of Science is much higher and only Candidates of Science may apply for it.

Warrior-internationalist *

When I analyzed Alexander Romanenko's book, I had no information on the author himself. In publishing his survey, Romanenko seemed to have fulfilled his task to the best of his ability, with nothing more expected of him. Yet, Romanenko himself did not hold that opinion. In the years of *glasnost,* he increased his activities to such an extent that he soon came forward as the leader of Soviet Zionology, leaving behind such notorious "scholars" as Vladimir Begun, Yevgeny Yevseev, and Lev Korneev.

Romanenko became indispensable at *Pamyat* rallies geared toward saving Russia from the Jewish-Masonic conspiracy. His book served as an eye-opener on the essence of Zionism for the historical-patriotic society. At a 1986 Leningrad rally, key speaker Muscovite Dmitry Vasiliev praised and thanked Romanenko for authoring the best book on Zionism.[6]

Subsequently, Romanenko started to participate frequently in Moscow rallies.

Thus, he was a key speaker at a notable meeting commemorating Alexander Kosarev, a Komsomol (Young Communist League) leader repressed by Stalin in the late 1930s. The emotional gathering took place on November 19, 1988, at the Youth House in Moscow. It was organized by the *Kosarev Club* and included one-time Komsomol members as well as Kosarev's relatives. It was difficult to believe that this rally could be related to Zionism or Russian chauvinism. It turned out, however, that the *Kosarev Club* was just another name for *Pamyat,* whose members occupied most of the seats in the audience. Alexander Romanenko, who acted as the key speaker, turned the memorial event into an anti-Semitic inquisition.[7]

The scandalous witch-hunt caught the attention of the press. According to the newspaper *Sovetskaya Kultura,* the delighted audience burst into applause at Romanenko's arrival and avidly followed his speech despite its disjointedness. "Evidently, they were like-minded people who could catch the meaning at once," the newspaper reported. With shouts of encouragement from the audience, Romanenko accused Zionists of the destruction of the environment and historical monuments. He denounced the horrors of a lawless past which victimized Kosarev and, exonerating Stalin, he blamed Kaganovich, Rappoport,

---

*During the war in Afghanistan, official Soviet propaganda claimed that Soviet troops in Afghanistan fulfilled their "international duty" by helping the Afghan people to save socialism. Accordingly, Soviet troopers who had served in Afghanistan were called warriors-internationalists; this title would also apply to the Soviet participants of the Korean and other Third World wars.

Shvartsman*, and other high-ranking officials of Jewish origin. Stalin, he theorized, had come under their influence and simply danced to their tune. "The audience broke out applauding," reported *Sovetskaya Kultura*, "and again it was not clear what this man, coming out recently as Stalin's zealous supporter and voluntary advocate, has to do with Alexander Kosarev, shot by Stalin's orders."[8]

Romanenko found some inaccuracy in the newspaper report and filed suit against the *Sovetskaya Kultura* to defend his "honor and dignity." The newspaper printed a humorous account of this trial in the form of an *Explanatory Note* by its photographer:

"I cannot go again to the trial at the Sverdlovsky district court and take pictures for the newspaper because a day earlier I attended this trial and only by a miracle did I manage to preserve intact the photo-equipment I was entrusted with. The hand by which I kept covering my *Nikon* hurts immensely.... In the courtroom many 'patriots' voiced their calls, such as 'Stop taking pictures!', 'Spoil his film!', 'The Kike's newspaper!' ... The plaintiff was giving rude answers even after the judge repeatedly rebuked him. The audience gave stormy approval to Romanenko's every remark.

During the intermission, several 'activists' with goggle eyes caught hold of me, trying to snatch the camera out of my hands. Somebody shouted: 'Destroy the film, or else we shall break your camera!' Fortunately, there were several young 'non-patriots' in the room who encircled me and took me out of the building.... It is clear that these 'fighters against Zionism' make use of any pretext to give vent to their emotions, which are not peaceful at all.... I ask to relieve me of such missions until they become safe. I am not afraid for myself but for my *Nikon*. Out of two of us, the camera is non-Russian..."[9]

I came across an unpublished account of a Leningrad exhibition held by the *Society for the Encouragement of Artists,* one of many informal organizations that emerged thanks to *glasnost*. The public devoted its attention to the work of painter Igor Borodin.[10] The ideological message of his works impressed the viewers far more than his artistic talents. The author of the article quoted several entries in the visitors' book which are very impressive.

---

* Lazar Kaganovich was the only Jewish Politburo member in Stalin's times, so modern anti-Semites claim that he orchestrated all Stalin's purges and other crimes. Rappoport and Shvartsman were secondary figures of the security bodies and could act only under orders from above.

"Igor Borodin's paintings are needed very much and are well-timed, too," wrote two soldiers on behalf of their entire detachment in the visitor's book. "... It is high time to tell the truth about Jewish fascism in the Soviet Union."[11] "Igor Borodin's works cannot fail to evoke a response in every Russian soul," noted another visitor, who did not sign his name. "They point to the main danger facing our Fatherland—the network of Yid-Masons. Hold your ground, Igor! All the patriots are with you." "The painter-patriot has exposed Satan's secret service by his works. We shall try to bring up our children to fight against the genocide of the Russian people and to respond to Zionists in the same manner."[12]

Although such "patriotic" sentiments prevailed, the visitors' book expressed other attitudes as well. "Igor Borodin's works are a model distortion of historical facts, a breach of elementary human ethics, a direct propaganda of pan-Orthodoxy and the ideas of the Union of Archangel Mikhail[*] ... I believe that Igor Borodin's works are nothing else but an infamy and shame for Holy Russia."[13] But this "anti-patriotic" attack was resolutely rebuffed as "malicious slander," and not by some anonymous visitor, but by Alexander Romanenko himself. "We hear the sound of approval in these wild shouts of animosity!" he stated.[14]

Romanenko led the foremost Leningrad "patriots" in a discussion which took place in an overcrowded conference room of the exhibition hall. In his lengthy speech, he paid special attention to Borodin's painting on a Biblical subject under the title *A Warning*.^{**}

"Igor Borodin threw light on one of the ancient Judaic reactionary legends about Judith in his most convincing, well-grounded, courageous, and ideologically correct manner," Romanenko said. "In the appraisal of our Soviet scholars, Zionism presents dogmas of Judaism in a politicized form.... Judaism has been carrying through centuries this reactionary idea that proved to be quite acceptable to modern Zionism. The idea that the Israelites must rule over the non-Israelites lies at the heart of the Zionist conception nowadays."[15]

---

[*] The *Union of Archangel Michael* was one of the major Black Hundreds organization, detached itself from the *Union of the Russian People* in 1908. The head of the *Union*, Vladimir Purishkevich, was a prominent right-wing deputy of the State Duma.

^{**} See more about this and other Borodin's works in chapter 8 (pp.147-148).

58   Chapter 3

   As Romanenko spoke, passions in the conference room ran increasingly high. Shouts of protest and support accompanied his words. However, advocates of the speaker and the artist dominated. Finally, the discussion disintegrated into a major brawl that ran along the lines of a classic Nazi gathering.

> "I saw a young guy who, taking no notice of the passions around him, was calmly clicking his camera," reported M. Glikman, the author of the quoted account. "I was not the only one who saw him. Riverov* was the first to stand up: 'Young man, I demand that you stop taking photos and expose the film!' Then came Romanenko's voice: 'On behalf of the army veterans, I demand that you destroy the film!' At the same moment, young and tough 'connoisseurs of art' jumped up in different sides of the room and, shouting 'Destroy the film,' rushed at the man with the camera. I saw that there would be no further talk about the arts and moved to rescue him. When I managed to squeeze my way through to him, I said, 'Come on!' He understood me at once. The camera was in my hands now. I dashed toward the exit past very strong hands. In the corridor, another group of 'connoisseurs' in military boots was twisting the arms of [my friend] Misha Kazakov in an attempt to seize his bag with a tape recorder. While running, I snatched the bag from his hands and rushed downstairs."[16]

Romanenko versus Katerli

   Both the meeting organized to commemorate Alexander Kosarev and the exchange of opinions about Borodin's paintings were dramatic but limited events on Romanenko's agenda. However, his other activities showed that he was equally fit for marathon races, such as the suit of "protection of honor and dignity" he brought against Leningrad writer Nina Katerli to counteract his failure in two suits against the newspaper *Sovetskaya Kultura*.[17]

   In October 1988, Nina Katerli published an article in the daily *Leningradskaya Pravda* (Leningrad Truth) in which she pointed out that Romanenko in his book "had no scruples about falsifying quotations from Marxism-Leninism classic works or appallingly distorting the truth or using the ideas and nearly exact excerpts taken without quotation marks from Nazi theoreticians."[18]

   Responding to Romanenko's petition, the Dzerzhinsky district court of Leningrad set up a commission of three independent experts who arrived at a single conclusion about "the obvious resemblance of certain assertions in the

---

* Leader of Leningrad division of the *Pamyat'* organization.

[Romanenko's] book to propositions found in Nazi literature," especially to "speculations of Nazi theoreticians about the Jewish-Masonic conspiracy against mankind."[19]

Yet, after the court declined his suit, the warrior-internationalist did not lay down his arms. He brought in an appeal, which resulted in the setting up of another commission of experts, and the cycle repeated itself. By October 1989, when I was in Leningrad, the district and city courts had held three sittings each to which Romanenko had brought along a crowd of thugs from *Pamyat* and *Patrioty* (Patriots), an organization he had created himself. They had turned every sitting into an uncontrolled anti-Semitic rally, putting the judges in an uncomfortable situation. They had to keep in mind that Romanenko's book "was published by *Lenizdat,* the official Communist Party Central Committee and the Leningrad Regional Party Committee Publisher" as the author had clearly stated in his petition.[20]

Rejecting the appeal implied that the Communist Party approved and supported Nazi-like publications. Since the judges were party members themselves, the safest course of action was for them to delay, postpone, and move the case from one court to another—a tactic they accomplished rather skillfully. Meanwhile, Nina Katerli received frequent threatening letters and telephone calls. After Romanenko informed the world that "Zionists" had assassinated his colleague Vladimir Begun using a heart attack as their "terrorist" tool, Nina Katerli, as she told me personally, prayed for one thing only. She asked God to protect Romanenko, an elderly and unhealthy man, from a heart attack since in this event she would undoubtedly be charged with murder.

Numerous court investigations led to the same conclusion: Since Romanenko's book had a Nazi outlook, Nina Katerli inflicted no insult on the author's "honor and dignity"—she only stated a fact. In September 1990, Romanenko withdrew his suit "as a sign of reconciliation."

On the breastwork

By examining the military exploits of the warrior-internationalist, we can put the finishing touches on his portrait.

When asked once from the audience what he had been doing during World War II, Romanenko replied that he had served as the Komsomol leader of a regiment. "Front-line soldiers know what it means," he said. "'Guys, for the Motherland! Go ahead!' Who is to mount the breastwork first? The Komsomol leader of the regiment ."

However, according to his official record that became public, Romanenko had been enlisted in late 1944 and sent to a training infantry regiment deployed in the Ural mountains. Positioned deep in the rear, he did not have a chance to fight during World War II at all. In 1949, he graduated from the military-political school in Gorky (currently renamed back to Nizhny Novgorod) and was sent to the Baikal region in Siberia and later to China. During the Korean war, Romanenko served in a detachment defending a Chinese military airfield from American aviation raids. Since the Americans did not make a single raid, Romanenko never smelled any gunpowder or raised anyone "to the breastwork."[21]

The personnel file of Alexander Romanenko, Lieutenant Colonel of the reserve, carries vivid censures.

"For deceiving the command and the forgery of certificates, the Baikal military district party commission decided to give A. Romanenko a reprimand. Protocol No. 39"[22]

The article "From the Sly" by journalist Gennady Rubinsky contains other indictments as well—for breach of discipline, for petty hooliganism, for removal of unwanted documents from his personnel file, and getting decorations for exploits in battles in which he had never engaged.

* * *

In 1992, Alexander Romanenko published another book in which he denounced the Bolshevik revolution as a Judo-Masonic conspiracy. After the failure of Communism in the USSR, the dedicated communist, who had repeatedly described himself as "infinitely loyal to the cause of the Great October, to Leninism, to our Soviet motherland," did not hesitate to replace all his views and values with the opposite ones—except for his views on Zionism, Judaism, Jews, and liberals.

CHAPTER 4

THE YEMILIANOV CASE

Zionologist No. 1

The name Valery Nikolaevich Yemelianov became known to me in December 1975, in connection with the 150th anniversary of the "Decembrists' Uprising."

This significant event in Russian history marked the beginning of the country's revolutionary movement. The young enlightened officers' and intellectuals' uprising, which took place in December 1825, strove to put an end to the Czar's despotism by introducing constitutional rule and abolishing serfdom. Czar Nicholas I severely crushed the rebels. Five of their leaders were hanged and hundreds sentenced to life or almost lifelong imprisonment and hard labor. But their heroic sacrifice for the sake of freedom had a major impact on Russian society. The Decembrists inspired several generations of Russian intelligentsia, and when the Bolsheviks came to power in 1917, they claimed to be the Decembrists' successors. Hundreds of scholars and writers studied the uprising, and their numerous books—biographies, historical novels, poems—sold in millions of copies. Children learned about the heroic patriotic act from textbooks. Everything related to the Decembrists was tantamount to the greatest of national treasures.

But in the late 1960s, the most "patriotic" publications started to articulate some reservations about the Decembrists. Emphasizing the affiliation of many of the rebels to Freemason lodges, some authors began to express the general notion that the Czar's regime had not been too bad after all, while the uprising had attempted to encroach on the stability of the state structure and impose Western values incompatible with traditional Russian lifestyle.

Nevertheless, the popularity of the Decembrists remained mostly undiminished and the press highlighted the jubilee. *Pravda*, the official newspaper of the Communist Party Central Committee, featured the opening of a Decembrists' museum in Moscow. According to the article, many original items and documents would be displayed in the exposition, including Masonic symbols of the movement's most radical leader, Pavel Pestel.

A day after the article appeared, a man presented himself at the office of the director of the museum. He delivered a statement that Masons "as it is universally known" were apprentices of Zionists, so to exhibit the Masonic symbols constituted a disruptive Zionist act. Committing his statement to paper, he signed his name: Valery Nikolaevich Yemelianov, professor, Moscow Institute of Foreign Languages.

Yemelianov's action immediately gave rise to a wave of jokes among Moscow intellectuals. But this amusement died when the director of the museum received a telephone call from the Moscow City Communist Party Committee.

"We have received a complaint from Dr. Yemelianov about your Masonic display," the party boss said, chuckling. "This professor is crazy, but it would be better to remove those signs from the exposition."

Encouraged, Yemelianov aggressively exposed "Zionists" (namely Jews) at his own university, where he taught political economics. He also moonlighted as a lecturer on Zionism at other institutions and organizations.

A couple of my friends attended some of his public lectures and gave me a detailed account of him. Yemelianov, they observed, did not lack for bulk or physical strength, yet he appeared a nervous 50-year-old man with a slight stoop. His closely cropped dark hair glinted with streaks of silver and his knitted brows furrowed close to the bridge of his nose. A convinced and zealous speaker, he could inflame his audience. I was anxious to see him with my own eyes, to witness his fury; but as luck would have it. I always learned of his public lectures after the fact, never in advance.

Sometimes he ran into trouble. The "Zionists" at his university demanded protection from his assaults. Following one such complaint, a special commission reviewed his lectures. The commission found lacking his contention that the Zionists had concentrated all world capital in their hands. His arguments, these critics maintained, did not adhere to a "Marxist approach."

It was a serious accusation, and Yemelianov had a hard time clearing himself. He received a party reprimand for ungrounded attacks against his colleagues and was even discharged from his job. He remained unemployed for about two years, then the Central Committee intervened and ordered him reinstated with retroactive pay for the entire period of his suspension.

In 1978, I read Valery Yemelianov's 35-page memorandum entitled *Who Stands Behind Jimmy Carter and the So-Called Euro-Communists*?* The document, addressed to the Communist Party Central Committee, widely circulated in the *Samizdat* press.[1]

Samizdat means "self-publishing." It was a unique political and cultural phenomenon in the USSR. Dissidents could not express their ideas through the media, so they typed their materials in four or five carbon copies for their friends, who retyped or photocopied them in ever-widening circles. Some of these documents had an extensive circulation.

The KGB never stopped persecuting Samizdat. The secret police treated those who kept and distributed manuscripts as criminals—searching their homes; confiscating all their papers, typewriters, and photo equipment; arresting, trying, and sentencing them to long terms in prisons and labor camps.

At the same time, the KGB tolerated some of Samizdat publications and even used the same techniques to distribute desirable materials that could not be printed in the official press. Yemelianov's memorandum fell into this category.

In his work he put forth and zealously insisted on a theory that apparent or disguised organizations of Masons and Zionists seeking world supremacy stood behind Jimmy Carter, the then United States President, behind Euro-Communists, Social-Democrats, Soviet dissidents, and everyone in the world who opposed the Soviet Union and its Communist Party. Thus, he urged the Central Committee to give the highest priority in all Communist Party activities to the tireless exposure of the disguised nature of Zionism. He sought to expose the Talmud, the Bible, and other Judaic books as promoting Jewish world supremacy and all Jews holding influential positions as henchmen of world Zionism—including those who pay lip service to fighting it. He decried all dissidents as Masons carrying out secret orders of the "Zionist government" and charged that French, Italian, and other Euro-Communists were on a Zionist mission to split the world Communist movement.

---

* At that time, the most influential Communist parties in the West (Spanish, Italian, and partly French), in an effort to attract more voters, insisted on their independence from Moscow and sometimes cautiously criticized the Soviet leadership, especially for their invasion of Czechoslovakia and human rights violations. The Soviet authorities reacted nervously to the "misunderstanding between comrades."

In short, Yemelianov expressed Vladimir Begun's anti-Zionist sentiments in a much more direct and uncompromising way, clearly outlining specific conclusions. He urgently suggested the introduction of a special obligatory course on "Zionism and Freemasonry" in all Soviet high schools and universities. He called for the establishment of a research institute to study and denounce Zionism and Freemasonry and specified that Jews be excluded from its staff. Finally, the memorandum called for preventive measures against Soviet Jews, who were "bound" to betray their motherland in a future world war. Yemelianov urged immediate action since it would be too late once the country was at war. His proposal paralleled the treatment of "traitor-nations" during World War II, when Stalin deported Crimean Tartars, ethnic Germans, Chechens, Kalmyks, and other ethnic minorities *en masse*. Yemelianov cited as positive precedents the Communist government's driving of nearly all the Jews from Poland in 1968-69 and even the systematic Nazi extermination of Jews in Central Europe during World War II.

Such direct solidarity with the German Nazis—not to mention the Stalin's most cruel crimes—was so unusual at that time that, of course, this work could not appear in any censored publication. At the same time, however, the authorities might see a certain value in letting the Jewish and liberal intellectuals—the main readers of Samizdat—know that such views existed in the society so that they would think twice before deviating from the mainstream politics and ideology.

I read and reread the Yemelianov memorandum several times. The convinced and passionate tone of his work left no doubt that the author really believed in the "Zionist conspiracy." But at the same time, he failed to provide a viable basis for his conclusions. He obviously juggled facts. While, on the one hand, he was clearly aware of his lies and distortions, on the other, he appeared to accept his own lies as the absolute truth. I questioned his stability.

Meanwhile Dr. Yemelianov continued his heroic fight against the Masons and Zionists. He enlarged his memorandum into a book-sized manuscript under the title *De-Zionization* and submitted it as his doctoral dissertation. Then he asked his Arab students to translate the thesis into Arabic—a task they performed with great enthusiasm. As a result, a Syrian daily newspaper published a serialized version over the course of two months. *De-Zionization* came to the attention of Israeli and European scholars, who regarded the work as an example of present-day Soviet anti-Semitism. The BBC and other foreign radio stations covered Yemelianov's work in Russian. The original Russian version of the book was also published in France,[2] and rumors circulated that Yassir Arafat himself brought one thousand copies of the book to Moscow and presented them to the author. All this started to annoy the party bosses. According to them, Yemelianov's extremism was useful for domestic consumption, but not for provoking international scandals. Thus, some kind of reprisal could have followed.

Still, it came as a shock to me, when rumors started to circulate that Valery Nikolaevich Yemelianov had been arrested. I could not believe it at first. I was sure that the authorities—especially the KGB—strongly supported the zionologists. When the rumors were confirmed, I was suffused with questions. If Yemelianov had gone too far, the KGB had the means to put him back on track without going to such extremes. Perhaps, I mused, I myself had become overzealous in my conviction that a kind of conspiracy existed between the zionologists and the KGB.

Soon, however, it turned out that the story took an unexpected and bizarre twist. Yemelianov had indeed been arrested, not by the KGB, however, but by criminal police—and not for his anti-Semitic activities, for murder!

The suspect

One September morning in 1980, when I was working in my Moscow home office, I got a call from a friend who told me that the hearing of the Yemelianov case had started at the Moscow City Court.

I canceled all appointments and plans for the day and rushed to Kalanchovka Street where the court was located, anticipating the last chance I could have to see Yemelianov with my own eyes. Soviet Criminal Code was extremely severe, especially to murderers. It followed the principles of the Old Testament literally: Life for life. I knew that if he were convicted, Yemelianov would face the death sentence, and get a bullet in the back of his head.

The Moscow City Court occupied an old three-storied building with long, dismal corridors and rows of empty chairs running along empty walls. The courtroom was crowded, and a small but thick group of people clustered near the wide-opened doors. I tried to look above their heads, and the first thing that met my eyes was the face of a man in smoke-colored eyeglasses. He sat in the very middle of the second or third row and would have had a good view of the trial, but he did not look in that direction. He stared instead at the entrance, taking note of everyone who appeared in the doorway. He had a big, kind-of-torn mouth, a protruded chin, and a flat forehead that, in contrast, slanted backwards, giving the impression that his head was tossed back in a most unnatural manner. However, what struck me most about his face was his guarded and suspicious gaze. I could feel his leaden inspection even through his smoke-colored eyeglasses.

A doorpost blocked my view of the right side of the courtroom, where the litigation actually took place. All I could see above the heads were three tall, long-haired youths near a window in the opposite wall and the dark-suited prosecutor. He looked dull, impenetrable, and half-asleep, lodged at a table with his back to the window.

When I squeezed closer to the doorway, I also saw the edge of the judges' dais. In a high-backed leather chair sat one of the *people's assessors*—a man with his hair carefully parted on one side. Approximately the same age as the prosecutor, he appeared equally dull and impenetrable. Although I kept squeezing through the crowd, the judge, the second assessor, the counsel for the defense and the dock remained hidden from me.

Soviet court procedures differed from the American and pre-Revolutionary Russian jurisprudence where a twelve-person jury determined the guilt or innocence of the suspect. The Bolsheviks considered the jury system "bourgeois" and substituted a three-person court consisting of a judge and two people's assessors. This judge not only tried the case, he also participated in identifying the guilt and passing sentence. In theory, he shared responsibility with two assessors—the "popular representatives"—and could not force a judgment since their two votes counterbalanced his one. In practice, however, the judge's law education and court experience made it virtually impossible for the people's assessors to oppose his authority. As a rule, their participation served only the decorative function of implying a collective decision, when, in fact, the judge had the final word.

All this applied to routine criminal cases of no political or public significance and of no concern to influential people. In other instances, the "telephone law" was involved. According to the Soviet constitution, judges were independent and irreplaceable, but in actuality they were controlled by the city or regional party leaders, who in turn might often come under pressure from high-ranking relatives of the suspect or from the prosecutor's office. In this event, the party boss might "advise" the judge. If the case were directly or indirectly concerned with politics, the KGB secretly passed sentence and the court's function was purely *pro forma*.

While I observed the courtroom from the doors, the first witnesses gave their evidence. The three youths I had noticed before were testifying. They were called in by turns. A loud, distinctive woman's voice asked them to give their first, patronymic, and family names; warned them of the consequences of providing responsibility for false evidence; and asked them to tell what they knew about the case. The woman's voice reached far and I could hear her well, but I could not make out what the witnesses were saying. Only from the judge's questions could I understand that a construction site and a fire on it were at issue.

Dismissed, the three young men hurried out of the courtroom. Thanks to the movement they caused in the crowd near the door, I was able to push my way farther ahead until I could see more of the courtroom. The judge, a nice-looking woman with fluffy henna-dyed hair, wore big, stylish eyeglasses. The second people's assessor, also a woman, looked absolutely indifferent to the proceedings. The counsel for the defense, a somewhat obese old man in a shabby suit, sat with his sides turned to the audience and judges, right across from the prosecutor. The dock behind the counsel for the defense remained hidden from me. Silence reigned there.

The judge began to call out new witnesses. She would pronounce a name in a loud voice. The name would resound in the audience, flow around the courtroom, and flutter out into the corridor but produce no effect. The judge went through a list of several names, but no more witnesses emerged. She announced a 15-minute break.

The crowd at the door dissipated and I could at last get into the courtroom to take a close look at the suspect.

But the black bench behind the low barrier was empty!

What could that mean? Could the suspect himself actually be absent from the trial?

It was all so absurd. A Kafkian absurdity. An empty place was on trial—not Valery Nikolaevich Yemelianov, professor of the Moscow Institute of Foreign Languages.

Meatheads

Bewildered, I looked around and for the second time ran up against the gaze of the man in the smoke-colored eyeglasses. Most people had left the courtroom during the break, but he continued to sit in the same place, his head turned toward the door as before. His whole attitude was forbidding. One would not venture to ask him questions. In the next instant, I met the eye of a red-haired woman standing next to me. Her green eyes were glimmering with impatience, and her freckles made her young face nearly childlike.

"What do you think about these *meatheads?*" She turned to me.

"What *meatheads?*" I asked, perplexed.

"I mean these *witnesses!*" She pronounced the last word with scorn. "They are idiots. Don't you see? Degenerates. What did they see there? They saw absolutely nothing!"

"What did they say? I could not make out a word from where I stood." I pointed to the door.

She waved her hand in annoyance.

"There was a fire. They found an empty container. What of it? There was a man leaving the site. What man? Maybe, it was not *him!*"

"Did they say it was?"

"They saw his back. And it was dark at that! They saw nothing, in fact!"

"The court will figure it out," I said reassuringly.

"Don't be naive!" she retorted with conviction. "All they want is a conviction."

"Can you tell me why he himself is absent?" I ventured the question that most intrigued me.

"That's it! They say he is ill."

"So what is the rush? I thought a hearing should be postponed in such case."

"No, it is not that," she answered, now in a whisper. "They say he has a disease. A *mental* disease. It means he is *crazy*. That's what they *say*."

"Now I see! He is insane. But are the insane supposed to be tried?"

"It appears they are," she said in a whisper again.

Schizophrenia

Although I could now see the reason for the absence of the accused, I still found it hard to believe. If so important a question as the sanity or insanity of the suspect had been solved prior to a court examination and without judges, the entire process had no purpose. It did not take a lawyer to understand that. If the suspect were in so grave a condition that he could not be brought to the courtroom, at least the psychiatric experts who pronounced him insane ought to be questioned. But they were not summoned either; they were only named at the end of the sitting. They were physicians from the *Serbsky Institute of Criminal Psychiatry,* headed by Dr. Morozov, a member of the Academy of Medical Sciences. When the KGB wanted to punish a certain dissident, bypassing the court procedure, this group of doctors examined him and routinely pronounced a diagnose, *slack schizophrenia,* that allowed the authorities to send the person to a special mental hospital for a forceful treatment. Most of the patients were absolutely normal. The close ties between these "doctors" and the KGB was not a secret.

But, perhaps, in this case, I thought, the KGB experts did not have to act completely against their conscience.

What had happened to Yemelianov before his arrest was already common knowledge. After his book was published abroad and attracted undesired publicity there, he, as a party member, was summoned to the Party Control Commission to account for his actions.

In such cases, the offender was supposed to repent, admit his mistakes, and promise to be more discreet in the future. But Yemelianov took a different course. He started "unmasking" Jews in high spheres, stating, for example, that commission chairman and Politburo member Arvid Pelshe's wife was Jewish; that a daughter of another member of the commission was married to a Jew; and that a third commissioner was Jewish on his grandmother's side. It was too much even for the party chief ideologist Mikhail Suslov. He became livid with anger. The party expelled Yemelianov from its ranks.

When Yemelianov's wife, Tamara, learned of his disgrace, she had a fit of hysteria. She was confident that he would lose his job again, this time never to be restored. Weeping, she reminded him of all the hardships they had undergone during the two years of his unemployment and reproached him for ruining their life. Yemelianov came to the conclusion that a Zionist plot had penetrated his own family.

Convinced that his wife had become a secret Zionist agent, he determined to deliver a forestalling blow. He developed a direct and simple plan, and put it in action at the earliest convenience.

Bas-Relief on the Rock

"Look at the mother. What a bearing she has! What a wonderful bearing she has!" My young freckled companion changed the subject.

The old woman sat in silence, looking straight ahead. I could readily see her profile. Her features were large: a big, slightly curved nose; thick, fleshy, sharply cut lips; a massive chin. The whole profile looked as if carved of stone. It was not a living face but a bas-relief. A bas-relief on a rock.

The old woman wore a severe, dark-blue dress. She positioned a handbag on her knee and her hands above it. Those hands, with senile knotty fingers and crooked twigs of veins visible through the dry skin, never moved. They lay motionless on the bag in a show of confidence and calm.

The old woman seemed aware of my gaze. She turned around, and I could see her eyes. They were large, pale gray, and the same confidence and calm reigned in their depths.

"She seems to be taking it calmly," I remarked.

"Who can guess what this reserve costs her!" my companion replied.

"Please, tell me, has he been absent from the very beginning?" I returned to my main concern.

"Don't expect them to show him here. He would tell the whole story!"

"You mean, you don't believe that he is mad?"

"Think about it. The man used to be quite normal, but now that he's come to trial he's gone mad?" My companion's sympathies were fully with the suspect.

"You probably knew him well," I suggested.

"No, I only saw him once at a public lecture in our Construction Bureau. He spoke on Zionism. Do you know what kind of man he is? A remarkable character! Not like anyone else. Committed. That's what he is being punished for."

"I thought he was on trial for murder. What does his being committed have to do with it? I am afraid I fail to understand."

"It is quite easy to understand," my companion said, surprised by my naivety. "That is how they deal with people when they want to take revenge upon them. They killed his wife and palmed her off on him. To conceal the truth, they declared him mad—and none will be the wiser! These witnesses are handpicked. Are they real witnesses? No. They are *meatheads!*"

I was astonished and could no longer continue this conversation.

Of course, I was suspicious about his insanity as well. The authorities never questioned his stability when he denounced the Jewish-Masonic conspiracy in his papers and lectures for more than a decade. At least, Yemelianov's alleged insanity could somehow account for his absence from the trial. But what this young woman was saying with full conviction was just too Kafkaesque.

Suddenly, I saw the man in the smoke-colored eyeglasses again. Now I knew what had struck me as peculiar and I understood why he sat as he did— watchful and bristling. His was the agitated attitude of a true schizophrenic haunted by maniacal apparitions. Even the air in the courtroom seemed to be permeated with special exhalations, infecting people with the same schizophrenic attitude even if they were quite sane by nature but not immune to the poison of suggestion.

"Zhenya, I am not guilty!"

The "15-minute" break had already lasted for over an hour when an official announced a postponement until the next morning due to the absence of necessary witnesses.

On the following day, far fewer onlookers crammed the courtroom, many of the gossip-mongers having been disappointed by the slackness of the trial's first day. Though all the seats were occupied, there was plenty of room in the aisles.

As on the previous day, the man in smoke-colored eyeglasses sat in the middle of the courtroom, his pale lips pressed tightly together. He continued his vigil, staring steadfastly at the door. I did not find my loquacious woman-companion, but I saw at once Dmitry Zhukov, a long-standing acquaintance, sitting solemnly in the first row. He was a voluminous literary scholar, a translator as well as an author of numerous books, surveys, articles, and reviews on subjects ranging from Russian satire of the 19th century to Hinduism. However, he enjoyed a certain celebrity not as a writer but as a fighter against "Zionism."

The film *The Secret and the Evident* conceived by Zhukov raised much speculation and became a cult sensation although it never ran in the movie theaters and was viewed only behind closed doors. I did not have a chance to see the film myself but was familiar with its content from many firsthand accounts. Years later, a Russian-émigré newspaper printed an article written by a person who had seen the film. According to the author, it had been "a mixture of sequences and photos grubbed up from different sources and glued together with the only purpose of proving the existence of a world Jewish conspiracy. The pseudo-documentary held the Jewish capitalists responsible for every world crisis from Lenin's assassination [in 1918] to Hitler's rise to power and from initiating [the 1961] Caribbean conflict to counter-revolution in Czechoslovakia."[3]

Like Yemelianov, Zhukov often went beyond the official Soviet propaganda limits, thus some of his most extreme works remained unpublished. However, he found a supporter in Yemelianov. In his paper *Who Stands Behind Jimmy Carter...*, he called for immediate publication of the hitherto unseen works of Vladimir Begun, Yevgeny Yevseev, and Dmitry Zhukov. Without a doubt, Yemelianov's familiarity with their manuscripts could have come only from a familiarity with the authors themselves—the three like-minded writers. So, Zhukov's appearance in the courtroom did not surprise me. Very possibly, Begun and Yevseev were also sitting in the courtroom, but I had never seen them and would not have recognized them.

Only two witnesses were absent from the day's proceedings—the Bakirovs. The couple had gone on vacation and was, the judge noted, "nowhere to be found." Clearly, these two witnesses were essential to the case; but rather than postponing the hearing, the court chose to have the couple's depositions incorporated into the trial from the record of the preliminary investigation protocols.

An incredibly appalling crime unfolded before the audience.

The premeditated offense had occurred in April, five months before the trial. In no way could it be condoned as the unexpected impulse of a madman.

Yemelianov had carefully chosen a day when his mother, who lived with him and his family, would be away, visiting a friend, until late at night. His wife Tamara dropped the children at kindergarten and headed for her own mother's home in Podolsk, a small town near Moscow. Yemelianov admonished her to return early since he had only one lecture scheduled and would be back by 1:00 p.m.

Tamara's mother saw her off on the 3:00 p.m. train from Podolsk, at the same time that Yemelianov tried to reach his friend Bakirov, leaving a message with the man's wife. He was very insistent that they should be at home that night since he would come to them to consult on urgent business. Thus, two hours before Tamara's return, he already knew his schedule for the rest of the day.

Tamara came home about five o'clock; and at seven, Yemelianov left the house carrying a rucksack, a suitcase, and a 12-liter metal milk jug. He took a taxi to the Bakirovs', who lived in a 12-story apartment building at the outskirts of the city. But when he arrived, his friend had not yet returned from work. Talking to his wife, Yemelianov told her that he turned to them for assistance in a matter of life and death. With Zionists hot on his heels ready to "murder or arrest him," he urgently needed to destroy the damning Zionist literature. Since he could not make a fire in his own neighborhood in the center of Moscow, he wanted to do it here, at the nearby construction site, where workers often burned scrap. He hoped that Bakirov would help him, but in the meantime he needed a place to conceal his "literature."

Deeply touched by the story, the woman gave him the keys to their car, which was parked in front of the building, and Yemelianov put his load into the trunk. Then he sat with her for about an hour, drinking tea and discussing Zionism.

When Bakirov arrived, the two went downstairs. Suddenly Yemelianov decided he would do everything by himself and asked only for a container of gasoline. (At the trial, the prosecution presented both the milk and gas cans as evidence.)

Within ten minutes, according to the couple's testimony, Bakirov was back home. Yemelianov returned almost an hour later, his bags gone, his shoes and trousers badly smeared with mud. He spent a great deal of time in the bathroom washing up, but then the three of them sat at the table, drinking tea. Yemelianov appeared absolutely calm. As usual, his conversation focused on Zionism and he did not deviate from his customary conduct.

The next day, a police officer canvassing the neighborhood spoke to Mrs. Bakirov. He explained that a fire had broken out at the construction site the previous night, but the second-shift workers (the very same *meatheads* who testified at the trial) had extinguished it and then found the charred remains of a human body. Now the police officer was making the rounds of the 12-story apartment house to find out whether the residents had noticed anything suspicious or out of the ordinary.

Mrs. Bakirov denied any knowledge of the incident. But at night, when she told her husband about the investigation, he called the local police station and informed them of Yemelianov's visit and his "Zionist literature."

Meanwhile, neither Yemelianov nor his mother reported Tamara's disappearance. When Tamara's mother, in an agony of suspense, had come from Podolsk and demanded to know her daughter's whereabouts, her in-law replied that Tamara had gone to the hospital for an abortion. She refused to give any further details, however, and her account was so confused that Tamara's mother, all the more worried, went to the police. Shortly afterward, she was summoned to identify the body. Although the corpse had been cut into pieces and was charred from the fire, she identified Tamara through intimate marks and scars known only to the family.

Yemelianov was arrested.

Soviet legal proceedings were such that the accused, as a rule, was kept behind bars prior to going to trial. While the investigation was underway, he was not allowed to contact the outer world, not even his own lawyer. However, before official charges were brought against Yemelianov, the investigator was so kind that he broke the rule and allowed him to make two calls from his office.

He called his mother. "Valera," she advised him, "stay steady!"

His second call went to his "comrade-in-arms in his struggle with Zionism," historian Yevgeny Yevseev. "Zhenya [short for Yevgeny]," he said, "I am not guilty!"

But only one day later, Yemelianov admitted to the murder of his wife Tamara in a detailed confession.

A man with a tape recorder

As the trial disclosed a picture of Yemelianov's crime in vivid detail, the tension in the courtroom heightened—but not because of the cold-blooded atrocity of the murder. No one seemed at all keen on the particulars or displayed the slightest sympathy for the murdered woman, her relatives, or her two small orphaned children. On the contrary, a sense of enmity arose. The poisonous atmosphere of irrational hatred intensified as malicious whispers circulated through the courtroom, ultimately converging in one word that reverberated ominously: Zionists.

"Zionists?" Tamara's mother, who was giving evidence, stopped speaking and faced the audience. "Why did they kill her, not him?"

She was an unsophisticated, country woman with good common sense. Her words were colorful and emotional. Her speech was so vivid that I, making hasty scribbles in my notebook, was beside myself with annoyance that I had no command of shorthand.

At her questioning, the half-sleepy prosecutor suddenly awakened and addressed the judge.

"A man over there is tape-recording!"

"Man with a tape recorder! Stand up!" The judge's voice thundered with alarm.

Dmitry Zhukov rose to the full length of his tall body. He had positioned a portable tape recorder on his knee.

"Tape recording is banned! Turn the tape in to the court!"

"Why should I?" Zhukov asked defiantly.

I heard a click as he removed a cassette from the tape recorder. I saw him thrust it furtively into his pocket like a thief.

"Be quick. Turn in the tape!" repeated the judge.

"No," Zhukov replied. "I will not."

"Then, you must leave the courtroom!"

"Why should I?" He held his ground, refusing to leave.

"I shall call the police!" the judge threatened. "You will be taken out."

"Go ahead!"

Tense silence hung in the air for several seconds. Although the judge undoubtedly wanted to avoid a confrontation, she had to maintain the dignity of the court.

"We shall have a ten-minute break," she announced after a visible hesitation.

The audience met this wise decision with relief. Chairs scraped against the floor as the courtroom emptied. Zhukov came up to me in the corridor.

"Why on earth can I not tape-record the proceedings?" he demanded.

I grinned. Clashing with the authorities must not have been easy on him if he turned to me for sympathy.

I had often encountered Zhukov when I worked at the *Lives of Remarkable People*. A frequent visitor to the editorial office, he had achieved favored-author status after Sergei Semanov replaced Yuri Korotkov. But after my forced departure and Zhukov's elevation to the glorified role of militant-fighter-against-Zionism-and-Freemasonry, neither of us was anxious to pursue a friendship. Zhukov's increasingly frank chauvinistic publications kept appearing, and I tried to refute his claims in the press.[4] All my attempts failed; my "controversial" articles, rejected by all magazines and newspapers to which I submitted them, remained unpublished. But Zhukov had wide contacts with most leading periodicals and was sure to have known about my efforts to oppose him.

"The hearing is open," he contended, prattling. "I am a writer. I am interested in psychological details."

"Dmitry Anatolievich," I said, making a helpless gesture. "Should it all depend on me, I would allow you everything."

Diffused, he went in search of someone who would allow him to argue his point. Left alone, I fell prey to another loquacious woman. She was much older and plumper than my previous informant, but equally talkative.

"Did you know Valery Yemelianov well?" she asked, cutting immediately to the heart of the matter.

"I have never met him," I replied honestly. "But I am familiar with some of his literary efforts."

"I have all his works," she said with noticeable pride. "He himself presented them to me." Her voice dropped conspiratorially. "We were great friends. He always confided in me."

The conversation promised to be interesting, but we were interrupted all too soon when the hearing resumed.

Zhukov must have failed to make his point since he was no longer in the courtroom. I soon forgot all about him as Tamara's mother returned to the witness stand. She gave a detailed—and emotional—account of her daughter's family life.

Tamara had not had an easy life with Valery. He had forbidden her to work and had often beaten her black and blue. Although her mother had seen the bruises on her body, Tamara herself was afraid to complain.

The overwrought mother related especially striking story about her daughter's wedding ring. Valery's mother told her that the ring "had disappeared" with Tamara. But when the body was found, the ring was absent. Tamara's mother became even more demanding until, finally, her in-law "found" the ring. Apparently, the "insane" murderer had not forgotten to take off all valuables before dismantling the corpse.

Yemelianov's mother was the last to take the stand. As a witness she presented the same calm bearing she had maintained when sitting in the audience. She would ask the officials to repeat their questions, complaining that she had hearing problems; but she never raised her voice the way deaf people often do. She spoke under her breath in a simple and trusting tone, as though confident that her voice reached everyone.

According to her testimony, Valery and Tamara had lived in harmony and never quarreled. Though she had shared the apartment with them, she had tried not to interfere in their life.

The judge asked what she knew about her son's first court conviction.

"He was never on trial before. This is the first time," Yemelianov's mother answered.

"What do you mean, the first time?" the judge persisted. "He himself mentioned another."

"Did he? I might not know about it. He is very secretive. When he was expelled from the Party, he never told me anything about that either."

Could she then, as his mother, account for this unsavory turn of events? She could, indeed, and her tone grew confidential as she voiced what for two days had been in the air, in the tense and poisoned atmosphere of the courtroom:

"He never killed her," she asserted. *"They* brought her to him in a sack."

The first court conviction

When the court recessed for lunch, I invited Valery's talkative woman-friend to join me. She readily complied; and as we searched for a food stand or cafe, I learned a great deal. She repeated her claim that she had known Yemelianov for years.

"Then, you must know about his first court conviction," I said casually.

"That case was never brought to court," she replied.

"What do you mean? The judge specifically referred to a court conviction."

"Take my word for it. I know every detail."

But I also knew a thing or two.

A friend of mine had once brought me a clipping from the *Literaturnaya Gazeta* of February 1963—17 years before the murder. This report, under the heading *From the Courtroom*[5] gave an account of the trial of post-graduate student Valery Yemelianov. The article said that this young scholar had copied a considerable portion of another man's thesis on India's economy and used it in his own thesis on Lebanon's economy, changing only one word—"India" to "Lebanon." After defending his dissertation and obtaining the degree of Candidate of Science, he submitted his work for publication. Failing to earn a single favorable review for his manuscript, he started to attack editors and reviewers in numerous letters and complaints to the authorities. The article did not reveal the character of Yemelianov's accusations, but stated that all of them had proved to be false. Thus, the court sentenced him to one year in prison for plagiarism and libel.

"That case never went to court," my companion insisted. "Nobody knows better than I."

I was ready to argue, but she stopped me with an apparent *non sequitur.* "I knew that woman myself!" she declared emphatically.

"That woman!" Her words flashed like neon through my mind. What a surprising turn of subject! We were speaking about different cases. My companion knew nothing about Valery's plagiarism, but she knew plenty about an incident unknown to me.

Among the numerous rumors that circulated about Yemelianov, his first wife's suicide frequently rose to the fore. Although he had come under criminal investigation, nothing had come of it. I never treated such rumors seriously: Odious individuals often attract sensational chatter. However, I questioned my companion:

"You mean his first wife?" I asked. "Is it true that she hanged herself?"

"That's what people say when they are ignorant!" My companion grew angry. "First, she was never married to him. They were only going to get married."

"But she did commit suicide?"

"No. Of course, not. That is all nothing but slander. I know for sure. She died." My companion hesitated for a moment. "She died during sexual intercourse."

"How so?" I was shocked. "Was it a heart attack?"

"No, it was not." She seemed at a loss for words. "They turned out to be physically incompatible. They did not fit each other. She was all torn inside."

I stared at my companion. Was she fully aware of what she was saying? If she spoke even a shred of truth, then her friend was more than a murderer—a sexual deviant who had raped to death a woman he had planned to marry!

I thought back to the evidence that Tamara's mother had presented. She had alluded to a story about a group of students hiking in the mountains under Yemelianov's supervision. The professor, she said, had either killed one of them or been responsible for his death. Unfortunately, neither the judge nor court representatives had pressed the issue, so it remained unclear whether such an accident had really taken place. Maybe this, too, was not an idle rumor?

Death, I observed, courted this man.

"Did he look like a madman?" I asked curiously, and my companion replied quickly, requiring no time to consider question or response.

"No," she assured me. "I never noticed anything out of the ordinary in his looks. He was very nervous; yes, he was. And easily excited, too." She had a clear vision of him. "Self-assured," she continued. "You could not argue with him. At the first hint of opposition, he would jerk his head up and gesture with his hands as if he were astounded that you would disagree. But I never noticed any streak of craziness about him."

I found her judgment credible enough to consider it seriously. The court did not discuss Yemelianov's insanity, but took it for granted, relying on the KGB "psychiatrists." If the KGB unblushingly used their "expertise" to prosecute dissidents undesirable to the regime, it could use the same technique to save from the death penalty such "dissidents" as Yemelianov. He had been useful for the KGB in the past and might come in handy in the future. Of course, he was mentally abnormal. But the court did nothing to find out if, at the time when he had committed his terrible crime, he were not in his right mind to the extent of insanity.

Sentence

Once the court reconvened, the performance did not last much longer. All the witnesses had been questioned, and pertinent evidence read *in absentia*. The results of the examination had been presented. Only the final speeches of the two sides and the pronouncement of the sentence had been left for the last act of the show.

The prosecutor delivered a brief speech—sluggish, but aggressive. In his summarizing, he proved clearly and easily that the accused, Valery Nikolaevich

Yemelianov had killed his wife, Tamara Yemelianova, in their apartment between 5:00 and 7:00 p. m.; that Yemelianov subsequently dismembered the body and took it to the Bakirovs, and that he then tried to burn it at the construction site where the charred body was found. The prosecutor did not question the insanity of the accused, which made meaningless, he said, any discussion of the motivation of the crime. But he described Tamara's murder as premeditated and committed with "particular savagery" and said that, in accordance with the Soviet criminal code, such a crime was punishable by death. But, given the mental conditions of the accused, the prosecutor suggested confining him in a mental hospital for forced treatment.

The counsel for the defense took more time to make his point. He could not deny the obvious, but emphasized the incomplete character of the investigation. The taxi-driver who had taken Yemelianov to the Bakirovs was not identified, and the key witnesses, the Bakirovs, failed to appear in court. He termed their role "very suspicious" because of their close involvement with his client and evident controversies in their testimonies.

He questioned the Bakirovs' honesty. If Yemelianov really had told Mrs. Bakirov that Zionists had sought to "kill or arrest" him, she should have been puzzled by such a strange statement, but she had not been. Instead of asking her friend to give her every detail of the danger—the lawyer noted—she had given him the keys to the car for the safekeeping of his "literature." And why had she so readily accepted that the burning of the literature could prevent an attempt on his life?

She might be utterly stupid, counsel conceded, but her husband had not pursued this line of thought either! Certainly friendship is sacred, but could not Bakirov have offered to keep this "literature" in his apartment to prevent its destruction?

With all these questions remaining unanswered, one more possibility surfaced. Perhaps nothing had happened at the Bakirovs as described. After he had accompanied Yemelianov to his car, Bakirov might have returned home not 10 minutes but much later. Perhaps, he had come back together with Yemelianov from the construction site.

The counsel for the defense did not try to deny that his client was the killer, but he pointed out that Bakirov might be a possible accomplice to the crime. He found Bakirov's actions extremely suspicious. All the more so, he added, since Bakirov was not an ignorant, semi-literate person, but a KGB officer.

With this last revelation, many pieces of this multifaceted puzzle fell into place.

Dmitry Zhukov had once been a state security officer, too. He had long been retired; but when he happened to be a bit drunk, he took delight in showing his major's uniform to his friends. I had not the slightest doubt that he remained in contact with the organization that had nurtured him. Involvement with the KGB could not be stopped; it was a lifelong obligation. Zhukov had scripted a film about the secret, crafty designs of Zionism at the behest of this powerful institution.

The KGB and the "patriots" had worked together for years, so the connection was obvious when, after committing his crime, Yemelianov had immediately rushed to a KGB officer for help and protection. Furthermore, the Bakirovs' vacations could have been deliberately timed to the trial to justify their absence in the courtroom, although, under the Soviet passport system, authorities could easily locate any person—unless they chose not to.

But all these sophisticated tricks did not help much. Ultimately, the desperate elements of Yemelianov's case established publicly a connection between the KGB and anti-Semitic Mafia.

The judge and two silent people's assessors withdrew to confer. Leaving through the main entrance, they had to cross the entire courtroom. When the judge approached the first row, she said in a low but distinct voice, "There are only schizophrenics here, too."

She must have had precise instructions to adhere strictly to the scheme of a routine murder case and not to yield to possible Zionist "provocation." But, contrary to expectation, the "Zionists" (i.e., the Jews) were not present in the courtroom. "Patriots" had occupied almost all places, creating this schizophrenic atmosphere. The judge had remained calm and balanced with great effort, leading the show trial in compliance with the instructions.

Healthy again

Six years later, soon after liberal trends became visible in the Soviet political landscape, Valery Yemelianov re-appeared on the public scene. Mysteriously pronounced "recovered" from his schizophrenia, he was released from a Leningrad mental hospital. The action was taken without the consent of the Health Ministry or even that of the sinister Serbsky Institute of Criminal Psychiatry, whose experts had pronounced him insane.

Once at large, Yemelianov immediately joined the *Pamyat* Society and soon became one of its leaders. However, despite his record, other leaders of *Pamyat* were unwilling to yield him command. All the more so, as some differences started coming to the fore, Dmitry Vasiliev, the society's most charismatic leader, insisted that the basic crime of the "Zionists" against Russia was that they had destroyed Russian Orthodox temples and eradicated the Christian religion. Yemelianov stood his ground, entertaining a theory that the Zionists imposed Christianity on Russia a thousand years ago and that that was their most perfidious act of subversion.[6]

These contradictory views proved to be beyond reconciliation, and Yemelianov with a group of his supporters set up a *Pamyat* of his own.

On March 18, 1990, a Moscow heathen community held a religious service in a Moscow park. Priests clad in ancient Slavic attire performed the rites. Two dozen people expressed a wish to convert into the new faith. The priests gave each of them a piece of planed wood and instructed, how to burn it ceremonially in the fire right on the spot. Classes in Slavic wrestling followed. Several children were among the newly-converted, while among the adults, someone recognized a 50-year-old man who had laid flowers on Stalin's grave at the Kremlin wall a fortnight earlier.[7]

Valery Yemelianov did not attend the service, but it was he who headed the community. Those present each received two leaflets bearing his signature. One of them was directed against the Jews, communists, and the "circumcised comrade Christ"—though, as we well remember, prior to his "treatment" in a mental hospital, Yemelianov regarded any negative opinion of communists as a Zionist conspiracy. The second leaflet came as an even bigger surprise. Yemelianov devoted it to his friend Yevgeny Yevseev, whom he had called ten years before from the investigator's office to say: "Zhenya, I am not guilty."

By that time, Yevseev was no longer among the living. During the years of *glasnost*, he had considerably increased his "patriotic" activities, setting up and directing a number of "anti-Zionist" organizations and committees.

In February 1990, traffic police stopped Yevseev's car near Moscow's beltway. He got out of his car to confer with the inspector, but a passing vehicle knocked him down. The vehicle allegedly had no license plates and safely outstripped its pursuers.

The enigmatic circumstances surrounding Yevseev's death added much speculation to Moscow's rumor mill. No one believed that it was an accident. *Pamyat* staged a march of protest against "Zionist terror," but a different opinion prevailed in liberal circles: Yevseev had gone too far in his activities and the KGB had removed him permanently.

In his leaflet, Yemelianov strove to clarify the issue. Yevgeny Yevseev, he explained, had been a "hidden Zionist" and that was why "Peroun's* arrow" had struck him. Was it not this same arrow that ten years earlier had struck down another "hidden Zionist," Tamara Yemelianova?

Valery Yemelianov remains very active. He is a leader of one of the most extreme groups of *Pamyat* and a permanent participant of the rallies, meetings, and other gatherings of right-wing nationalists. National radio and TV stations often interview him, and his message is always clear:

"Every Jew is a criminal and should be shot."[8]

---

* Peroun is the leading God in the Russian pre-Christian mythology.

PART TWO

FREEDOM TO HATE

CHAPTER 5

METASTASIS OF NAZISM IN THE ERA OF GLASNOST

Astafiev-Eidelman duel

The correspondence between historian Nathan Eidelman and prose writer Victor Astafiev depicts a vivid picture of Soviet intellectual life at the start of the *glasnost* era. Its significance is most apparent in the wider context of the prominent role that fictional literature and its creators have traditionally played in Russia.

The country's cultural tradition spawned few original philosophers. Almost all 19th century Russian thinking followed Schelling or Hegel, Comte or Marx. The Russian Orthodox Church, under strict government control since the time of Peter the Great (1672-1725), served mostly as an administrative "department of spiritual affairs." Before the Revolution—and especially after the Revolution—literature, too, endured severe restrictions; nevertheless, the literary world attracted the most talented and independent spirits. Through the artistic form of the novel, poetry, and drama, writers could indirectly challenge official ideological doctrines, uncover the evils of tyranny, and give their readers hope for change. Literary works that combined real artistic talent and independent thought had a special place in society, creating a quasi-legal spiritual resistance. This social literature helped the Russian people maintain their pride and self-esteem in spite of the humiliations they experienced under the despotic regime. These works enjoyed extraordinary popularity and became an inseparable part of the national heritage.

Consequently, literary critique also encompassed a broader canvas than mere artistic commentary. Analyzing fiction, a reviewer got an opportunity to express publicly views that could never be published as direct political criticism. The most popular literary critics of the 19th century taught their readers to see literature as not just a source of entertainment, but as the textbook of life. Writers were called "the rulers of thoughts."

The prestige of the best Russian writers reached a height unimaginable in Western societies. Writers themselves regarded their efforts as a mission—not just a profession. They saw themselves as political thinkers, philosophers, moralists, psychologists, priests, and—only after that—as entertainers.

The extraordinary high status of Russian literature forced the Bolsheviks to treat it seriously. After they came to power, censorship increased substantially from what it had been under the Czars, but prohibitions and purges were not enough. The new government was building a "proletarian" state and needed a "proletarian" literature. Those writers who did not emigrate but were critical of the Soviet regime were subject to ostracism. Many of them were arrested and executed or died in prisons and labor camps. Those who were hesitant became subjects of "re-education." They were sharply criticized and persecuted for the "bourgeois" elements in their works and rewarded for everything "proletarian." Simultaneously, committed party activists, some of them absolutely ungifted and poorly educated, were encouraged to create "proletarian" prose and poetry. "Socialist realism" forced writers to describe all aspects of life from the Communist point of view and to indoctrinate readers in the "advantages of socialism" and the final victory of Communism throughout the world.

The party control was tightening from year to year. By the last years of Stalin's life, Russian literature had turned into an endless flow of boring illustrations of the latest party decisions and the sayings of the Great Leader.

The most obedient writers were well-rewarded. Every year, hundreds of authors won Stalin Prizes, which made their works immune to any negative critique. Books of the "laureates of the Stalin Prize" were printed and reprinted again and again in millions of copies, bringing them fame and big money. They were granted free luxury apartments and country houses when the average Soviet family occupied a small room without toilets and running water. They could ride in elegant cars with chauffeurs, ordering them for free from government garages, when their countrymen had to wait hours in the cold for overcrowded trams and buses. They had access to "special" hospitals with the best medical care available at that time, to "special" department and grocery stores filled with a countless variety of imported products when average people had to stay in long lines to buy stale bread. Their lifestyle was equal to those of the Western multimillionaires while most of their readers had to live below the poverty line.

But even serving Stalin's regime faithfully—and getting all the privileges of the elite in exchange—some writers, especially the most talented of them, were ashamed of their miserable role. Right after Stalin's death in 1953, and even more after Nikita Khrushchev denounced Stalin's "errors" in 1956, the voice of Russian literature began to be heard again.

The party immediately took counter-measures against this new trend. The most-known became the story of Boris Pasternak, who had published his uncensored novel *Doctor Zhivago* abroad. After the novel won him the Nobel Prize (1958), the party leadership started a campaign of ostracism against him. Pasternak was accused of anti-patriotism; Khrushchev threatened to exile him from the country. In order to stay, the elderly writer publicly refused to accept the Nobel Prize. He was expelled from the Writers Union and was never published again in the USSR until his death in 1962.

The monthly literary journal *Novy Mir* and some other publications with the courage to print talented works, even if they did not meet all the requirements of "socialist realism," had a lot of trouble with censorship and party bureaucracy.

The situation was controversial. The party leadership, on the one hand, did not want to return to Stalinism, but, on the other, did not want to lose its control over people's minds.

In 1962, Khrushchev personally approved publication of the novel *One Day of Ivan Denisovich* by Alexander Solzhenitsyn, which for the first time described life in a labor camp. Only a few years earlier, the work would have been regarded as anti-Soviet; but, with Khruchshev's endorsement, the official press unanimously praised the novel as the greatest achievement of the Soviet literature for decades. Its influence on the society was enormous. The novel was nominated for the Lenin Prize, the highest official award.* Yet during the same era, the much-less-challenging-the-regime memoirs by Ilya Erenburg could be approved by the censors only after major cuts—and even then they became a subject of sharp criticism for "political incorrectness."

In 1966, under Brezhnev's government, Andrei Sinyavsky and Yuli Daniel were sentenced to a concentration camp (for seven and five years respectively) for publishing their "anti-Soviet" novels abroad. This severe persecution provoked protests in the West, and many Soviet writers also signed

---

* After Stalin's death, the numerous Stalin Prizes were replaced by a few Lenin Prizes, which were much more prestigious.

letters in support of their colleagues. After that, the authorities avoided such severe treatment—at least against officially recognized authors (like members of the Soviet Writers Union). Gradually, more and more suppressed works began to appear in the West or in the Samizdat. Put on the defensive, the authorities had to loosen their restraints, and many works that would have been forbidden even a few years earlier started to get a real chance for publication.

Certainly, direct criticism of the regime was still forbidden; and in some important respects, censorship became more restrictive than it had been under Khrushchev. For example, it became almost impossible to criticize Stalin again or even to mention his merciless purges. Solzhenitsyn's attempts to publish his new works about GULAG made him persona-non-grata and led to his exile from the country. At the same time, many works were issued in which there was not a single word about the "wisdom" of the Communist Party or about the "advantages of socialism." The characters in these novels lived the difficult lives of common Soviet citizens, often suffering the cruelty and injustice of those who were more powerful and were cruel to those who were weaker. Much was revealed by innuendo, according to the traditions of 19th century Russian literature. The Aesopian language made it possible to express almost everything forbidden. Writers were becoming the "rulers of thoughts" again.

Of course, such works were only a small part of literary production, but their paucity made the prestige of their authors even higher.

Victor Astafiev was one of these authors. The publication of his novel *The Czar-Fish* in 1976 catapulted him to fame. The story gives an accurate picture of a miserable life in today's Siberia. The novel displays cruel people surrounded by cruel circumstances. The writer's eye is precise and penetrating. He draws truthful characters, his language is vivid and lively.

Astafiev's renown received a further boost in 1985 with the release of his novel *A Sad Detective Story* in which he depicts the decay and degeneration of a provincial Siberian town. The novel heralded *glasnost,* an open exchange of ideas that radically transformed the Communist superpower a few years later.

Glasnost also brought to light the attitudes of Russia's current spiritual leaders and revealed their true beliefs and attitudes. The Aesopian language that might be (and often was) interpreted differently by different readers became obsolete, and Astafiev was in the vanguard of change.

In May 1986, *Nash Sovremennik* published several short stories by Victor Astafiev of no particular literary value. Despite the author's famous name, the stories would have gone unnoticed. But one of them, *Fishing Gudgeons in Georgia,* shocked its readers. They did not expect to find such blunt inspiration of chauvinistic and anti-Georgian sentiments in a work of this liberal and almost dissident author.

Shortly afterwards, a Congress of the *Soviet Writers Union* convened in Moscow. In the past, the party had employed such conferences for political propaganda. Outwardly these meetings demonstrated the unity of Soviet writers and their enthusiasm in the service to the "most advanced and progressive ideas of communism." Behind the scenes, party officials orchestrated the entire event, blocking any unorthodox activities at every turn.

But this Congress was the first to meet under *glasnost*, and some writers had the courage to deviate from the pre-planned scenario. The Georgian delegation protested the publication of the insulting Astafiev's story and demanded a public apology from the *Nash Sovremennik's* editorial board, threatening to walk out. After that, one member of the editorial board presented apologies on his own initiative. The conflict was softened, but not ironed out. Astafiev, who was a member of the editorial board as well, resigned from the journal shortly after the Congress.

Nathan Eidelman was also a well-known author and a member of the Writers Union. His brilliantly written books about great Russian writers, political thinkers, and dissidents of the 18th and 19th centuries were very popular. When describing the horrible past, the author always kept the present in mind. Since he never wrote fiction and had a Ph. D. in history, he viewed himself more as a historian than a writer. Considering Astafiev one of the best free-thinking authors, he wrote him a letter that I extensively quote here as one of the most spectacular documents of the Russian intellectual life of the beginning of the *glasnost* era:

> "Esteemed Victor Petrovich! I have read all, or nearly all, your works and now I would like to outline my opinion of them. But let me introduce myself first. Eidelman, Nathan Yakovlevich: historian, writer (member of the Writers' Union), born in 1930, Jewish, a Muscovite. In 1910, my father was expelled from a gymnasium* for a slap in the face of a Black-Hundreder teacher. Later, he became a journalist writing about theater. He fought in World War I and World War II. From 1950 to 1955, he was a labor-camp inmate. My mother was a teacher. I graduated from the Moscow State University, worked in a museum and as a schoolteacher for many years, then became an expert in Russian history of the 18th and 19th centuries. . . .

---

* High school in pre-Revolutionary Russia.

Some of these biographical particulars are not likable to you, but the writer cannot choose his reader. Now, let me express my thoughts about Victor Astafiev as a writer.

"His, I believe, are the best descriptions of nature over the decades in Russian literature *(The Czar-Fish)*. In his [recent] article published by *Pravda,* he spoke of World War II as no one ever did. Of major importance is that the writer is honest, not cynical, and concerned. His mental suffering for Russia is genuine and intense. The pictures of ruin, disintegration, and lack of spirituality are most merciless. Neither is he reticent about the most guilty [for all misfortunes]. They are parasite-intellectuals, 'tourists' and, finally, non-Russians.

"One can say that Astafiev does not flatter his own people either: the Russian peasants or the city-dwellers. It is true and not true. When it comes to the 'root of all evil,' there necessarily appears the sinister city-dweller Gogi Gertsev (his first and last names are not Russian, and Gogi will later appear in connection with Georgia). Horrible are both the life and the soul of the characters in *The Czar-Fish,* but Gogi is by far worse than all drunkards and murderers taken together since all misfortunes come from him ...

"In this time, under our circumstances, only the Georgians may write about themselves in such or even tougher terms (which they, by the way, do—their literature, theater, arts, cinema are as honest as the Russian ones). A lyrical digression of this kind, written by a Russian pen, is that very spoonful of tar that is not to be made up for by many barrels of the Russian-Georgian feast honey.*

"Alexander Pushkin said, 'I, certainly, despise my fatherland from top to toe—but it will hurt me if a foreigner shares this feeling with me.'...

"Let us continue. Why do many critics mention only the 'Georgian' hurt feelings in the story [*Fishing Gudgeons in Georgia*] when you insulted other minorities even in a greater degree?

"'In keeping with their barbarous custom, the Mongols fixed stables in Orthodox churches. They decided to profane this marvelous and austere [Christian] temple (Gelati), too. They drove their shaggy horses into it, made fires, and started gorging the under-fried bloody horseflesh, tearing the horses right there in the temple; and drunk from the bloody debauch, they fell down one after another with their slanting-eyed mugs into the

---

* A metaphor making use of a Russian proverb "a spoonful of tar in a barrel of honey"—equivalent to "a fly in the ointment."

stinking horse shit, unaware yet that the creators for eternity on earth build eternal temples.'

"How can one comment upon this? Surprisingly, the Kazakhs and Buryats are keeping silence. It would not be out of place to remember here other Mongoloids—the Kalmyks and the Crimean Tartars—who, in 1944, were driven out of their native homes, steppes, and hills and got 'their slanting-eyed mugs into the shit.'[*]

"One hundred seventy years ago, Nikolai Mikhailovich Karamzin,[**] quite oblivious to the feelings of the Mongols or other 'non-Russians,' gave a different account of the Batu[***] invasion. After vividly enumerating the horrors of the invasion (children crushed by horses, girls raped, free people enslaved by barbarians, 'the living envious of the peacefulness of the dead'), the historian-writer, as we can guess, started to think that, in fact, there are no bad nations, but there are tragic circumstances—and added a surprisingly balanced conclusion: 'Russia underwent at that time all the disasters endured by the Roman empire, when the Northern savage tribes smashed up its blossoming regions. All barbarians act under the same rules and differ only in force.'

"Karamzin, grieving the awful disaster suffered by his homeland, still is wary of betraying his habitually humanistic outlook, his high objectivity. He compares the horror of the Mongol invasion to the raids on Rome by 'Northern barbarians,' to the ancient Slavs playing a major role—the Slavs, the direct ancestors of those who are now pillaged and plundered by Batu.

"Will this example not suffice? Here is another one. You, Victor Petrovich, are sure to remember the lines from *Hadji Murat*[****] giving an account of a Chechen village after the Russian army had devastated it:

"'The fountain was polluted, evidently on purpose, so that nobody could use the water. The mosque was polluted the same way. ... Old men gathered on the plaza and discussed their situation. No one spoke of hatred of the

---

[*] Kazakhs, Buryats, Crimean Tartars, Kalmyks, and several others ethnic groups currently inhabiting Russia and other former Soviet republics are descendants of the Mongols, who invaded Russia in the 13th century. In 1944, Crimean Tartars and Kalmyks as well as several other ethnic groups were declared "traitors." Their entire populations (with children, elderly, and the sick) were deported to Siberia or the Central Asia under such wretched conditions that almost half of them died on the way.

[**] Nikolai Karamzin (1766-1826), a prominent Russian historian and novelist, composed the 12-volume *History of the Russian State*.

[***] Batu-Khan (1208-1255) was a Mongol ruler, grandson of Genghis Khan, who conquered Russia and other countries of Eastern Europe.

[****] *Hadji Murat* by Leo Tolstoi is a historical novel about the Russian conquest of the Caucasus in the mid-19th century

Russians. The feeling experienced by all the Chechens, from the youngest to the oldest, was stronger than hate. It was not hatred, for they did not regard those Russian dogs as human beings; but it was such repulsion, disgust, and perplexity at the senseless cruelty of these creatures, that the desire to exterminate them—like the desire to exterminate rats, poisonous spiders, or wolves—was as natural an instinct as that of self-preservation.'

"Leo Tolstoi could impress by his writings! But let us imagine that a Chechen, Georgian, or another non-Russian had written these lines.

"It makes me sad to conclude that the notion of a *people's writer* is changing nowadays. In the past he was, first of all, the mouthpiece of high ideas, aspirations, giving the lead to the people; now he can also be a herald of popular malice, prejudices, one who does not raise people to his level but goes down with them.

"Against this background, one takes as a mere nothing a phrase from *A Sad Detective Story* about its character who studies Lermontov's[*] translations from German in the Pedagogical Institute along 'with a dozen little Jews.' I am only curious to know—what do they imply in the story, if neither before this phrase nor after it they ever appear again?

"As a reader and an expert in Russian history, I will draw your attention, Victor Petrovich, to this: You (and not only you) are violating ... the main tradition of Russian thought and Russian literature. The greatest masters bequeathed the tradition, which requires that, while reflecting on the bad and the horrible, we must, first of all, prior to any explanations, *put the blame on ourselves,* take the responsibility. They teach us that it is impossible to give to the people more freedom from outside than they are free internally (Alexander Herzen's[**] saying, which Leo Tolstoi liked so much). As to all personal, public, or popular misfortunes, the greater and the more horrible they are, to the greater extent their cause lies inside, not outside. Only such a moral approach can lead to a genuine, high mastery [of a writer]. A different view is suicidal for an artist, since it dooms him to a malicious barrenness. Forgive my harsh words; but by your works, you

---

[*] Mikhail Lermontov (1814-1841), a Russian poet and prose writer.

[**] Alexander Herzen (1812-1870), a Russian writer and political thinker, an enemy of the Czarist regime. Czar Nicholas I exiled him to the remote Eastern province of the country, where he spent six years. In 1847, Herzen emigrated from Russia and founded an independent Russian émigré press that had an enormous influence on the Russian intelligentsia. Herzen sharply criticized serfdom; but after Czar Alexander II abolished it in 1861, Herzen emphasized that the mentality of the Russian people, caused by hundreds of years of serfdom, could not be changed by decree and remained the major obstacle to creating a civil society in Russia. The characteristic feature of this mentality is considering oneself an object—not a subject—of the political process, not taking responsibility for one's own fate, and blaming others for all personal failures and misfortunes.

yourself teach us how to show things in their true colors. With respect, N. Eidelman. August 24, 1986."[1]

I have come across different opinions about this challenging letter ranging from a complete and unconditional approval to an equally complete censure. Some of Astafiev's admirers argued that Eidelman interpreted the quotations out of context, unjustly opposing the writer's ideological stand to that of Tolstoi, Karamzin and Herzen. Others believed it had been improper to "beat" a modern writer and his works by comparing them to the classics.

Artistic endeavors always offer room for different interpretations, so Eidelman's view is not infallible. However, whether or not he gave an objective appraisal of Astafiev's works does not seem to be the key question. Something else puzzled me. What grudges could Eidelman have had against Astafiev, as a writer, if he never called into question his intelligence, talent, and honesty? The attitude toward the non-Russians expressed in Astafiev's novels and stories was unacceptable to Eidelman, but could it be helped if the author had precisely these feelings toward them? Did he have to mask his attitude by the hypocritical demagogue of official "internationalism"?

Nathan Eidelman was a good friend of mine. When we parted in 1982 because of my emigration, we had no hope of seeing each other again. Thanks to *glasnost,* however, we ran into each other several times both in Moscow and Washington before his unexpected death in December 1989. I asked him about his stance, but never received a clear answer. His letter to Astafiev was an emotional impulse, not a rational act.

Like most assimilated Jewish intellectuals in the Soviet Union, Eidelman believed that only mentally retarded or dull Russians could be obsessed by chauvinism and hatred for non-Russians, making up for their own inferiority. This notion provided a psychological background for the Soviet Jews to see themselves as individuals whose talents, knowledge, and professional achievements were needed and appreciated by the Russian society regardless of their ethnic origin. Thus they could slough off anti-Semites and chauvinists as mere annoyances. Nathan Eidelman was positive that a gifted and honest Russian writer could not help being a humanist and a democrat like Leo Tolstoi or Alexander Herzen. Victor Astafiev's works, however, testified that this was not necessarily true, undermining the most basic of Eidelman's beliefs—thanks to which he, being Jewish, could regard himself as a Russian historian with no contradiction implied. His letter was the outgrowth of a tragic confusion. An assimilated Jewish intellectual, he had devoted his life to Russian culture only to discover that this very culture (personified by one of its most respected representatives) hated him as an insolent "little Jew" interfering in other people's business.

However, Eidelman had overestimated both Astafiev's intellect and integrity. The tough and unprejudiced scenes in his novels merely imitated honesty. In fact, he barely outlined his genuine attitude toward the non-Russians in his books. Perhaps this accounted for the relish with which he splashed out his most cherished sentiments in his personal correspondence.

"Nathan Yakovlevich! You can hardly imagine how delighted I was by your letter," he answered. "Everybody everywhere is speaking and writing about the national revival of the Russian people. But to speak and write is one thing while to actually revive—not in words or on paper—quite another.

"Every national revival—all the more so, the Russian one—must have its opponents and foes. While reviving, we can go so far that we shall start singing our own songs, dancing our own dances, writing in our native tongue, instead of the 'Esperanto' imposed on us and called with 'subtlety' a 'literary language.' In our chauvinistic aspirations we can go so far that literary scholars studying Pushkin and Lermontov will also have to be Russian, and—how horrifying even to think of it—we Russians shall compose collected works of our home classic writers all by ourselves; we shall 'take in hand' encyclopedias and all kinds of editorial offices, theaters, and cinema, and.... Oh, how horrible! How awful! We ourselves shall comment on Dostoyevsky's *Diaries*.

"This summer near Zagorsk,* my wife's aunt died. She was like a mother to both of us. Before she died, she told me about the comedy played by the Georgians at the Congress [of the Soviet Writers Union]. 'Do not answer evil by evil, and it will not multiply...' I'll follow her advice and won't answer with evil to your black letter, overcrammed with not simply malice but with the boiled pus of the Jewish high-brow haughtiness. ...

"The sea of malice in your letter shocked me most. What is it that you, an elderly person, are carrying in your soul? What burden of spite and hatred is swirling in your maw?

"I will wish you what our last Czar's daughter wished in her verse put into the gospel: 'God, forgive our enemies. God, take them into your embrace.' Both she and her sisters and her little brother, who in exile finally lost the ability to walk, and her father and mother—were all shot, by the way, by

---

* Zagorsk is a small town not far from Moscow.

Jews and Latvians headed by inveterate and double-dyed Zionist Yurkovsky*.

"So, you'd better, in your moments of peaceful contemplation, give thought to the fact that you were kept in camps for Yurkovsky's and his associates' crimes, too; that you were languishing by orders of the 'Highest Judge' not only through the undue of Yezhov** alone.

"As you can see, we, the Russians, have not lost our memory yet and we are still *The Big People* and it still does not suffice to kill us, but you must bring us down first. ... I give you my best regards. Let gracious God enlighten your soul! September 14, 1986."²

As is evident from this letter, Astafiev did not have the slightest doubt as to who were the deadly enemies of the "national revival of the Russian people." His unrestrained energy of hatred was aimed not at the person whom he could have regarded as his offender. He insulted neither Eidelman the reader, nor Eidelman the historian, nor Eidelman the writer. He declared the Jews (Eidelman as only one of them) to be the foes of Russian culture. He made them responsible for the ruin of Russia—in fact, for all the evils of the 70-year Bolsheviks' rule, starting with the murder of the Czar's family in 1918.

Eidelman gave a short reply.

"Victor Petrovich, seeking to insult, you only aggrieved me. In my most horrible dreams I could not have imagined in one of the 'rulers of thoughts' such a primitive savage chauvinism, such an elementary ignorance. The point is not that the shooting of the Czar's family (in which, don't doubt it, most instrumental were Yekaterinburg workers) was headed not by 'Zionist Yurkovsky,' but by Bolshevik Yurovsky (while the Zionists sought a quite different goal—the creation of a separate Jewish state in Palestine—as you, apparently, don't know). The point is not that you follow the logic of [Hitler's] *Mein Kampf* about the hereditary national guilt (though if my father were in prison for the sins of 'Yurkovsky,' then your personal

---

* In July 1918, Czar Nicholas II and his family, under arrest at what was called a "House of Special Purpose" in Yekaterinburg (Ural region), were executed. Although the secret order came from Moscow, officially, Yekaterinburg Soviet authorities passed the death sentence and ordered the guards of the "House" to carry it out. Yakov Yurovsky (not Yurkovsky) was commandant of the "House" and commander of the guard. Astafiev knew so little about the event that he misspelled the name of the executioner, but he did not hesitate to call him a Zionist and to claim the participation of other Jews and Latvians, which was not true at all.

** Nikolai Ivanovich Yezhov was chief of the Soviet secret police from 1936 to 1938, when Stalin's purges and terror achieved the highest point. In 1939, he himself was executed.

misfortunes must come as retaliation for the partition of Poland, the humiliation of minorities, Jewish pogroms, and other things). The point is that you could find much malice in my letter only in quotations from your works, Victor Petrovich. Maybe you mistook them for my words and crushed down on them? Several times you unctuously mentioned Christian values; but, in reality, your attitude is always that of a furious, 'eye-for-eye,' Old Testament-minded Israelite. ...Farewell, unfortunately, we have nothing to say to each other. September 27, 1986."[3]

Eidelman did not make this correspondence secret. It was widely distributed in the Samizdat and found its way abroad. Under the circumstances of relative publicity, some information about it penetrated the Soviet press. Right-wing critic Vladimir Bondarenko stated in one of his articles that he never reads someone else's private letters and cannot comment on them. Nevertheless, he called Eidelman's action a "provocation" which "caused certain moral damage to a well-known writer."[4]

Soloukhin and pseudo-Soloukhin

However, Bondarenko's commentary did not put an end to the responses to the Eidelman-Astafiev correspondence. A second answer to Eidelman started circulating in the Samizdat, and it is so descriptive that I cannot restrain myself from another extensive quotation.

"You rebuke writer Astafiev that he gave an unfavorable description of Georgians-profiteers, of barbarian Mongols, though much more shameful accounts have been written in Russian literature about all of these, and by Pushkin, too. You, as Pushkin's literary scholar, must be fully aware of it. In Jewish literary studies, only those quotations are picked up to prove a point that are most instrumental at the moment.

"'In our century, under our circumstances, only the Georgians can write about themselves in such a manner,' you say to us. Can I ask you, who gave you the right to judge and humiliate the Russian people? If you feel like it, judge the Jewish people! But you will not have the heart to do so. Your Zionist leaders will not allow you to do that—one is risking one's head by this. What are these 'our' circumstances that you keep harping on here? These circumstances have been created exclusively by you, the Jews.

"What delight you are taking while quoting Pushkin and Tolstoi when they say bitter things about Russia and the Russian people! Here lies their force. Whose writers are also capable of the same? I do not think I know anything of the kind about Georgian, Mongolian, or Jewish writers—while the latter write all bad things only about Russians. You also, in your letter, wrote sternly about an alien nation. ...

"Can you tell me why Jewish Heine* in his poems and articles violently abused Germans? Read our modern Yunna Morits,** who breathes hatred for everything Russian. The Jews insulted everybody, but most of all, those on whose land they used to live. And, certainly, there is no need to point out to you what the Palestinians are thinking of you. You personally don't care a bit about Georgians. It was the 'little Jews' from *A Sad Detective Story* that jarred upon you. That is why you caught hold of 'poor Georgians' to take revenge on the writer, to voice your—so to speak—indignation. You seemed indispensable here, too. Start censuring Georgians, and a Jew is quick to appear. He feels from afar that something is in the air and tries to benefit from any scandal, to capitalize on any problem. And how hurt a look he has—as if it were he who was called a petty-profiteer! The Georgians have long calmed down through their natural kindheartedness while the Jews keep making a hubbub and beating the air.

"Now a word or two about some facts of the letter. Zionist Yakov Yurovsky directed the shooting (he was a jeweler and had his eye on the Czar's family jewels that they had managed to take along in case they got a chance of escape). You know it as well as I do. You also know that a Bolshevik does not mean a non-Jew. Shaya Goloshchekin,*** also an ardent Zionist, maintained general control in Yekaterinburg at that time, while Beloborodov (Waisberg)**** was a chairman of the local council.

"You feign naiveté, saying that 'Zionists sought a quite different goal—the creation of a separate Jewish state in Palestine.' This is baby-talk that makes one laugh. Whom are you taking us for? Even schoolchildren are laughing at you! Somebody else might be unaware, but not you, that the goal of Zionism is getting power over all mankind, over the entire world, and turning

---

* Heinrich Heine (1797-1856) was a German poet of Jewish origin.
** Yunna Morits is a contemporary Russian poetess of Jewish origin.
*** Philip Isaevich Goloshchekin (1876-1941) was a leading Bolshevik in the Ural region. In 1918, he traveled several times from Yekaterinburg to Moscow and back and allegedly brought Lenin's secret order to shoot the Czar. Anti-Semitic "scholars" use three different Jewish manes for Goloshchekin—Shaya, Isaac, and Isai Isaacovich—although there is no reliable data that he was Jewish and that Philip was his party nickname, not his real name.
**** Alexander Petrovich Beloborodov (1891-1938) was a Chairman of the Executive Committee of the Ural Soviet Region, a Russian who signed the order to shoot the Czar and his family. He never was known as Waisberg or Waisbard, as more sophisticated anti-Semites claim (see chapter 7).

Russia into one of the 'provinces of the Zionist Great East.' The Jewish 'paradise on earth' in Palestine has long been created, but you are in no hurry to go there."⁵

The letter ends as follows:

"The Russian people are becoming increasingly aware of the situation, and hatred is ripening toward those who have been systematically ruining Russia over the last century. A huge role in this awareness is played by writers who have stuck with their nation in all times, unlike you—Jew Eidelman. You have provoked this correspondence. Now, don't you complain that the Russian people have started responding."⁶

The letter was signed by the name of another well-known writer, Vladimir Soloukhin, and followed by Eidelman's home address and telephone number so that the readers could call and write to him. The readers, however, bombarded with telephone calls and letters not as much Eidelman as Soloukhin, who at last begged for mercy from the pages of *Literaturnaya Gazeta*.

"It is necessary for me to say one thing. For me, this is like ... running to a public place and calling for help. Over the recent months, I have received many letters and telephone calls testifying that in circulation is an 'open' letter allegedly written by me. This letter causes either ardent approval from some readers or sharp censure from others. Both attitudes cause moral damage to my reputation as a Russian writer. ...In due time, thanks to God, I managed to inform the addressee that I am not the author of this libelous letter. But I am not able to explain to everyone that I have never written any 'open' letters to anyone and have never distributed such."⁷

Indeed, the letter is so primitive that it is difficult to imagine that Vladimir Soloukhin, a professionally established author, could have really written it. However, it was no accident that the anonymous writer had picked his name.

For many years, Soloukhin has been persistently propagating the values of the traditional Russian culture neglected and destroyed by Bolsheviks. Nobody has done as much to attract public attention to Russian ancient art, to decaying temples and icons that profiteers and scavengers were buying up in old villages for next to nothing. For these activities, the public admired Soloukhin, and many liberal intellectuals treated him with great respect. But his close ties with *Nash Sovremennik* and other similar publications have been known as well.

He revealed his real views on the Russian tragedy only several years later, in 1992, in his book *In the Daylight,* about Vladimir Lenin.

For more than 70 years of the Soviet regime, Lenin could be portrayed in Russia only as the kindest, the most just, the most patriotic, the most altruistic person that ever lived, and as the greatest genius on Earth, who fought for the well-being of the working people. After *glasnost* brought to light the enormous crimes of the Communist government, some liberals started to speak out that Lenin, as a founder of the Communist one-party system, had also been responsible for them. However, nobody dared to go as far as Soloukhin. His book describes Lenin as the vicious enemy of Russia, who, in cold blood, murdered millions and millions of Russian people from all classes of society, destroying the Russian culture, spirituality, economy, and environment. Soloukhin connected his emotional—and partly truthful—descriptions of Lenin's villainies not with his Bolshevik fanaticism, however, but with his alleged Jewish (and Kalmyk!) origin.[*]

To see the book by Soloukhin in historical perspective, we have to keep in mind that while Vladimir Lenin was Soviet God and his family was the Holy Family, nobody in the USSR questioned that he was the flesh and blood of the Russian people. Even Black Hundred ideologists, who had fled Russia after the Civil War and permanently denounsed the Soviet leadership as dominated by the Jews, never dared to declare Lenin himself Jewish. Alexander Solzhenitsyn, in his book *Lenin in Zurich,* published in the West after the author's exile from the USSR in 1974, gave a very negative portrait of Lenin, exposing him as a traitor financed by the German military command to destroy Russia from inside and get her out of World War I. But, according to Solzhenitsyn, Lenin was a kind of a "Russian fool" seduced by Alexander Israilevich Parvus, a Jewish political advanturer, who forced him to accept German money.

For Soloukhin, such interpretations are too complicated. According to him, Lenin himself had Jewish blood in his veins, which made him a malicious

---

[*] The author refers to an archive document, discovered by one Jewish (sic!) historian several decades ago. It is a certificate issued to a certain Jew, Israel Blank, which confirms that he had been baptized in St. Petersburg in 1820 and was given a Christian name, Alexander. However, Soloukhin provides no subsequent biographical data of this baptized Jew. In theory, he could have become the father of Maria Alexandrovna Blank, wife of Ilya Nikolaevich Ulyanov and mother of Vladimir Ilich Ulyanov (Lenin). But the same might be true about any Alexander Blank living at that time. Thus, all speculations about Lenin's alleged Jewish extraction remain a mystery. His claim that Lenin's father, Ilya Nikolaevich Ulyanov, was a product of incest between a baptized Kalmyk and his daughter is highly speculative as well.

hater of everything Russian and that all his activities were motivated by one overriding passion: to destroy this beautiful country and her people.*8

In heaven and on earth

An anonymous article entitled *The Chosen Character of the Jewish People* circulated for years in the Samizdat. This intriguing document did not address the "purification of Russia from the Jewish dominance" or exposing of all Jews as inciters. It neither threatened nor abused, concentrating on theological issues. But the ideas remained the same.

> "The religion of those professing Judaism is directed to the future, to meeting the Messiah (not Christ), i.e., the anti-Christ who would establish mastery of the Jews and Judaism over the entire world. Here lies the difference between the Judaic idea and the concept of Christianity. Christians seek the Kingdom of Heaven while the Jewry, a kingdom on earth dominated by the Jewish people. ... That is why the Jews crucified Christ—for failing to become their idea of the Messiah by providing for prosperity on earth. Instead, Christ preached the Kingdom of Heaven, an unworldly Kingdom."[9]

There is hardly any point in starting a theological argument with the author. The expectation of the Messiah has for the Jews approximately the same religious implications as for the Christians, the expectation of Christ's second coming. The basic moral principles of Christianity—such as *thou shall not kill; thou shall not steal,* and *love your neighbor as you love yourself*—are drawn from the Old Testament, from Judaism. (Oddly enough, Nathan Eidelman seemed unaware of these affinities when he drew an irrelevant parallel between a malicious anti-Semite and a "furious Old Testament-minded Israelite"). It is all the more curious that the just-quoted work of an anonymous author from Moscow found refuge on the pages of *Pravoslavny Vestnik* (The

---

*In 1924, after Lenin's death, the Politburo decided to embalm his body and place it in a mausoleum in Red Square in Moscow. It was a unique honor repeated in the Soviet Union only with Stalin, who died in 1953. Several years later, however, after Stalin's "mistakes" were denounced, his body was removed from the mausoleum, leaving Lenin the only dweller once again. On the advanced stage of *glasnost* era, some most brave liberals started to speak out that the time had come to take Lenin out of the mausoleum, too, since he also made "mistakes." There is little doubt that his body will eventually be removed. But, most probably, the removal will not symbolize the final liberation of Russia from despotism as the liberal intellectuals hoped. The bitter irony is that Lenin was placed in the mausoleum as the greatest Russian genius, patriot, and Savior of the Russian people, while he will be taken out as a little Jewish degenerate who destroyed Russia.

Orthodox Herald) published in the United States by one of the Russian Orthodox Church groups. "The tone of the article is calm, reserved, and reasonable" expounds an editorial note. "Its ideas are deep and clear and quite in keeping with the teaching of the Orthodox Church and Holy Fathers."[10]

Pravoslavny Vestnik is outside my regular reading. I received the quoted issue and some other materials from Vadim Shcheglov, a Russian Orthodox believer and a former Soviet dissident residing in Boston.

Vadim Shcheglov, a professional mathematician, worked at the Central Institute of Economy and Mathematics under the Academy of Sciences of the USSR and then at the Ministry of Health Computing Center. Like most Soviet intellectuals, he grew up as an atheist. When he became deeply disappointed with the official Communist ideology, and with atheism as a part of it, he started to search for a different outlook. On his own, he studied non-Marxist philosophy in a search for the meaning of existence. Gradually, he started to realize that the religious teaching of how to be good and brotherly and how to love one's neighbor could provide the spiritual support which he needed so desperately.

At the age of forty, Shcheglov was baptized. This path to Orthodoxy had been long but profoundly conscious. However, he discovered that the Russian Orthodox Church in the Soviet Union was under strict Communist control as any other official institution, and most clergymen served the Government more than their flock. Shcheglov had developed close contacts with a dissident-priest, Gleb Yakunin,[*] and had started contributing to the work of the *Committee for Protecting the Rights of Believers,* primarily comprised of Yakunin, deacon Varsonafy (Boris Khaibulin), and Victor Kapitanchuk, layman. The KGB persecuted all of them.

In 1970, Yakunin was arrested, tried, and sentenced to five years in a labor camp and five years in exile. Victor Kapitanchuk was also arrested. The KGB managed to break his spirit so that he abandoned any further activity. Varsonafy had to give up his dissident work because of an illness. But the work of the Committee never stopped. It was taken over by Vadim Shcheglov, Vasily Fonchenkov, and Nikolai Gainov. Though all the Committee members belonged to the Orthodox faith, they fought for the rights of all religions—Catholic, Baptist, and Jewish. Vadim Shcheglov's human rights activities lasted until 1983, when the KGB threatened reprisal through his children and forced him to emigrate.

---

[*] Gleb Yakunin is now one of the leading figures in the Russian democratic movement.

In the United States, Shcheglov joined the Russian Orthodox Church Abroad. And here, he had discovered that part of the Church-goers and hierarchs inherited the believes of those Russian immigrants, who shared traditional prejudices against the Jews. Thus, Vadim Shcheglov became a dissident again.

The article in *Pravoslavny Vestnik,* in Shcheglov's opinion, not only disagrees with Christian values but stands in glaring contradiction to them.

"I was particularly grieved and insulted by the editorial board's attitude toward this article, by its assertion that such is the viewpoint of the Orthodox Church and the Holy Fathers," he commented. "This is the editorial board's opinion, which does not correspond to reality."[11]

He pointed to the Christian commandment "love thy neighbor" as well as to the celebrated psalm of David, "The hating of Zion will be put to shame by God," a required component of the daily morning prayer of Orthodox Christians.

However, only a fraction of Russian Orthodox believers, both in Russia, and abroad, shares views similar to those of Vadim Shcheglov and Gleb Yakunin. The majority does not. It is amazing that so many Orthodox Christians were always ready to "be put to shame by God" and continue to be so now. As a Russian philosopher Nikolai Berdyaev observed, "For us Christians, the Jewish question is not by far whether the Jews are good or bad, but whether we, the Christians, are good or bad."[12]

Dozens of millions of Russians who have been educated and brought-up as atheists have been joining the Orthodox Church in recent years, disappointed in the Communist ideology. But what kind of spiritual guidance do they find in the temples?

Formerly classified KGB files now reveal that most of the top hierarchs of the Russian Orthodox Church were secret KGB agents. Not one metropolitan or bishop has been asked to resign his standing in the Church after such public disclosure, and they continue to play a leading role.

Different "patriotic" organizations actively compete with each other for the influence over the Russian Orthodox Church. The "patriots" need the church not as a house of repentance and prayer, purification, and a source of spirituality, but as a ready-made organizational structure through which to achieve their political goals. In one of his speeches, Alexander Kulakov, leader of *Pamyat Orthodox National-Patriotic Front,* one of the most extreme branches of *Pamyat*, proclaimed a spiritual war between Russian Orthodox ideals and perceived Zionist encroachments.

"The destruction of evil forces on earth, i.e., of Zionism, will start with the revival of the Orthodox spirit among the grass roots," he said. "We believe that the victorious march of the forces of light intending to liberate the entire world will start in Russia. Now we are witnessing an attempt to establish democracy and capitalism in this country and weaken the executive authorities of the Ministry of Interior and the KGB. We regard it as the result of hostile Zionist actions on our soil.

"The destruction of the Orthodox faith, of the Aryan genotype, and the ruin of Russia is the basic credo of Zionism. The Fathers of the Church as well as the Vedic pre-Christian texts* say that it is Russia that will have to arrest and destroy the world evil in the form of Zionism.

"Liberalism, humanism, communism, democracy are the weapons by means of which Judaism is trying to destroy and defile the Aryan world, reducing the Aryans to their level. Faith in God is, above all, the vision of light; but at the same time, it is a vision of darkness; while Judaism is part of darkness. It means that anti-Judaism and faith in God are inseparable.

"The secret power, this bloody vampire that fed Lenin and that is seeking now to take control of the entire world, we regard as international Free-Masonry on the payroll of Judaism. It has been openly legalized by the United Nations.**

"The secret power of Zionism and Free-Masonry is a cancer sucking all sound forces out of mankind from Talmudic atheism (Marxism) to reducing human beings to the level of cattle. Our ruined economy and agriculture are the result of a huge mass grave created by Zionists on Russian soil.

"Generalissimo Stalin was the first to break the backbone of the bloody Leninist guard. Stalin was the first to raise his sword against cosmopolitan Bolshevism (Zionism); and his cause, the cause of combating Zionism, is still underway throughout the world. For example, in such countries as Libya, which confronts international imperialism and world communism

---

Vedas are the ancient Hindu scriptures originated thousands of years before Slavs and Russians appeared on the historic scene, thus nothing could be found there about Russia. Current Russian racists, however, claim that Russians are direct ancestors of the Hindu-German (Aryan) tribes that created *Vedas*.

** The speaker, most probably, refers to the revocation of the shameful 1975 UN resolution that declared Zionism a form of racism.

practically single-handedly, or Iran, where the deceased Ayatollah Khomeini never allowed insults to the religious sacred tenets of his nation."[13]

While we might consider these the ravings of a madman, the essence of his message has no difference from the perceptions of Victor Astafiev, Vladimir Soloukhin, or some other Church-oriented intellectuals.

After being destroyed almost completely during the first decades of the Communist regime, the Russian Orthodox Church started slowly to regain its strength during Brezhnev's time, when more and more people became disenchanted with the Communist ideology.

The party leadership was not concerned very much with such a development since the Church demonstrated its loyalty to the government and often served the party political interests, both on international and domestic arenas. As was mentioned above, many high-level hierarchs of the Church were secret KGB agents; thus, the party could control all activities of the Church and its members. Those few courageous priests and activists who represented more independent Orthodox believers were often persecuted not only by the KGB, but by the Church itself as well.

All these processes intensified dramatically during the *glasnost* era. Paralleling the decline of the power of the Communist Party, the influence of the Russian Orthodox Church increased both in terms of growing membership and in its role in social and political life. Some former religious dissidents, especially the most outspoken among them, like Father Gleb Yakunin, Father Alexander Men, and a few others, became very popular as articulate promoters of universal Christian values. However, the predominant trend in the Russian Orthodox Church was Russian nationalism. This was the common ground for most Church leaders and the *Pamyat* society.

In 1990, priest Alexander Men, who not only had preached religious liberalism, but had the bad luck to be of Jewish origin, was brutally murdered on his way to his church. The killer did not rob him and did not leave any signs of non-political motives for the assassination. The entire society was shocked. The KGB leadership promised to do everything possible to find the killer, but did nothing. When another priest, Father Lazar, organized an independent committee to investigate the murder, he, too, was killed—in his apartment, without an apparent cause. Father Gleb Yakunin was finally disfrocked in 1993 for his refusal to abstain from political activities.

So when new believers come to the church looking for peace of mind and the Christian values of love and brotherhood, they more often than not find a different kind of "Christianity" than what they seek.

According to Metropolitan Ioann, who is the head of the Church in St. Petersburg and Ladozhsky Province, the entire world, and especially the "Zionized" West, seek to destroy Russia and the Russian Orthodox Church.

"'Let us look around,' he wrote in one of his numerous articles. 'What kind of additional proof do we need to understand that a foul, dirty war against the Russian people is under way? This war is generously funded and thoroughly pre-planned. It is continuous and merciless. We have to fight it to death because its devilish inspirators' goal is to destroy our entire country and to kill the entire nation—for our faithfulness to our historic mission and to our religion. The enemies seek to eliminate the Russian people because, in spite of many centuries of disturbances, rebellions, and wars, we preserved the sacred things of the [Orthodox] religious ethics, Christian values, and our firm belief that eventually the good will prevail over evil."[14]

The situation in the church merely exemplified the anti-Semitic and anti-Western attitudes in all spheres of life. The cancer of hatred, developed under a decaying Communist rule, gave metastasis in all sectors of the society.

CHAPTER 6

DMITRY VASILIEV AND IGOR SYCHEV

Smoke of the fatherland

October-November 1988. For the first time after six years of exile, I am back in Moscow and I catch myself whispering time and again the same line of poetry, "The smoke of the fatherland is sweet and pleasant to us."

This verse comes from a classical early-19th-century Russian comedy *Woe from Wit* by Alexander Griboedov in which the main character, Alexander Chatsky, returns home after several years spent abroad.

The difference between that character and me was, however, fundamental. He traveled as a wealthy tourist, just learning foreign countries and lifestyles, confident that he would return as soon as he wished. Meanwhile, my family and I were driven out of our homeland with four suitcases and no money, deprived of our citizenship, and strictly warned by officials that never, under any circumstances, would they allow us to come back.

Gorbachev's *perestroika* opened new opportunities, and I was wandering through familiar and somewhat unfamiliar streets; pushing my way through a usual yet somehow unusual crowd; entering lobbies of apartment buildings familiar from old times but gloomier now, with their smell of cats*—the same,

---

* A special smell of dirty lobbies and staircases being produced by rotted mud mixed with urine. Moscow humorists call it "a smell of cats."

but somewhat different, too; embracing my friends, who have not changed a bit and at the same time have irreparably changed; coming across the habitual but a-bit-forgotten caddishness and luring a taxi-driver to the curb with a pack of cigarettes Camel in my hand lifted toward the gloomy autumn sky.

The main purpose of this visit (as well as the subsequent ones) was to get a firsthand feeling and uncover information about the new stage of the "patriotic" movement, for which the policy of *glasnost* and *perestroika* opened as many or even more opportunities as for democrats. Of special interest to me was the historical-patriotic society *Pamyat,* the most visible front-runner of all patriotic forces at that time.

In Moscow, I met with many people from various unofficial groups and movements who closely followed *Pamyat* activities, were familiar with its history, and had numerous documents from *Pamyat* and about *Pamyat* at their disposal. They generously shared them with me and also spoke at length about concepts and situations not addressed in official publications or in the Samizdat press. Thanks to them, I acquired a well-rounded view of *Pamyat* and its key figures.

The most "charismatic" leader of the *Pamyat* society was certainly Dmitry Vasiliev.

A professional actor, photographer, and painter, he was patronized by Ilya Glazunov, a "people's artist" and a unique figure among the Soviet elite. Despite his close ties with the KGB and high party officials, Glazunov, for dozens of years, created and maintained his image of a half-dissident artist persecuted for the patriotic substance of his art. But after Vasiliev parted with Glazunov, he started to denounce his former patron for a lack of patriotism. He found that on one of Glazunov's paintings, an ancient Russian warrior held his sword down, not up. According to Vasiliev, this was evidence of an anti-patriotic stand.

A thorough, confident, and inspired speaker, Vasiliev can expound for hours on end, working his audiences into a frenzy.[1] He has a well-trained voice, strong and wide-ranged, and he lards his speech with quotations drawn from a wide variety of sources. This adds a certain imposing character to his addresses, but does not mean that he delivers a rigid discourse. On the contrary, he frequently improvises, spontaneous and passionate in his tirade. He often loses his train of thought or gets lost in a maze of subordinate clauses. Sometimes, he betrays an elementary ignorance of facts, though at other times, he deliberately falsifies them (for example, when he declares that Hitler, Eichmann, and most of the leaders of the Third Reich were Jewish.*).

Yet, Vasiliev's vivid temperament, conviction, and acting skill more than compensate for those drawbacks. Given the peculiar character of his audiences, which regard him as an expert on the Zionist-Masonic conspiracy, his charisma is doubly ensured.

Vasiliev quotes extensively from a "secret document" that, according to him, proves the existence of the Jewish-Masonic conspiracy against mankind. This document, *Protocols of the Elders of Zion,* is the most virulent of all anti-Semitic forgeries.

In 1903, Pavel Krushevan—writer, publisher, and one of the leading ideologists of the *Union of the Russian People*—was the first to print the *Protocols,* serializing the work throughout ten issues of his newspaper *Znamya* (the *Banner*).[2] Decades later it was discovered that the foreign branch of the Czarist secret police had fabricated the *Protocols* in France. Unknown authors slightly modified a rare satirical book that ridiculed the regime of Napoleon III and never was in circulation. The original French manuscript of the forgery (it disappeared later) was translated into Russian. Krushevan claimed that he had obtained the actual record of a meeting of the secret World Jewish Government. This alleged body supposedly had full authority over all Jews and Masons and planned to destroy the traditional values and governments of all other nations in order to take over the world and turn the gentiles into the slaves of the Jews. In this "document," an anonymous Jewish leader explains in detail how the Jews were destroying the governments and enslaving all nations. The "very deep thoughts" of *the Protocols* impressed Nicholas II himself. Later, however, when the Czar learned that his own police had devised the hoax, he forbade the use of the *Protocols* by his government officials. He said, "Good deeds should not be done with dirty hands."

But the *Union of the Russian People* was not a government organization. In 1905, Gregory Butmi and Sergei Nilus published two different book versions

---

* Of course, in a racist anti-Semitic society, some people concealed their Jewish or other "non-Aryan" roots, so real ethnic background of almost anyone is uncertain. Some top leaders of the Third Reich might have a portion of Jewish blood, too. Adolf Hitler himself is a suspect. His father, Lois Hitler, was the "illegitimate" son of an unmarried woman, Maria Anna Schicklgruber, who never revealed the name of her baby's father. He might have been anyone from the neighborhood, although there is a slight possibility that a Jew named Frankenberger or Frankenreither impregnated her when she worked as a maid in his wealthy Jewish household at Graz.

the *Protocols*.* From 1905 to 1907, Butmi's edition had four print runs, while Nilus reprinted his version in 1911 and in 1917.

After the 1917 revolution, the Nilus' version of the *Protocols* became known abroad and was translated into dozens of languages. *Protocols* impressed many leading politicians in the West, including Winston Churchill; but in 1921, the London *Times* presented clear and definite evidence that it was counterfeit.

Nevertheless, the *Protocols* remained linked with anti-Semitic propaganda throughout the world. In the 1920s, a scandal erupted in the United States after Henry Ford published *The International Jew*, a book based on the *Protocols*. The publication sold in hundreds of thousands of copies, but strong protests from the Jewish leaders and some influential intellectuals compelled Ford to apologize publicly and to renounced his authorship. In the mid-1930s, the Swiss courts debated the origination of the *Protocols*. After hearing expert testimonies from throughout Europe, the court came to the conclusion that the *Protocols* were a virulent anti-Semitic forgery.

Thus, in spite of the damage to the Jewish people, this "premier lie of the century," as some experts subsequently dubbed it, could not overshadow truth in the democratic countries. But Hitler's Germany was another story. Nazis reprinted the *Protocols* again and again while no true information about them was accessible. With millions of copies in circulation, the book became a *warrant* for Nazi genocide.**

The USSR represented another extreme. Here the *Protocols* were banned and absolutely unknown. The iron curtain shielded the country from any Western information about them, while Soviet scholars never studied the origin, history, or concomitant controversies connected to the document. In the late 1970s, anonymous anti-Semites—perhaps, after secret KGB aproval—started to distribute it in Samizdat.

Dmitry Vasiliev seems to be the first who began quoting the *Protocols* publicly, and he shrewdly exploited his countrymen's ignorance. He emphasized that Vladimir Lenin's personal library had included several books and booklets about the *Protocols,* evidence—he claimed—that "the leader of the

---

* I have compared these two versions with each other and with the text published in Krushevan's newspaper, *Znamya*, and found that the Butmi's version is almost identical to the newspaper's while Nilus' version is stylistically different. That suggests that there were two independent translations of the *Protocols* from French. Most likely; it was Butmi who brought his translation to Krushevan. Thus, Butmi deserves recognition as the translator of the first published edition of the *Protocols*—not Nilus, as scholars contend.

** *Warrant for Genocide* is the title of the most complete and accurate study of the *Protocols*, conducted by Norman Cohn.[3]

world proletariat" took the *Protocols* seriously. All "true Leninists," he maintained in his speeches, had a right to know this book which their leader studied so carefully. At the same time, Vasiliev did not disclose that those who accepted the *Protocols* at face value considered the Bolshevik revolution itself the fulfillment of the secret plan outlined in them.

In 1985 and 1986, Vasiliev repeatedly declared his loyalty to the Bolshevik Party and extolled Gorbachev in all possible ways. He accused the "Zionists" of trying to "play off *Pamyat* against the party." Later, he started to speak sharply against "secret Zionists" within the party leadership, including Politburo member Alexander Yakovlev. Still later, when the party lost its control of the country, Vasiliev labeled Mikhail Gorbachev a "Zionist" as well. During the same years, Vasiliev turned from an atheist and Leninist into a Russian Orthodox Christian believer and found a lot of friends and supporters among the clergy.

This super-flexibility of the leader failed, however, to save *Pamyat* from internal differences and an eventual split.

There had long been signs of that. In February 1988, the Soviet newspaper *Vechernyaya Moskva (Evening Moscow)* printed an interview with two members of *Pamyat*, Doctor of Chemistry Stepan Zhdanov and painter Igor Sychev. Both argued that they represented the "good" *Pamyat* while Vasiliev represented the "bad." A vivid cartoon of Vasiliev saying "*Pamyat* is me" accompanied the interview.[4]

Given that at that time the party still maintained control over the press and that *Vechernyaya Moskva* was one of the most compliant newspapers, the appearance of such an article suggested an urgent need to respond to the escalating criticism of *Pamyat*. Left-wing publications had described it as a pro-Fascist, chauvinistic organization, and the liberal part of the party chieftains encouraged such censure.

The conservatives opted to preserve *Pamyat* by sacrificing one of its most odious figures, but their plan proved only partly successful. Vasiliev still had a sufficient margin of support to preserve his leadership. Indeed, a significant part of Moscow *Pamyat* remained loyal to him, and he even assumed control over the organizations in Leningrad, Novosibirsk, Sverdlovsk,* and several other cities, creating a historical-patriotic *front Pamyat*. However, another part of the historical-patriotic society broke its ties with Vasiliev and formed the **movement** *Pamyat*, with Igor Sychev at its head. I decided to interview him.

---

* Now and before the revolution—Yekaterinburg. The city was renamed after a prominent Bolshevik, Yakov Sverdlov, but after the collapse of communism returned to its original name.

In the beginning was the Word

Igor Sychev lived at Bolshaya Filevskaya Street in a standard one-bedroom apartment on the second floor of a typical *khrushchoba*.*

He shared the flat with his son and two nice-looking small dogs—who raised a ruckus upon seeing me. Although in apple-pie order, the rooms betrayed the absence of a woman. Uniquely male, his lodgings preserved an austere, almost military tone. Two strictly symmetrical rows of equal square posters on the wall looked like troops on parade. Their selection was scrupulously determined and told me a lot about the host. The portraits of all the great Russian generals, whose names Stalin had listed in his historic November 7, 1941, speech at the Red Square military parade (with German troops several miles from the capital), stared severely down at me.

"Let the courageous images of our great ancestors, Alexander Nevsky, Dmitry Donskoi, Kuzma Minin, Dmitry Pozharsky, Alexander Suvorov, and Mikhail Kutuzov,** inspire us in this war," Stalin said. The Supreme Commander-in-Chief could offer little more encouragement to the hastily mobilized Soviet recruits after four-and-a-half months of war. Almost the entire Red Army pre-war personnel (four million soldiers and officers!) had been slaughtered or taken prisoner—to a large degree because of Stalin's poor leadership. Later, he acknowledged his military inadequacies and blunders.

> "Our government had made many mistakes; there were a few moments of despair in 1941-1942. Some other people could have said to the government, 'You fell short of our expectations; go away. We shall set up another government.' But the Russian people did not choose to do so because they believed in the right policies of their government and they chose to make sacrifices."[5]

---

* A combination of two words: *Khrushchev* and *trushchoba* (slums). *Khrushcheba* refers to the shabby, four-entrance, five-storied walk-ups. They were built in large numbers at Nikita Khrushchev's direction in a vain effort to solve the housing crisis. These tenements had low ceilings and extremely small kitchens and bathrooms.

** *Alexander Nevsky* (1220-1263) was the Grand Duke of Novgorod who—allegedly—successfully fought against German invaders. *Dmitry Donskoi* (1350-1389) was the Grand Duke of Moscow; he defeated Mongolian (Tatar) troops in 1380 at the Don River. *Kuzma Minin* (?-1616) and *Dmitry Pozharsky* (1578-1642) helped to restore Russian statehood in the early seventeenth century after many years of anarchy, civil war, and foreign intervention resulting from a dynastic crisis. *Alexander Suvorov* (1729-1800) was a Russian field marshal (generalissimo) who won many battles and never lost a single one. *Mikhail Kutuzov* (1745-1813) was the Russian field marshal who won the war against Napoleon

Nevertheless, "the courageous images of our great ancestors" helped Stalin to win the war and later they were glorified in hundreds of books, poems, movies, and paintings. Now I saw them again in the apartment of the new Russian patriotic leader. The faces of the generals, in harmony with several banners strung in the corners of the room, imbued the flat with a strong sense of the battlefield.

But we were talking peacefully.

We sat at a small table pushed close to the wall—I to the right of my host, his son to the left. The boy, a lean fellow in his early twenties, never uttered a word during the entire two hours of our talk. I presumed that his training prohibited him from engaging in conversation with his elders or expressing his opinion.

Igor was about 45. He had a pleasant, ordinary face with a clean forehead. A small beard did not make him look older. His blue eyes had a straightforward gaze that nevertheless betrayed a certain excitement. He had given interviews more than once, but he was not accustomed yet to guests from as far away as I had come.

"Tell me, please, about yourself, about the *Pamyat* Society, about its history," I asked him.[6]

"I am Sychev, Igor Sergeevich," he began, "a member of the Union of Soviet Artists. A painter. Mostly I paint landscapes and old Moscow."

He spoke slowly, choosing his words with care.

"For this and other reasons," he continued, "I feel a particular affinity to the ideals propagated and fought for by the *Pamyat* Society. In our opinion, memory[*]—as such—never disappeared from popular consciousness. It has always existed in different manifestations because, if it were not for this memory—the great memory of our land and our history—there would probably have been no great exploits, no great courage of the Russian people and the other peoples of the Soviet Union in World War II."

Sychev glanced at the tape recorder that I had put on the table. The overseas device noticeably embarrassed him; but, on second thought, he said that he did not object to tape-recording. I asked him to give a more detailed account of the emergence of *Pamyat*.

"The *Pamyat* Movement started taking shape in the early 1980s," he explained. "It was prompted by the publication of the novel-essay *Pamyat* by

---

[*] In Russian, *pamyat* means "memory."

Vladimir Chivilikhin,* which gave impetus to public consciousness for the revival of memory about everything that is sacred for the nation, without which no nation can exist."

I failed to learn from Sychev anything more definitive about the origin of *Pamyat*. But later on, burrowing through numerous materials I had acquired from a variety of sources, I did come across a collective interview with several *Pamyat* activists that detailed its evolution more precisely. The contributors included T. Ponomareva, a member of the Writers Union; Doctor of Law G. Litvinova; engineer G. Frygin; Doctor of Chemistry, Professor S. Zhdanov; Assistant Professor A. Vasilenko; Russian language and literature instructor A. Svyatozarsky, and Igor Sychev himself. The list of participants suggests that educated circles were actively involved with *Pamyat*. Engineer Frygin, said, "I am among those who stood at the sources of the *Pamyat* Movement that emerged in the late 1970s, when we organized the first *voskresniks*** to restore cultural and historical monuments. ... The name *Pamyat* for our movement was on everybody's lips, including mine."[7]

According to another version, *Pamyat* appeared in the early 1980s under the umbrella of the Ministry of the Aviation Industry.[8] A Muscovite, who requested anonymity and who kept a close eye on the movement, confirmed that *Pamyat* was, indeed, set up at the Ministry—but much earlier (in 1972-1973), with high-ranking officials included on its roster. According to my source, two charter members later became ministers, while another became a member of the Academy of Sciences Presidium.[9]

Thus, it became clear to me that *Pamyat* was not one of numerous "informal" organizations which had sprung up spontaneously after the *glasnost* era made it possible. Under *glasnost*, *Pamyat* only came out of the closet, but it had started to function much earlier, when no one group could appear without authorization. At the same time, nobody could say for sure who had authorized it and when, where its headquarters were located, and who financed its activities. All this secrecy indicated the direct involvement of the KGB.

Sychev claimed that his *Pamyat* Movement united hundreds of organizations in 30 Russian cities. These figures coincide with those given by Dmitry Vasiliev. I could see that each man laid claim to the same membership body as his organization: Vasiliev insisted that they belonged to his Historic-Patriotic *Front*, Sychev—to his Historic-Patriotic *Movement*.

---

* Vladimir Chivilikhin (1928-1984) was a second-rank Soviet writer with Stalinist and "patriotic" views. His book *Pamyat* is a boring and inaccurate two-volume piece, but the officials widely used it to promote "patriotism" among the youth.

** Voluntary collective work on Sundays; *voskresnik*—from *voskresenie*, which means Sunday.

Sychev also emphasized that he was at the head of the patriotic union *Russia*, which he characterized as the most active core of the *Movement*.

I wanted to know what the difference was between the *Pamyat* Front and the *Pamyat* Movement in terms of their visions, goals, and tactics, but it was not easy for Igor Sychev to outline that in clear words. He just told me his story.

Standing at Manezh Square

Initially, he said, *Pamyat conducted* mostly cultural and educational activities, collecting facts and documents about forgotten historical figures or neglected architectural monuments; but, in Sychev's opinion, it was insufficient. He was keen on action. The *standing* at Manezh Square on May 6, 1987, marked the turning point in *Pamyat* activities for Igor Sychev.

The authorities had approved the construction of the Monument of Victory (in World War II) at *Poklonnaya Gora* (Bowing Hill). Here, Napoleon, according to legend, waited in vain for a deputation of Muscovites to hand him the symbolic keys to Moscow with a humble bow. No one consulted the people about the implementation of the project, which included leveling the entire hill to build a museum. *Pamyat* did not approve.

About 300 members of *Pamyat* attended a meeting at the Komsomol (Young Communist League) Moscow City Committee in April 1987, when Sychev urged them to stand against the construction at Poklonnaya Gora. Thus the idea of "standing" came into being. Vasiliev proposed May 6, the feast of St. George the Dragon Slayer, for the rally since St. George's image served as the emblem of *Pamyat*.*

Vasiliev brought about two hundred people to the square; Sychev, 150—among them artists, writers, poets, and other members of the "artistic community." They crowded into Manezh Square, banners unfolded and placards held high. The slogans spoke volumes.

"Do away with the saboteurs of *perestroika!*"
"Stop the construction at Poklonnaya Gora!"
"We demand a meeting with Gorbachev and Yeltsin!"
"The memory of the people is sacred!"
"We demand a legal status for the historical-patriotic society *Pamyat!*"

Just a few years earlier, an unauthorized demonstration could have not gathered more than a half-dozen people and would have lasted only a few sec-

---

*The same picture of St. George the Dragon Slayer (Georgy Pobedonosets) was also the emblem of the *Union of the Russian People*.

onds. All dissidents or Jewish *refuseniks* who might have had the courage for such an action would have been under constant KGB monitoring, all their mail, contacts, and telephone conversations under strict control. Thus, the authorities would have know exactly from the beginning the time and place of the planned gathering. That day, the police would not have allowed most of potential participants to leave their homes; those few who managed to elude the police, come to the site, and unfold their placards, would have been immediately attacked and arrested. The only hope would have been that within these few seconds, foreign correspondents (informed by the demonstrators in advance) would have been able to shoot a couple of pictures and tell the world about their protest.

In 1987, however, such a brutal crackdown was not in line with the new, liberal government policy. At the same time, the demonstration was not authorized and the slogans challenged the authorities. Later, unauthorized demonstrations became routine, but this was one of the first; thus, the confused authorities failed to instruct the police. Without authorization, the police could not or did not want to disperse the gathering and responded only by putting barriers along the sidewalks. Curious passers-by crowded close to the barriers, only creating more problems to the pedestrian traffic in one of the most crowded intersections in Moscow.

"I took the flag of the Russian Federation," Sychev said, "came to the barriers, and urged people to be active—to join our standing for the Russian land, for everything that is sacred. And people, plucking up their courage, overthrew the barriers and joined us. I brought three groups, each of 60 to 70 people, thus enlarging the total number to over 400, or maybe 500, people.

"Valery Saikin, chairman of the Moscow City Council Executive Committee, turned up and suggested that we submit our complaints to him and leave the square. We answered that we were asking for a meeting with Gorbachev or Yeltsin, as one of our slogans said. Saikin disappeared, but later appeared again. Finally, we were invited to fold the slogans and banners and quietly march to the Moscow City Council. We said that there was nothing wrong in our slogans and we would not fold them but would stand on the square all day long and throughout the night."

The authorities had to yield again. The marchers formed a column five or six people wide and, holding high their banners and placards, marched about half a mile to the Moscow City Council, where in the big assembly hall they were received by Boris Yeltsin, the then first secretary of the Moscow City Party Committee.

"Who actually participated in the meeting with Yeltsin?" I asked.

"All of us!" Sychev said. "All of us, with our placards, found seats in the assembly hall. We did not delegate any special group to meet him."

"All of you were received?" I asked, surprised.

"Yes, up to 400 people filled the hall."

"But you could not have spoken—all of you together—with Yeltsin. Who spoke on behalf of *Pamyat?*"

Igor Sychev did not find this question very much to his liking.

"They suggested that I speak, too," he said nervously, "but I decided against speaking as one of the preceding speakers had already said all that was necessary about Poklonnaya Gora."

I persisted and asked him again who had stated *Pamyat's* claims to Yeltsin. Sychev named Dmitry Vasiliev with reluctance.

"In fact," he hurried to explain, "Vasiliev was instructed to maintain conversation. My functions involved pure organization. To organize the people, to arrange them accordingly, to take them to the necessary place. I fulfilled my task."

Uncomfortable with the historical reality, Sychev unwillingly admitted that in this meeting with Boris Yeltsin, he, the head of the *movement*, had remained in the background while Vasiliev had played first fiddle.

Sychev remembered that Yeltsin had answered all the questions but one—whether Poklonnaya Gora would be restored. But at least, Yeltsin assured the audience, the construction work would cease.

"In fact, the construction never stopped for a single day. In the daytime it was stopped, but at night it was resumed," Sychev said to me. "In the following two days, a big part of Poklonnaya Gora was hastily removed. That's why *Pamyat* organized another standing, on May 9, this time at Pobeda* Square."

At noon they raised their signs and placards. One can easily imagine the officials' alarm at a non-authorized demonstration—on the official Victory Day at that!

Street-watering machines appeared shortly on the square and started to push the marchers aside. However, Igor Sychev assured me, he himself never gave in. With the flag of the Russian Federation, he stepped forward under the streams of icy water, forcing the machine to stop. Retired Colonel Levshov, who "had stormed the Reichstag," followed Sychev's lead, compelling another street-cleaner to shut down. The "standing" lasted until 4:00 p.m.

---

* Pobeda means victory. The square was named in honor of victory in World War II. Thus, the gathering in Victory Square on Victory Day had an additional symbolic flavor.

"We wanted to wait for the Victory fireworks but could not go on as some people were all wet and it was horribly cold. Besides, Vasiliev and his group failed to back us."

"Do you mean that he was not there?"

"No, he was not. Neither he, nor his people were present. Except for a few who refused to obey his instructions and attended as private citizens, not as representatives of his organization."

"Why did he give such instructions?"

"Yeltsin promised to be positive about granting a legal status to the *Pamyat* Society, so Vasiliev was afraid that their participation in any action could provide an excuse not to keep the promise."

Following actions

Sychev said that in 1987, they carried out approximately fifteen "patriotic actions," as he called their activities.

"Thus, there was a movement of setting up a monument to Sergius of Radonezh[*] near Zagorsk.[**] The patriotically minded public contributed greatly. In September, I headed a breakthrough to Radonezh of a team consisting of approximately 300 to 400 people following me from the railway station. At first, there were not many of us activists, about 50 people. But gradually, people joined us as we marched, our red banner flying. We forged a sizable column which broke through police cordons almost effortlessly."

As he continued in his calm, almost indifferent tone, the story became more and more dramatic.

"The last cordon was near the bridge leading to Radonezh. We stopped chest to chest with the police on the bridge when suddenly we heard a thunderous *hurrah!* The cheer came from those who, by hook or by crook, had already reached Radonezh and were now greeting us. Renewed by their enthusiasm, we pushed further and broke through the cordon."

The monument was not erected at that time, however. Afraid that the situation could got out of control, the authorities stopped the truck with the sculpture on its way to Radonezh. They turned it back to the studio of Fyodor Klykov, the sculptor, also a member of *Pamyat*.

---

[*] Sergius of Radonezh (1321-1391)—the guardian saint of Russia. He founded the Sergian Monastery of the Trinity in the forest of Radonezh. It became the center and symbol of Russian religious renewal and national unity. Sergius rendered considerable support to Moscow's Grand Duke Dmitry Donskoi, who instigated the liberation of Russia from the Mongol yoke.

[**] See footnote on page 90 (chapter 5).

"We displayed our patriotic determination in Radonezh," Sychev said with pride. "We were two thousand strong and we stated that we, the public, wanted to commemorate the spot. Officials from the Ministry of Culture and local authorities showed up. They assured us that there would be a monument there eventually. I said that we would come back the next year and see whether they had fulfilled their promise."

While telling his story, the leader of the *Pamyat* Movement repeatedly mentioned that Dmitry Vasiliev—disapproving of the demonstration—did all he could to undermine it. At first he insisted that an overt activist stance would result in the crushing of the patriotic forces and the discrediting of Klykov (the sculptor), putting him in opposition to the authorities. Later, he said that he was against a monument to Sergius of Radonezh since it was not in keeping with religious canon to erect a statue of a holy man. And finally, he tried to discredit the monument itself.

"The work depicts an old man, with an adolescent in front of him holding an icon of the Trinity," Sychev explained. "Vasiliev imposed his interpretation that the sculpture represent a Jewish ritual murder. The old man looked Jewish, he said, while the boy looked as if he were murdered."

But, despite Vasiliev's opposition, the monument was erected on May 29, and more than five thousand people came to Radonezh to attend the unveiling.

On September 18, *Pamyat*, as it had promised a year before, held a celebration in the town. Once again, the people were confronted by police cordons which, this time, acted more decisively. Three leading figures, including Sychev himself, were arrested and detained for a couple of hours.

Although Igor Sergeevich described this clash as an attempt to crack down on the patriotic movement, I learned that a simple misunderstanding had actually sparked the altercation. Just prior to the rally, the government had endorsed a new procedure for public assemblies, requiring advance permission to hold a demonstration. Sychev did not secure the required permit.

A few days later, he organized a rally at the Staroye Simonovo monastery, and all went smoothly. According to Sychev, the *Pamyat* Movement "revenged itself for the failure it had experienced in Radonezh."

"We thought that the new regulation of public rallies would put an end to our activities," Sychev said. "But it did not happen this way because ours is a patriotic stand since we believe in all that is sacred. In a year and a half, we held about sixty public rallies and demonstrations."

He handed me an annotated list of these activities. When I looked through the list—peppered with well-known and barely known historical figures, anniversaries, streets, cemeteries, and monasteries—I was impressed.

We should keep in mind that when the devastating fire of revolution, civil war, collectivization, and the terror of state security bodies burnt out the lives and souls of millions of people, not only the living but the dead as well were devoured by this inferno. The creators of a "new world" blew up graves, confiscated church property, arrested clergymen of all religions, and destroyed temples or turned them into clubs, storehouses, or latrines. Clearing the site for a new communist religion, the Bolsheviks dealt severely with old religions. "Our motto is do away with rabbis and priests!" crowds of militant atheists repeated cheerfully. This barbarism erased so many events and names from Russian history that future generations of scholars will have to work tirelessly to restore them. What is wrong with some people and groups which are concerned and try to do something about that?

"Perhaps, Sychev's *Pamyat* is really different from Vasiliev's," I thought. "Perhaps they are honestly preoccupied with the revival of the Russian traditional culture—not with exposing Masons and Zionists."

Sychev and Vasiliev

I did not question Sychev about his principal rival, Dmitry Vasiliev, but he himself kept digressing to this sore subject. No matter where I tried to direct our conversation, Sychev returned to Vasiliev until at last I implored, "Let us finish with Vasiliev!"

Delighted, Sychev replied, "He is already finished!"

But when I made the transcript of the tape recording, I realized that Vasiliev had permeated our discussion from beginning to end.

For instance, when we talked about *Pamyat's* regular meetings in the early 1980s in the Gorbunov House of Culture in Moscow, Sychev examined the cross purposes of the separate *Pamyat* factions.

"Here, at these meetings, something emerged that led the patriotic movement astray. Vasiliev read out excerpts from the *Protocols of the Elders of Zion* and, in fact, declared the existence in this country of the Zionist-Masonic conspiracy. His point was that if the conspiracy succeeded, Zionists would enslave the country, would enslave and destroy the nation. Since then, *Pamyat* has acquired this coloring, which was not intrinsic to it. Given the situation that we, our people, and our fatherland are facing now, it is simply provocative to speak of searching for enemies and liquidating them. Our people are lacking now to a large extent in spirituality and memory. Under the circumstances, how could one try to find enemies, liquidate, or neutralize them? Who has the right to decide who is the enemy and who is not, with the people unable to interfere!

Here lies the difference in the positions of the *Pamyat* Movement and the *Pamyat* Society headed by Vasiliev. He regards only one thing as of paramount: There are the enemies; and as long as they exist, Russia cannot develop as a full-fledged state."

"If Vasiliev's views are in such contradictions to those of *Pamyat,* how do you account for the fact that he is at the head of the organization?" I asked.

"He is not at the head!" Sychev exclaimed. "He heads only the *Pamyat society* here in Moscow."

"Were you also a member of the society?"

"I have never been a member of it; and when Vasiliev claims to have thousands of people under his leadership, he simply bluffs. Only a few people follow his lead. But the mass media highlighted him as the most important leader."

"What mass media do you mean?"

"Both in this country and abroad. They started speaking of *'Pamyat's* leader, Dmitry Vasiliev.' But what *Pamyat* do they mean? One must differentiate. He is the leader of the *Pamyat* Society. This organization, in our opinion, was put to the foreground with provocative purposes."

"With provocative purposes? Who might be interested in it?"

Since Sychev himself discounted the "Zionist-Masonic conspiracy," he was at a loss for an answer to this question.

"Well, who?" He hesitated. "Probably somebody is entertaining a wish to accuse *Pamyat,* I mean all *Pamyat,* of the mortal sin of nationalism. If they accuse the whole movement, then, in certain circumstances, the government machine could liquidate it with a stroke of the pen. This would mean, in fact, liquidating the patriots indispensable to any full-fledged, strong state."

"Whose purposes does Vasiliev serve?" Igor went on. "Deeds are what we never see from the *Pamyat* Society. We only see their demagogy and a desire to show off."

"But they hold crowded rallies." I tried to put in a word in Vasiliev's defense.

"Crowded rallies? They don't hold them!" Sychev became angry. "That is what we must be clear about: Who holds what. I will put it plainly. After that meeting when Vasiliev declared the existence of some dark forces, a split took place."

"When did it happen?" I asked.

"I believe ... probably ... in 1985 or 1986." Sychev was uncertain about the year. We changed the subject, but when he returned to it, I reminded him of his statement.

"You said that you split from him in 1985," I prompted.

"No!" he exploded. "The split took place in 1987. It was complete and final, and occurred when he started to label us as nothing short of enemies of the people for our activities."

Sychev's memory was inconsistent. In discussing secondary military battles that had taken place one, two, or even six hundred years ago, he was as fluid with dates as if he kept a reference book in his head. But when we touched upon recent events, uncertainty emerged in his eyes and his words became confused.

Meetings in the Gorbunov House of Culture, according to Sychev, had started in 1983. Then, following Vasiliev's statement about the existence of a Zionist-Masonic conspiracy, the organization had split down the middle. Since Sychev dated the division at 1985, 1986, and, finally, at 1987, either Vasiliev had never touched this subject for several years or his statements about the conspiracy had aroused no objections.

However, when we came back to the same subject for the third time, a completely different picture emerged:

"Several patriotic meetings were held at which Vasiliev showed himself as a good speaker, an active person. These meetings gathered huge crowds. By the way, these meetings were organized mostly by us painters."

"Was Vasiliev the key speaker at these meetings?" I wanted to be exact.

"He often acted as chairman of the meeting," Sychev replied, indicating, thus, that he and Vasiliev had run in one harness for several years. The differences between the *movement* and the *society* emerged only after the Manezh Square rally and the meeting with Boris Yeltsin (when Vasiliev decided to lie low for some time to get legal status while Sychev deemed it necessary to increase public awareness).

This triggered a rabid enmity between them.

"It was not that Vasiliev tried just to avoid activities," Sychev argued. "He stuck various labels on us, calling us Masons or Zionists. There is nothing else he can say. According to him, he alone personifies patriotism. Only those who follow him are genuine patriots. He regards it as inconceivable that some groups could emerge having nothing to do with him and still holding patriotic stands. He seeks to get everyone under himself and, by pursuing such a provocative line, jeopardizes the entire patriotic movement."

"Vasiliev makes frequent use of Adolf Hitler's arguments in his addresses," Sychev went on. "You will find them filled with anti-Semitism and chauvinism. He is aware that Russian culture and history have undergone an all-out beating and that, in response, people are anxious to find out who is to blame. Thus, he lays the guilt for all this at the door of the Jewish people. He calls them 'Zionists and Masons.' In our opinion, the historical evil that had taken place was the result of government and party policies. That is why now we say that the party and government officials must shoulder the responsibility for what was destroyed and outraged back in the 1930s or even in the 1920s. That is why there is no need to search for any concrete people of any concrete nationality. The percentage of Jewish presence in the government bodies was large. But the representatives of other ethnic groups also contributed to the destruction of sacred national values."

"These must be the Masons, from Vasiliev's point of view," I suggested.

"I don't think it is so." Sychev pressed his point. "Shall we presume then that the whole Soviet government was Zionist-Masonic? In our opinion, it was not. Such was the policy of a state allegedly creating a new culture and a new human being and thus cutting off the roots connecting this state's peoples with their great past. This cutting off took place. Coming out as a fighter against Zionism and Free-Masonry, Vasiliev acts as a voluntary or involuntary accomplice of the destroyers."

Sychev managed to disarm me again by putting things so definitely. I thought, why should we sound the alarm, saying that Nazi sentiments are on the rise, that extremists incite ethnic enmity in order to sink the Russian democracy (that comes into being with such pain) in the blood of Jews and other non-Russians?

"Tell me, please, Igor Sergeevich," I began as I posed my last question, "what about such people as Vladimir Begun, Alexander Romanenko, and Yevgeny Yevseev—who for about twenty years have been writing books and articles exposing the conspiracy of Zionists and Masons? Are they somehow connected with Vasiliev or, maybe, with you?"

"They are not connected with Vasiliev!" Sychev answered sharply. "He wants to stick everyone to himself as though all good people, scholars working for the benefit of our fatherland, serve as ideologists for his deeds. But these people do not want to be engaged in his swindle."

"Do you mean to say that Begun, Yevseev, and Romanenko are supporting you, not Vasiliev?"

"Certainly! They are within the sphere of the *Pamyat movement*, not society, do you see?"

Yes. I could see it all now. Romanenko, Begun, and Yevseev propagated in their books the very same ideas that Vasiliev disgorged before his numerous audiences. By enlisting their support, Sychev only acknowledged that the differences between the *Pamyat movement* and the *Pamyat Society* are nothing more than a family quarrel.

I do not know how this thought flashing through my mind was reflected on my face, but Sychev noticed it. He started to explain that the above-mentioned Zionologists "are professing creative principles and that there are more positive than negative aspects in their works."

Well, I appreciated his sincerity.

After the interview

I visited Igor Sychev on November 22, 1988. Soon I left Moscow and I was sure that I would not hear his name again for a long time. I was wrong. Almost immediately, reports started coming in about new activities of the *movement,* not society, *Pamyat.*

First of all, it turned out that the Alexander Kosarev memorial meeting mentioned in chapter three was organized by T. Ponomareva and G. Frygin, close associates of Sychev. The scandalous meeting had taken place three days before I interviewed Igor Sergeevich, but he did not mention this latest rally of his Movement. On December 13, right after the horrible Armenian earthquake, Igor Sychev spoke at the Moscow discussion club *Perestroika.*

> "We cannot take the responsibility for eighty thousand dead in Armenia away from the Jewish people," he stated. "There are three Jews in the state system. A great number of Jews who work in the field of geophysics did not foresee the disaster. That is why the full responsibility lies with the Jewish people." [10]

Hardly three more weeks passed before Igor Sychev reappeared in the public eye. This time he was not alone but with a team he called the Patriotic Union *Russia,* the most active link of the *Pamyat* Movement. The rally was staged at the club, where a meeting was scheduled in which Vitaly Korotich, editor-in-chief of the weekly liberal magazine *Ogonyok,* was to be nominated for a seat in the Congress of People's Deputies. For the first time in Soviet history, a semi-democratic process of election was in place.

Sychev and his Union occupied the gallery. When the meeting started, his team unfolded placards and stamped their feet, shouting and whistling. The team was well-trained and highly visible. "Their leader, sitting in the center," an eye-witness described, "shouted out, 'Long live *Pamyat!* Long live *Russia!'* After which he raised up his boot."[11]

It was not hard to recognize Igor Sergeevich in the picture that accompanied the publication. In the photograph, he was not sitting, but standing, and had his right hand—not his boot—above his head.

Another eyewitness reported no less impressive details:

"The microphones installed in the hall were surrounded by groups of people whose unity was conspicuous thanks to the badges with the picture of St. George the Dragon Slayer. They announced for the whole audience to hear:
'The people do not need Korotich!'
'We must expose the weathercock!'
'Shame on the alcoholizers* of Russia!'
...Then they started shouting out anti-Semitic slogans."[12]

The meeting could not proceed and was canceled.

Pamyat staged its next *action* on January 23 in the Kryliya Sovetov Sport Center. The editorial staffs and free-lance authors of the "patriotic" journals *Moskva, Molodaya Gvardia,* and *Roman-Gazeta* managed to attract a multi-thousand audience; thus, the gathering offered an excellent opportunity for Igor Sychev's Movement.

Representatives of the *Pamyat* Movement swung banners with the slogan: *"No* to cosmopolitans without kith or kin."** This meeting was notable for the complete mutual understanding between the audience and presidium. Small wonder, given that the three magazines together with *Nash Sovremennik* were just shaping *Pamyat's* slogans into a literary form.[13]

On February 19, a noisy rally took place near the Moscow TV center. Passions were high, since, for a long time, the "patriots" had demanded more access to the TV programs than they could receive. That was enough for them to claim that the TV was "occupied" by the Jews and served international Zionism. "Central television cripples the youth and destroys national culture!" one slogan read. "We are sick and tired of Tel-Avision!*** Give us a Russian TV-screen!" demanded another one.[14] As we can see, the slogans were not devoid of wit.

---

* One of the anti-Semitic prejudices in today's Russia is a widespread belief that Jews "alcoholize" the Russian people.

** As we know from previous chapters, "cosmopolitans without kith or kin" was the nickname of the Jews during the Stalin's anti-Semitic campaign in late 1940s and early 1950s

*** Neologism originated from Tel-Aviv.

One T-shirt-clad demonstrator—who appeared on the same placard-degraded *Tel-Avision*—carried a sign that read, "Down with the occupation of Jewish Nazis!" When asked about his attitude toward the liberal weekly *Moscow News,* he gave a simple answer: "Masonic News!"

The newspaper *Sovetskaya Kultura* carried a detailed quotation from a speech of Alexander Kulakov, one of the rally participants, who later became a leader of the *Pamyat* Orthodox National-Patriotic Front.*

"It is time to set up a Russian Academy of Sciences, a Russian Communist Party and its Central Committee.** Russia is the only Soviet republic that has neither. We must develop our economy on our own basis, close our borders to keep away from economic "cooperation" with the West, from foreign concessions. Free-Masonry is worming its way into the country under the cover of business. Of primary importance is introducing percentage representation of every nationality in the structures of management, science, the press, and others. Russia must be run by Russians. ... As to army reductions, we are against them! The army is the only lasting hope today! Eventually we must return to the traditions of Russian Orthodoxy."[15]

Wandering in the crowd, the reporter heard "the revived stories" about the Jews drinking "blood of Christian babies," and even that the execution of the Czar and his family was "a ritual Jewish sacrifice." The editorial note says:

"This rally was officially allowed and was carried out under police supervision. Our employee called the Dzerzhinsky District Executive Committee, where they confirmed that the not-unknown Igor Sychev had lodged a request to the Moscow City Council to hold a rally against the dominance of pornography on TV. The Council forwarded the request to the Dzerzhinsky District Committee, which complied with the request at its sitting on February 15."[16]

Thus, contrary to what Igor Sychev told me, the authorities had no intention of using the decree on holding rallies, meetings and demonstrations against the "patriots." If there were some misunderstandings between *Pamyat* and the authorities in the chaotic situation at the beginning of *glasnost* era, they

---

* Another speech of Alexander Kulakov was quoted in chapter five.

** Very soon these requests were met.

were successfully ironed out. And when some new disagreements occurred, the authorities—not *Pamyat*—went on the defensive.

For instance, when the Moscow City Court considered a retired KGB officer's suit against well-known author Ales Adamovich—according to his opponent, he had insulted the honor and dignity of Comrade Stalin—Sychev's *Pamyat* turned the trial into an arena for yet another "patriotic action."

"Roaring, hysterical sobs of the defenders of "democracy" and Joseph Dzhugashvili* rocked the austere walls of the building at Kalanchovka Street** during the interval. Hysterical people literally hunted out journalists and hurried to explain everything, to dot all 'i's for them, feeling free in their choice of words and gestures. One could see posters and slogans insulting the mass media, microphones 'on fishing-rods,' photo-flashes, and speakers changing—but the subject never changed."[17]

When Romanenko's suit against *Sovetskaya Kultura* was considered, as was described in the chapter three, Sychev's *Pamyat* played the main role in the show again.

"Some *Pamyat* representatives even wear T-shirts on which is printed 'De-Zionization of society.' As I could gather from their shouts, these fans of scandals and rallies in courtrooms are ready to stage pogroms right away, though racist propaganda is forbidden as a criminal offense. ... In Moscow, courtrooms are being turned into rostrum for non-sanctioned *Pamyat* rallies, but the authorities never take any measures against these 'patriots.'"[18]

Pamyat staged a noisy protest on July 18, 1989, the anniversary of the murder of Nicholas II and his family. The rally took place in Moscow near the monument to Yakov Sverdlov (1884-1919), a leading Bolshevik of Jewish origin, second in rank after Lenin.

"Nearly no one mentioned the last Russian emperor's family shot in Yekaterinburg in 1918," an eyewitness testifies. "About half-a-thousand cutthroats were shouting out these notorious slogans: 'Down with the Jewish fascism in the USSR,' 'Jews, go to Israel,' 'Down with russophobes,'*** and

---

* Stalin's real name.
** Where the Moscow City Court is located (see Chapter four).
*** This term is discussed in the next chapter.

'Down with the Zionization of Russia.' A bit later, for about ten minutes, they kept shouting, 'Down with the monument to Sverdlov.'"[19]

The demonstration ended with the laying of a barbed-wire wreath bearing the sign "To the organizer of mass terror" at the foot of the monument.

"Bearded people," the same eyewitness says, "continued to converse near the monument for another couple of hours on the subject of the Old Testament being a program of action for the exterminating the Russian people."[20]

Demoralizing public impact of such activities was enormous. After seventy years of strict ban on any deviation from the official party line, suddenly everything became allowed, if it sounded "patriotic." Even direct attacks on the most inviolable Saints of the Soviet Communist religion became possible, if these Saints bore Jewish names. "Patriotic" hatred toward Jews and other minorities rapidly filled the spiritual vacuum of the *perestroika* years.

CHAPTER 7

"RUSSOPHOBIA"

Heralds of the Big People

Until 1989, Igor Shafarevich was known much more in the West than in Russia. A child prodigy, he displayed extraordinary learning abilities very early on. At age of 16, he had already graduated from Moscow University.

He became a prominent mathematician, a corresponding member of the Soviet Academy of Sciences, and a member the U. S. National Academy of Sciences, the American Academy of Art and Sciences, the London Royal Society, and the German Academy Leopoldina. He holds many international awards and prizes. From the early 1970s, Shafarevich also authored a number of sociological works that sharply criticized the socialist system and ideology and were widely circulated abroad, reaching only a narrow circle of Samizdat readers in his own country. They brought the author worldwide repute as a brave and courageous dissident—and a lot of problems with the Soviet authorities. Unlike other leading dissidents, he has never been arrested; but the authorities forbade him to teach in Moscow University or to publish his works in the Soviet press.

In 1982, Igor Shafarevich wrote *Russophobia*, a book so explosive, as he believed, that he chose not to publish it—even in the West. The manuscript, however, had some narrow circulation in the Samizdat. Victor Astafiev, for example, indicated his familiarity with *Russophobia* in his letter to Eidelman when he wrote, "We are still *the big people* and it still does not suffice to kill us, but you must bring us down first."

The basic premise of the book (borrowed, according to the author, from a barely remembered French scholar) comes from the statement that every nation, and especially the Russian nation, consists of two antagonistic factions: *the big people* and *the small people*.

While *the big people* form a group that includes the vast majority of ordinary Russian men and women sharing the same beliefs and values and practicing a traditional lifestyle, *the small people* constitute a tiny minority of the nation made up of a liberal-minded intellectual elite, the most active and influential part of which is Jewish. *The small people*, according to this definition, are West-oriented highbrow snobs, liberal aristocrats. They have no roots within *the big people* and are not connected to their nation by common traditions, culture, or religion. *The small people* seek to impose on *the big people* values and institutions alien to their own way of life borrowed from the West. *The big people,* as a single body, is conservative and resists innovations, while *the small people* want to change the traditional life of the nation even against its will. *The small people* despise and hate the vast majority of their countrymen. Zealously pursuing their goal, they do not care about the damage they impose on their country. *The small people* are *russophobes;* they are deadly enemies of Russia.

Thus, in *Russophobia*, a well-known dissident with a long record as a courageous fighter against the totalitarian Communist regime, emerges as an opponent to democracy. He sees the Western system as a Jewish innovation that *the small people* are inflicting on Russia with no regard for her age-old traditions. In practice, he concludes, these efforts can only result in the enslaving of Russia by the West.

Not just a figment of Shafarevich's imagination, negative attitude toward the Russians existed in the Soviet Union for decades—primarily in non-Russian republics of this multinational country. Local ethnic groups associated the Communist totalitarian regime with the domination of the Russians. The regime itself strengthened such sentiments by infiltrating local ruling bodies with Russian bureaucrats. Moscow needed these watchdogs because those in Kremlin never had full confidence in local party bosses. Moscow also resettled millions of Russians in non-Russian republics by offering them good wages and some extra benefits if they agreed to work there on big industrial construction sites. Most of these transplanted nationals never returned. But they did not try to learn local languages or to adjust to local customs. Feeling themselves at home in any part of the Soviet Union, the Russians believed that the locals should adjust to them. Surely, such attitudes never helped to establish harmonious relations.*

While under the totalitarian regime nobody could openly express anti-Russian or anti-Communist sentiments, most people in the Soviet Union had no illusion about the existence of such attitudes. But Shafarevich does not discuss the implications of this government policy and a burgeoning public awareness and response. He does not even mention these real and very complicated problems in his book. He is looking for *Russophobes* in the circles of the Soviet liberal intelligentsia, especially within the tiny Jewish enclave, where they could never be found. Like Nathan Eidelman, most intellectuals of Jewish origin are completely assimilated within the Russian culture and consider themselves a natural and organic part of Russian society. Shafarevich's *Russophobia* justified only his own hatred of all liberally minded intellectuals, especially the Jews. While he tries to adhere to an objective academic style, his emotions burst through and he stoops to numerous lies and falsifications—which negate his credentials as a scientist.

As evidence that the Jews play first fiddle among *the small people*, he compiled a "Jewish list" that included such well-known gentiles as Spanish painter Pablo Picasso and American statesman George Marshall. Shafarevich is not bothered that genealogies clearly verify that they did not have a single drop of Jewish blood in their veins. Others, not as well-known or even completely forgotten historical figures, are further testimony to the unlimited scope of the author's imagination.

Thus, Shafarevich's interpretation of the murder of the last Russian Czar and his family laid the blame at the feet of the Jews.

The Bolsheviks conducted this terrible crime in Yekaterinburg, in July 1918, shortly before the White Army captured the city. The real circumstances are still unclear because the Black Hundreders conducted the investigation. They did not look for the truth, but for the Jews. Anti-Semites authored the first three books on the Czar's murder based on the inquiry: Robert Wilton, 1920; General M. K. Diterikhs, 1922; and Nikolai Sokolov, 1925.[1] All three generously "enriched" the already falsified materials.

According to their descriptions, almost all Bolsheviks connected to the crime were Jewish; and those few whose Russian origin was impossible to deny, they declared secondary or decorative figures. Even Lenin, these "investigators" claimed, was not the real head of the Bolshevik government, but just a

---

* After the Soviet Union collapsed, about 26 million Russians unexpectedly found themselves "abroad"—in new, independent, non-Russian states.

figurehead; "the Bolshevik's Czar," Yakov Sverdlov (a Jew), ruled the country and authorized the shooting of the royal family behind Lenin's back. Likewise, they pictured Alexander Beloborodov, Chairman of the Yekaterinburg City Soviet, who actually had signed the order of execution, a puppet in the hands of alleged Jews like Goloshchekin, Voikov, Safarov, Yurovsky, and many others.*

Later, the credibility of these interpretations of history faltered in the wake of fact even more. It became too obvious, for example, that Lenin ruled the country, with Sverdlov as his lieutenant. And Alexander Georgievich Beloborodov built such a successful party career, far above all the other Yekaterinburg Bolsheviks, that it became impossible to believe that he could have been manipulated.

The easiest way to overcome this obstacle was to make both Lenin and Beloborodov Jewish. We know from chapter 5 how later, in 1992, Vladimir Soloukhin handled Lenin in his book *In the Daylight*. But Igor Shafarevich pioneered in *Russophobia*, literally translating the name Beloborodov ("White beard") into Yiddish, turning him into Waisbard.** After making all killers Jewish, Shafarevich took the next logical step, declaring that the crime was not just a political murder, but a religious ceremony, a "Jewish ritual sacrifice."

In 1989, *Russophobia* appeared simultaneously in several Russian-émigré publications. Some contained apologetic comments, while others were sharply critical. Even at the time, the author evidently could not imagine that his work might be published in Russia, although the soil for it was already prepared and fertilized. Hardly had the issues of the émigré journals reached their subscribers, when a significant part of *Russophobia* appeared in the June 1989 issue of *Nash Sovremennik*, concluding in the November issue.²

Although this magazine—as well as dozens of other central and hundreds of local publications—was overflowing with anti-Semitic materials,

---

* In fact, only Yakov Yurovsky who carried out the Beloborodov's order was of the Jewish origin, but even he had converted to Christianity in 1904. The Jewish origin of all other Yekaterinburg Bolsheviks—including Philip Goloshchekin, who was described as a key figure—has never been proven.

** Shafarevich borrowed this idea from Russian-émigré, anti-Semitic "historian" P. Paganutstsi, whose book *The Truth about the Murder of the Czar's Family* was published in 1981. [See: P. Paganutstsi, *Pravda ob ubiystve Tsarskoy Sem'i*, (Georgedanwille, NY: St.-Troitsky Monastery, 1981)]. Paganutstsi was so ignorant about the theme of his research that he confused Beloborodov's patronymic name. But, as a "cautious" scholar, he left room for uncertainty about his last name in the notation: "Alexander Grigor'evich [instead of Georgievich-S. R.] Beloborodov (Waisbard?), 27 years..." (p. 62). Without mentioning his predecessor, Shafarevich just eliminated the question mark. Pseudo-Soloukhin (the anonymous author of the letter to Eidelman quoted in chapter 5) perhaps had read the Shafarevich's manuscript as had Victor Astafiev. But he had forgotten how Beloborodov was named there and turned him into Waisman ("White man"). Real names were never important to those detractors—only the evidence of ethnicity mattered.

Russophobia became an overnight sensation. The idea that *the small people* were destroying the nation from the inside, since all their activities were inspired by the *Russophobic* Jewish-Western cultural tradition, took the notion of a Jewish-Masonic conspiracy a giant step forward. No longer did the Russian "patriots" have to look for secret organizations, a world Jewish government, or a network of Masonic lodges ruled by Zionists.

In the thousands of years of their alleged destructive activities, these organizations have left no direct evidence of their existence and have not produced a single document other than the controversial *Protocols of the Elders of Zion*. Shafarevich solved the problem "scientifically," explaining that all these organizations and their conspiracies are not needed. Liberal intellectuals are deadly foes of the Russian people just because they are intellectuals influenced by the Jews. The Jewish element plays a significant role in their activities. The concept of *the small people* came closer to Hitler's racist theories than any other previous view.

Shafarevich is starring

The scandalous nature of *Russophobia* made the author famous across the country, and his articles appeared in countless publications. "Tel-Avision" broadcast his interviews, and he became frequent guest in many "patriotic" audiences. Shafarevich used these opportunities to extensively promote his views on a wide range of topics, using the same methodology as in his book.

Of special interest were his comments on *All is Flowing*, a novel by late author Vasily Grossman (1905-1964), one of the greatest Russian prose writers of this century.

Grossman's most significant novel is *Life and Fate*. In 1962, he completed the manuscript and submitted it for publication to the literary journal *Znamya*. The editor-in-chief of the journal not only rejected the manuscript, but provided it (with his comments) to the KGB. Although it was the peak of Khrushchev's liberalism—Solzhenitsyn's *One Day in the Life of Ivan Denisovich* was printed that year—the KGB regarded Grossman's work as the most anti-Soviet novel ever written. An unexpected search of the author's apartment resulted in the confiscation of four original typescripts and all carbon copies. But somehow, the author managed to save one copy. Many years after his death, the 800-page novel appeared in the West—and was determined one of the greatest masterpieces of Russian literature. No other work gives such a vivid insight into the deep resemblance between Stalin's and Hitler's regimes, which, despite their outward polarity, were based on the same principles—a false demagogue of unprecedented proportion, total lack of freedom, fanaticism, chauvinism and Judophobia. However, Soviet readers did not have access to *Life and Fate* until 1987, when—under Gorbachev's freer policies—the journal *Oktyabr* published the work.

While the journal was sharply attacked for this publication, the opposition was not as strong as might have been expected. Two years later, the same journal printed Grossman's last novel, *All is Flowing,* in which the author tried to answer the most fundamental question, "How could Stalinism succeed in his country?"

The novel's main character barely survives more than 15 years in Stalin's concentration camps. After his "rehabilitation," he meets a woman who endured food deprivation in the yearly 1930s, when millions of people died from famine. In their discussions and thoughts, the two try to understand the cause of their sufferings, concluding that Lenin's one-party system of government led to Stalin's crimes. Lenin succeeded in establishing the totalitarian regime because both Lenin and the regime were products of hundreds of years of Russian slavery under the Czars' despotism.

The publication of this work was a risky enterprise even in 1989; thus, the editorial board, to distance itself from Grossman's ideas, accompanied the novel with a thirty-page preface. Its author, Professor G. Vodolazov, saw his task as twofold—extolling the magazine for the decision to publicize a brilliant work of art, but critiquing the author's ideas.

> "Although I applaud the artistic merit of Grossman's novel," Vodolazov wrote, "I shall resolutely protest the author's (and his main character's) interpretation of the cause, roots, and sources of Stalinism; his putting Lenin on the same level with Stalin, and Leninism with Stalinism. In this sense, I protect Lenin. But above all (and it is of primary importance for me today), I would like to defend Grossman, to defend his right to speak his mind, his right to bring his ideas to the reader's notice."[3]

Thus, the purpose of the preface was to shield the magazine from possible accusations in anti-Sovietism or anti-Leninism. But an unanticipated blow came on a still-exposed flank.

Former dissident Igor Shafarevich led the crusade against the publication of Grossman's work. In *All is Flowing*, Shafarevich argued, the author expressed "sharply negative opinions" of "two characters"—Lenin and Russia. While Vodolazov's preface might "cushion the shocking assessments of Lenin," Shafarevich suggested, *Oktyabr* considered no less-negative appraisals of

Russia "as natural" and not requiring shock absorbers. "This contrast is of some interest as it objectively characterizes certain sentiments in society," Shafarevich remarked.[4]

According to Shafarevich, Grossman's alleged *Russophobia* was directly related to his Jewish origin. "Hatred for one nationality is most likely connected with a keen emotional experience of belonging to another," he stated.[5] This generalization corresponds with the central idea of his book. All assertions focus on it and proceed from it. Jews do not care about anyone but themselves, and they hate Russia and Russians just because they are Jewish. Period. Shafarevich was positively indignant about the worldwide significance of Jewish interests.

"There is only one nation, the concerns of which we hear nearly every day. Jewish national emotions make this country and the entire world feverish. They influence disarmament talks, trade contracts, and the international contacts of scientists. They cause demonstrations and sit-in strikes, and emerge in nearly every conversation. The 'Jewish question' has acquired incomprehensible power over people's minds, over and above the problems of Ukrainians, Estonians, Armenians, or Crimean Tatars. As for the existence of the 'Russian question,' it is not acknowledged at all."[6]

Surely, it was strange to read this in 1989, when in nearly all Soviet republics and ethnic regions, active national fronts urged independence for their people. In most of these fronts, liberals worked together with nationalists in their efforts to get rid of both communism and Russian domination. However, as we remember, Shafarevich had actually completed the book seven years before, when the Soviet Jews had voiced their discontent higher than anybody else. Shafarevich does not explore whether the Jews had any reason for this or whether they simply had invented their problems just to keep the Ukrainians, Estonians, and others silent. But when different Soviet nationalities started to speak out for independence, Shafarevich's reaction was unquestionably negative. "Most national movements have one thing in common," he said in an interview. "They are tough and aggressive. Should we take the statements of any Baltic organizations and, say, of *Pamyat* and change only the names of the nationality, we would have the same thing, in fact."[7]

Shafarevich becomes most indignant at the assertion that Russia—like any other country—has only one out of two major options of social and government structure: Democracy or dictatorship. Certainly, he reserves that he is not against democracy in general, but only against its "Western type." But

Lenin and Stalin did not oppose democracy in general either, only a "bourgeois" (i.e., Western) democracy. The Bolsheviks claimed they would create a better system—a socialist democracy. The result is only too well-known. A bitter joke has long been in circulation among Moscow intellectuals. Q: "What is the difference between democracy and socialist democracy?" A: "The same as between a chair and an electric chair."

Shafarevich also champions a special Russian way, but fails to explain why "Western" democracy is not fit for Russia. Instead, he reiterates his point: "The people will go along in the way they themselves will work out and choose (certainly not with the help of secret ballot, but through its historical experience)."[8]

Despite his extensive learning and mathematical expertise, the author of *Russophobia* is inconsistent. On the one hand, he insists that Russia, with her thousand-year history, is a living and developing body, not a mechanism; that her future is organically emerging from her past and the attempts of any "mechanic" to repair or damage her chassis are doomed to failure.

Yet, contradicting himself, Shafarevich tries to prove that Marxism-Leninism-Stalinism has no roots in Russian history, that *the small people* imposed it on the unfortunate country and now seek to impose an alien (and, thus, extremely dangerous) outlook once more. Going through "a keen emotional experience of belonging to his nation," Shafarevich is anxious to close Russia off again with an iron curtain and to separate his people from the rest of mankind.

These "phobias" are particularly manifest in his article *Phenomenon of Emigration.*[9]

The author depicts a horrible picture of a universal evil that emigrants have always produced and continue to produce. Shafarevich assumes that emigrants compose a special group of people. They are not attached to their native country emotionally because they are "least rooted in the life" of *the big people.*[*10] Thus, they do not take into account the needs of the people, do not hesitate to abuse them. According to Shafarevich, neither the Brezhnev regime nor the invasion of Czechoslovakia nor the persecution of dissidents and *refuseniks* who were fighting for the freedom of emigration brought about the current crisis in Russia. The free emigration movement itself was responsible for everything! And when *perestroika* began, the party *apparatchiks* or the

---

    * To understand better whom Shafarevich has in mind, we should remember that the Jews comprised the majority of emigrants from the former Soviet Union.

corrupt *nomenclatura* or the ultra-nationalists did not threaten it as much as the "Russophobic" emigrants did.

At the same time, Shafarevich interprets the notion of an "emigrant" in a very wide sense. "There exists an 'émigré-like attitude towards life' which may lead, and may not lead, to a departure," he stated.[11] According to this flexible definition, anyone who has said, written, or published something not to Shafarevich's liking, he may regard as an émigré, whose main goal is to destroy his homeland. Following this line of thought, the converse would hold equally true. Some emigrants, like Alexander Solzhenitsyn, whom Shafarevich praises and quotes on any occasion, should be regarded as true patriots because they have nationalistic views.

After outlining his definition of "emigrants," Shafarevich presents a vivid example of how they undermine Russian spirit.

"Many people could probably witness a method widely used by a united group, or 'Mafia,' when it takes over the control of some sphere of life. They 'test' someone who is of interest to them, 'feel through' him, making him do something he dislikes. If he submits, they can further bend or fully subjugate him. If he does not, it is necessary to wait a bit. He is not ripe yet. Entire social sections and nations undergo such tests in case of large-scale events."[12]

According to Shafarevich, for this terrible "testing" of the Russians, the émigré Mafia used *Oktyabr* again—because the journal published an excerpt from the book *Walks with Pushkin* by Andrei Sinyavsky.

Sinyavsky wrote the book secretly in the labor camp where he had spent seven years for publishing his works in the West. This activity after heavy-labor days helped him survive as a writer. After he served his term and emigrated, he published his book in the West, but only through the publication in *Oktyabr* did the work become available to the Soviet audience.

That publication forced Shafarevich to "unmask" the Russophobic "Mafia." It was not even émigré Andrei Sinyavsky (a Russian and Orthodox believer), but the journal's editor-in-chief, Anatoly Ananiev (Russian, former Communist, and high party official), who was the main "Mafia" agent. Shafarevich's argument goes like this:

"What would be the most effective way of 'testing' the Russians? Blasphemy, the insulting of Orthodoxy? It would be painful only for a minority now [since most Russians grew up as atheists]. To smear Russian history one more time? We're accustomed to that as well. But Pushkin is cherished by most Russians, and most of his countrymen will feel it if this spot is pricked. ... This publication is a test of our nation's vitality, of its ability of giving a rebuff."[13]

Alexander Pushkin really means a lot to the Russian consciousness. He is much more than a genius poet—he symbolizes the best part of Russian cultural heritage and spirituality. Andrei Sinyavsky, however, did not defame Pushkin in any way. Indeed, he expressed his love for the poet, who had helped him to survive in the camp. But some of his interpretations differed from traditional commentary. Several years before Shafarevich, Alexander Solzhenitsyn pointedly criticized Sinyavsky's book; but at that time, it looked more or less like a family quarrel within the Russian émigré community. Shafarevich went much further, demanding retaliation for this "Russophobic" act of subversion.

"Not long ago, a similar situation made a stir throughout the world. Salman Rushdie's notorious *Satanic Verses* are, apparently, a kind of Islamic version of *Walks with Pushkin*. I must say that the Islamic world again proved its great vitality by its response to this 'test,' by which it probably considerably weakened the pressure it might have come under in the near future. ... Its actual response manifested itself in huge demonstrations and hundreds of lives sacrificed in clashes with the police. As a result, they managed to have the book banned in many countries."[14]

This reasoning made clear what kind of regime, in Shafarevich's opinion, is more appropriate for Russia than "Western" democracy.

Shafarevich and Pamyat

Since public scandals accompanied activities of *Pamyat*, nobody outside the organization wanted to express publicly his or her sympathy or support of the "patriotic" front or movement. Recalling Igor Shafarevich's remark that *Pamyat's* platform was indistinguishable from the aggressive slogans of any (!) Baltic organization, we might expect his equally negative attitude toward *Pamyat*. Yet, his statements testify something different. When a reporter asked him directly about *Pamyat*, Shafarevich at first said that he "knew only a little" about this organization; then he put its program on the same level with Baltic movements, and finally he said:

"I do not have the slightest idea whether anyone can imagine the real picture of the scale of the *Pamyat* movement. From all indications, it is not large at all. Its rallies are not crowded. It has no press of its own. A single newspaper does not support the movement, and yet its role has been inflated to a significant proportion. The explanation? A desire to artificially create an 'image of the enemy,' an image of a huge monster which everybody must be afraid of as they would fear the awakening of Russian national trends."[15]

Thus, by avoiding publicizing his direct support of *Pamyat*, Shafarevich attacked those concerned by *Pamyat's* growing strength. He simply turned all known facts upside down. According to him, it was not *Pamyat* that created a false "image of the enemy," but those who were against *Pamyat*. It was not *Pamyat* that tried to arouse fear and hatred for the mythical Jewish conspiracy against Russia, but rather her detractors who instigated suspicion of the "Russian national trends." It was not *Pamyat* that created the image of "a huge monster," but somebody else.

"Even the European parliament adopted the resolution to disband *Pamyat!*" Igor Shafarevich exclaimed ironically. In order to fully convince his readers that *the small people* had invented *Pamyat*, he even resorted to the assistance of an "American sovietologist" whom, he claimed, he had met in Moscow but whose name he did not disclose. This sovietologist allegedly said to him, "There is a joke: four Russian words are most well-known in America—*sputnik, perestroika, glasnost,* and *Pamyat.*"

The flavor of the joke might be understood only within the context of Shafarevich's reasoning. The Russian word *sputnik* became known in many languages after the Soviets successfully launched the first man-made satellite of the Earth in 1957. *Perestroika* and *glasnost* symbolized Gorbachev's policy of reforms and "new thinking" that had changed the international climate. Thus, these three words were associated with events of historic proportion. Meanwhile, the fourth Russian word, *Pamyat,* represented an organization, whose real significance, according to Shafarevich and the alleged sovietologist, was next to nothing.

A funny joke, is it not? However, it would have become even more piquant, if the "sovietologist" had reminded Igor Shafarevich of a fifth Russian word so widely known in America that it entered English dictionaries long before all other words of the Russian origin. This word is POGROM.

From words to deeds

When the article *Phenomenon of Emigration* first appeared, the author's speculations about an émigré Mafia testing the limits of a society could be construed as nothing but a poetic metaphor. Nevertheless, soon the "patriots" began to look to it for instruction. In December 1989, the Plenum of the Russian Federation Writers Union held in Moscow turned into a *Pamyat*-like rally.

Those speaking at the meeting were angrily creating the "image of the enemy" in the likeness of Vasily Grossman, Andrei Sinyavsky, and—most of all—Anatoly Ananiev, who printed their "Russophobic" works in his journal.

Here are a few fragments from speeches.

Anatoly Znamensky: "Who could have guessed only two or three years ago that ... the disintegration would manifest itself so completely and clearly and in the journal having the purely ideological title *Oktyabr*[*] ... that they would start to defame national holy objects and that novels and essays would appear, such as *Walks with Pushkin* or a rough draft under the vague title *All is Flowing?* In the pages of his journal, the editor blessed the repeated and malicious defamation of the Russian people and the things sacred to them. In the last novel, *All is Flowing*, he openly spat in the face of all Russians—the past, the present, and probably the future."

Anatoly Builov: "Let us speak about the Jews. The Jews are evidently the only ethnic group interested in strife. ... Now the *Pamyat* society has emerged. I am not a member of this society, but I like many things about it. Earlier I was unaware of this Jewish question. But why are they in every profitable place? I was told that they are clever. Well, I agree, they are clever. But if they are so smart, why have they brought us into a dead end?"

Tatiana Glushkova: "I did not hear Anatoly Builov's speech yesterday. Later, I asked several people, 'Did he speak badly?' They told me, 'He specifically said the word *Jews!*' I asked, "Did he use any insulting epithets?' No, no one confirmed that he inflicted a direct ethnic slur."[16]

Perhaps, the most remarkable was the address of G. Pinyasov, a Mordovian writer.[**] This "ruler of thoughts" asked "to excuse himself before

---

[*] The journal's title *Oktyabr* means not so much the month of October, as the October Revolution.

[**] Mordovia is an autonomous republic within the Russian Federation.

those present and before Russian literature as represented by them because the *Walks with Pushkin* had been written on Mordovian land, in the Mordovian political labor camps."[17] Thus, the Mordovian writer perceived his guilt not because Russian writers had to languish in camps "on his land" (which, by the way, was not Mordovia's fault), but because some inmates had enough physical and spiritual strength to continue to write!

It is necessary to mention, though, that some other voices could also be heard at this Plenum. Prominent literary scholar and critic Andrei Turkov, who wrote dozens of books about classic and modern Russian writers, tried to calm the audience down with clear, succinct arguments.

> "At moments of great grief, annoyance, and bitterness, different people have used strong—even repugnant—expressions, castigating the very places and people of whom they were most fond. 'The devil contrived that I be born in Russia, with my brains and talent!' Do you remember this phrase [by Alexander Pushkin]? ... 'Good bye, unwashed Russia, country of slaves, country of masters!' expressed the sentiments of one of our greatest poets [Mikhail Lermontov]. ... In a moment of horrible bitterness, shortly before his death, [Alexander] Blok wrote to [Kornei] Chukovsky,[*] 'Foul mother-Russia, as a sow, has gobbled up her sucking-pig.'"[18]

Turkov could have added similar "Russophobic" quotes from Nikolai Gogol, Pyotr Chaadaev, Mikhail Saltykov-Shchedrin, Ivan Turgenev, Anton Chekhov, and other classic writers to demonstrate that the "patriots" placed the hateful "Russophobes" in good company. But the audience did not let him speak and drove him from the rostrum.

Immediately after the Plenum that "had adopted a resolution" to dismiss Anatoly Ananiev from the position of editor-in-chief of *Oktyabr* and appointed its own editor, the "patriots" tried to storm the editorial office. Besieged, the entire staff could not leave the office for several days. The party, government authorities, Moscow city officials, and the police observed complete neutrality.

Liberal literary critic Andrei Malgin summarized the polarization. "The forces of reaction are still strong, unpunished, and vengeful in the Soviet Union. And I am not sure that they will lose in the ideological struggle now sweeping the entire society, the entire country."[19]

---

[*] Alexander Blok (1880 - 1921) and Kornei Chukovsky (1882 - 1969) were prominent Russian writers of the 20th century

It has since become clear that these concerns were justified. Victor Astafiev, speaking on Russian TV on February 19, 1995, said:

"I am annoyed and alarmed with the emerging of fascism in our country. We should be honest and clear about it: Fascism does exist here. Some people say that fascism may exist or may not, or perhaps, it is a different kind of fascism. [After seizing power], our fascism will become more cruel than the German fascism since Hitler ruled the country only 12 years, while we had more cruel rulers for 70 years. They taught us atrocities, spite, and fanaticism; thus, if we go off the track, then it would be much worse here [than in Germany]. The fascists call for new blood and violence. They call us to the 'bright past.' This is an incredible stupidity, but they do not understand that."[20]

To Victor Astafiev's credit, we have to say that after his correspondence with Eidelman, he began to distance himself from the ultranationalists. He did not join their organizations, did not publish his works in *Nash Sovremennik* or like-minded periodicals. Sometimes, ultranationalists criticized him for a lack of patriotism. While he has never regretted publicly his letter to Eidelman or his chauvinistic publications, it seems that he reconsidered some of his views after the scandal. Finally, Victor Astafiev started to speak out against the growing danger of fascism. Well, better late than never.

However this was an extremely atypical evolution for modern Russian writers.

CHAPTER 8

INVASION WITHOUT ARMS

A landing in Washington

At the end of March 1990, the Kennan Institute for Advanced Russian Studies, based in Washington, DC, mailed out a list of its regular seminars for the forthcoming month. When I received the flyer, my attention was caught by the following entry:

TUESDAY, APRIL 17 SEMINAR, 3:00-5:00 PM

"Cultural and Ethnic Diversity
in the Soviet Union"
Stanislav Kuniaev
Editor, Nash Sovremennik
Vadim Kozhinov
Critic, Nash Sovremennik
Sergei Lykoshin, publisher
Lives of Remarkable People, a book series;
Valentin Rasputin
novelist and publicist;
Petr Palamarchuk
author of the book Edin Derzhavin;

Chapter 8

Svetlana Selivanova
editor, Literaturnaia Gazeta;
Leonid Borodin, writer;
Pavel Gorelov, critic and writer;
and **Evdokia Aleksandrovna Gaer**,
Supreme Soviet Deputy from Vladivostok.[1]

One glance at the names listed showed me that practically all the guest speakers had been selected from the same group of the most outspoken Russian Red-Brown ideologists whom I had followed for two decades.

It was not a bad idea at all—to introduce these writers to the U. S. academic community and to the public. America deserved to have firsthand evidence of the rapid nazification of Russian society.

But the topic offered for discussion—*Cultural and Ethnic Diversity in the Soviet Union*—indicated that the people who had planned the seminar had no knowledge of whom they had actually invited. Why on earth would the most extreme promoters of hatred of everything they considered "non-Russian" have to come here to teach us about ethnic diversity?

As a regular contributor to the Russian émigré press, I decided to share some background information about the participants of the forthcoming seminar with my readers. The Russian Los Angeles weekly *Panorama* printed my article "Soviet Nazi Landing in Washington." It is reproduced here in a slightly shortened translation.

"The members of this group call themselves 'Russian patriots'; but both in the Soviet Union and in the West they are more often referred to as Russian Nazis.

"Five out of nine guest speakers were among 74 signers of the notorious 'Letter' addressed to the Communist Party Central Committee, the Soviet government, and the President of the USSR and published last February by the ultranationalist weekly *Literaturnaya Rossia*.[2] The aggressive and anti-Semitic tone of the letter by far exceeded that of the manifesto penned two years ago by a Leningrad college professor, Nina Andreeva, who sought to defend Stalinism from an alleged Zionist plot.[*]

"The authors of the new manifesto brand the democratic reforms now underway in the Soviet Union as 'a historically unparalleled persecution and defamation of the country's native population.'[3]

---

[*] More about Nina Andreeva and her manifesto will be in the chapter 10.

"As far as they are concerned, Russia's main enemies are the Jews, half-Jews, and all those who support the democratic process.

"Soon after the 1917 Bolshevik Revolution, the authorities responded to a ground swell of pogroms against the Jews by adopting a decree that banned anti-Semitic activities. The 74 signers of the letter in *Literaturnaya Rossia* characterize that decree—not enforced since the early 1930s—as 'a selective national privilege' that, they claim, led to 'the genocide of the Russian people.'[4]

"The signers accuse those who speak out against anti-Semitism of 'an uncritical, mawkish, and essentially slavish attitude toward Jews—Jews past and present, foreign and domestic, including imperialists and Zionists.' They regard Zionists as Hitler's minions, responsible 'for many pogroms, including pogroms against Jews, for cutting off desiccated branches of their own national tree in Auschwitz and Dachau, in Lvov and Vilnius.'[5]

"The signers believe the rumors of impending Jewish pogroms in Moscow, Leningrad, and other cities to be totally unfounded and propagated by Jews themselves; but in the same breath, they warn of pogroms that may be started by Russians 'driven to despair.'[6]

"The letter, both in style and substance, bears a close resemblance to the ideology of the pre-Revolutionary Russian 'patriots,' whose creed stemmed the proverbial 'Kill the Jews, Save Russia' motto.

"The letter concludes with a clarion call, 'Let us walk tall. Let us take the fate of our Russian motherland into our hands.'[7]

"Five of the signers are invited to speak at the Kennan Institute. Their own writings, printed in newspapers and magazines controlled by their group (about half the official Soviet publications), are filled with hatred toward the Jews.

"Vadim Kozhinov, a literary critic, almost stopped writing about literature many years ago. He has become, instead, a preeminent leader of those Soviet commentators who are busy ferreting out Jews in the ranks of the Bolshevik leadership. Since millions of people of different ethnic backgrounds were involved in large-scale political violence under Lenin and Stalin, it is easy to find among them a few dozen Jewish names and, if needed, add to them the names of half-Jews, quarter-Jews, and those who were 'related' to Jews. By attributing to those individuals *all* the heinous crimes perpetrated by the Communist regime, Vadim Kozhinov and his followers are concocting a new blood libel against the Jewish people.

"Stanislav Kuniaev, a poet, is no less active in contributing to anti-Semitic mythology. A decade ago, he wrote poems about 'Jews in the Pentagon' plotting to destroy the Russian people. In more recent years, he has been uncovering the Jewish plot in a venue more appropriate to the task: articles and essays. Last year, Kuniaev became editor-in-chief of the magazine *Nash Sovremennik*, a leading publication of Russian ultra-nationalists and chauvinists. In his 'inaugural' piece, brought out just before he assumed his new responsibilities, Kuniaev spoke with horror and fascination of the *Protocols of the Elders of Zion*. According to him, this book is an 'iron brief for and a set of instructions in gaining power over the people of the earth. ... It is a fruit of painstaking examination of mankind's entire political history. ... Brilliant minds—evil, anonymous demons—created it. They were well-aware of the political teachings of their time. ... Reading the *Protocols*, one occasionally shudders from the horrific realization that much of what it predicted has already happened in the 20th century. ... The *Protocols* is a book of political and moral Apocalypse of our century.'[8]

"Until recently, even the most extreme Judophobes in the Soviet Union did not dare quote the *Protocols* in the press, leaving it to the firebrand gatherings of the *Pamyat* Society. Kuniaev showed that he had more guts than his colleagues. Was that the reason he was invited to descant on Soviet ethnic issues at the Kennan Institute?

"Sergei Lykoshin is not a publisher, as the flyer identifies him. He is a chief editor of the *Lives of Remarkable People* book series, a division of *Molodaya Gvardia* Publishing House. In the early 1970s, the series started to publish "patriotic" books. Sergei Lykoshin continues the same policy.

"The most prominent of the invitees is Valentin Rasputin. He is one of the leading village prose writers and a member of the Congress of the People's Deputies (parliament) and the newly created ruling Presidential Council, designed to replace the Politburo in the wake of the liquidation of the one-party system. Rasputin is a supporter of *Pamyat*, whose program he finds 'convincing on many points.'[9] To whip up hatred toward the Jews and other 'aliens,' Rasputin calls Russian writers a 'national minority, being offered for an immolation' to Russian-speaking (i.e., non-Russian by blood) literary forces.[10]

"According to the *Washington Post*, Valentin Rasputin 'is widely regarded as anti-Western and anti-Semitic ... and had even expressed some sympathy for *Pamyat*, an extreme nationalist group'[11] The *Washington Times* adds that 'Rasputin leads a group of like-minded authors who believe a sinister conspiracy of Westerners, Jews, and Masons is seeking to destroy the Russian people.'[12]

"Petr Palamarchuk is the author of a biography of Gavriil Derzhavin, an eminent Russian poet of the late 18th and early 19th century who was also a senior government official holding the rank of a minister and an expert on the Jewish question. He faulted the Jews for turning the Russians into drunkards and for exploiting the Russian peasants and also shared the belief in the ritualistic use of Christian blood by the Jews. In his book, Palamarchuk offers an apologia of Derzhavin's anti-Semitic activities and paints him as a victim of the Jewish plot.

"The other four speakers are not among the 74 signatories of the Letter in *Literaturnaya Rossia*, but not because of fundamental disagreements with the authors. These four include Svetlana Selivanova from *Literaturnaya Gazeta* (In an editorial environment not totally controlled by 'patriots,' she still seeks to carry forward the Russian nationalistic line); Pavel Gorelov, a lesser known 'patriot' and literary critic; Evdokia Gaer, a member of the Congress of People's Deputies from Vladivostok, who belongs to a group of lawmakers speaking *against* reduction of the military and the shift to market economy, and *for* 'equality' of the Russian people, allegedly victimized by Jews and other minorities.

"Only Leonid Borodin cuts a somewhat less one-sided figure. Under Brezhnev, he was a dissident hounded by the authorities. His brand of Russian nationalism did not share the Stalinist coloration of Kozhinov's or Kuniaev's variety. He was an anti-Stalinist then. But these differences are now merely of historical interest. With the advent of *glasnost* and *perestroika*, Russian nationalists of all types have banded together. The nostalgia for an 'iron fist,' hatred of the Jews, and a deep-seated fear of democracy unite them.

"Recently a group of Nazi-oriented writers organized several gatherings in Leningrad under the title the *Russian Meetings*. Leningrad's liberal press characterized the invasion of the 'patriots' as a Nazi landing which might inflame the explosive atmosphere in the city. In a few days, the same landing will occur in the U. S. capital, which, according to the 'patriots,' was conquered by 'Zionists' long ago and is a center of the Judo-Masonic plot against Russia." [13]

Usually émigré publications go unnoticed by the mainstream American public. Even leading sovietologists, fluent in Russian, mostly overlook them. This time it turned out differently, thanks to Si Frumkin, Chairman of the Southern California Council for Soviet Jews, who translated my article into

148   Chapter 8

English and distributed it as a Newsletter.* Si Frumkin conducted his own research to figure out who invited the group to the U. S. and why.

> "They are coming here as guests of the American taxpayers, with their trip sponsored by the U. S. Information Agency! I spoke to the people at USIA, who told me that the reason for the invitation was to acquaint these individuals with our country and that they have all been "screened" by the Moscow Embassy. Personally, I can think of several hundred million Soviet citizens who deserve a free luxury trip to the U. S. more than these neo-Nazi right-wing thugs.
>
> "Their appearance to discuss 'cultural and ethnic diversity in the USSR' is equivalent to having a group of Ku Klux Klansmen going to Russia to talk about blacks in the U. S. or Hitler's cronies about Jews." [14]

A few days later, Judith Havemann from the *Washington Post* approached me. She gave me the English version of my article, asking me to look through it and approve the translation. Of special interest to her were the quotations from the *Letter* of the 74 writers and from Kuniaev's article. I confirmed that the wording was accurate. I also translated more fragments for her orally to demonstrate that those few quotations I used in my article were in line with the spirit and context of the entire document.

On April 17, Judith Havemann's article appeared on the front page of the *Washington Post*. She quoted different people, from the USIA officials and leaders of some Jewish organizations to the Russian guests themselves, who had already arrived in Washington D. C. The article said that the group was invited to this country for a month-long tour that would cost American taxpayers $60,000 and include Pittsburgh; Iowa City; Urbana, Ill; Oxford, Miss.; San Francisco; Bozeman, Mont.; and New York City.[15]

The composition of the group had been significantly changed in comparison with the previous announcement. It was cut to eight persons instead of nine; and Oleg Mikhailov, Ernest Safonov, Victor Likhonosov, and Vyacheslav Rybas replaced Rasputin, Kozhinov, Lykoshin, Palamarchuk, and Gaer. The reasons for these changes remained unknown, but the goal in no way was to make the group more diverse in opinions. All the new members of the group were from the same camp. Two of them—Oleg Mikhailov and Victor Likhonosov—had also signed the "Letter of 74" while Ernest Safonov was the editor-in-chief of *Literaturnaya Rossia*, the weekly that had published the Manifesto. Oleg

---

* Si Frumkin's slightly edited translation is used here as well.

Mikhailov, by the way, back in the early 1970s, published a biography of Gavriil Derzhavin and was the first who handmade the poet a victim of the Jewish plot.[16] Palamarchuk only followed in his footsteps.

The seminar

An hour before the seminar was to start, the Kennan Institute library hall was filled to capacity. The administration provided additional accommodation where the discussion could be listened to on radio. When this hall was also overcrowded, the door was closed and the guard became implacable. I was told later that one journalist insisted on being let in, saying that she had unrestricted access even to the White House. She produced her press pass to no avail; the guard only reminded her of the address of the White House.

The crowd near the entrance did not disperse, however; and the *Washington Post* featured a report based on interviews with people in the crowd.[17]

Meanwhile, the show began.

Stanislav Kuniaev was the first to speak. He pointed out that he and his friends comprised a group of single-minded people united by the "idea of Russian revival, of the revival of Russian culture, spirituality, and statehood." At the same time, he indicated that every member of the group was a "personality, an artist, or a writer," stressing that they deserved to be judged individually.

Speaking of himself, Kuniaev emphasized his free-lance status throughout his career. Not until the previous year had he agreed to take on the position of editor-in-chief of *Nash Sovremennik*. In doing so, he yielded to the pressure of his friends—Valentin Rasputin, Victor Astafiev, Vladimir Soloukhin, Vasily Belov, and Yuri Bondarev*. He had taken this trip to the United States as a rest from the burden of editorial duties.

Once the other guests had introduced themselves, Marshall Brement took the floor. A former U. S. ambassador to Iceland and a U. S. embassy official in Moscow, he devoted a considerable part of his speech to Igor Shafarevich's *Russophobia*. Emphasizing the sacred right of freedom of expression, Brement quoted American jurist Oliver Wendell Holmes, who had said that freedom of

---

* Most of Kuniaev's listed friends were introduced in previous chapters. Vasily Belov will be introduced in chapter 10. Yuri Bondarev is a well-known contemporary prose-writer. During Khrushchev's *thaw*, he wrote the novel *Silence*, in which he truthfully described Stalin's repressions. The book made him very popular. Later, he became one of the most well-known hard-line Stalinists and ultranationalists and achieved a high position within the bureaucratic hierarchy: Second Secretary of the Union of the Soviet Writers of the Russian Federation. He was the actual leader of the ultranationalistic faction of the writers' community and, using his high administrative position, cynically promoted his friends and supporters regardless of their talents and creative abilities.

speech does not imply the freedom to shout out "Fire!" in an overcrowded theater, for it might cause panic.

Quotations from Shafarevich's book made the guest speakers uncomfortable. They were "surprised" that the "small" question of anti-Semitism should dominate the discussion when Russia now faced so many "big" problems. They were eager to speak at great length about hundreds of different things, including the economy and refugees from different zones of local ethnic conflicts, paralyzed agriculture and rising alcohol consumption. But they avoided the admission that at home their only "solution" to all these problems was to blame the Jews.

Repeatedly exposed as anti-Semites by the excerpts from Shafarevich's book, the Moscow guests chose not to uphold their views. Oleg Mikhailov proved to be the most dexterous. Declining to discuss *Russophobia* in the absence of the author, he added that in December 1989, he had stressed in an article in the *Literaturnaya Gazeta* that the Jews could not be called *the small people* since a nation that created the *Old Testament* would be great.

Later, I leafed through all December 1989 issues of *Literaturnaya Gazeta*, but failed to find his article. I also looked through the November and January issues—to no avail. So, probably, this article never existed or it was published somewhere else. In any case, Mikhailov's "disagreement" with Shafarevich was pure manipulation. There are populous—or big—nations numbering in the hundreds of millions of people, and there are comparatively scanty—or small—nations. When Shafarevich called the Jews "the small people," he simply stated a demographic fact. The inciting message of *Russophobia* lies in the fatal hatred for Russia that Shafarevich makes intrinsic in *the small people*, while urging *the big people* to fight back. Oleg Mikhailov did not distance himself from this inflaming concept.

The next question dealt with the *Letter* of the 74 writers. It was more difficult for the guests to dissociate themselves from this document since half of them had signed or printed it.

Trying to justify its publication, Ernest Safonov addressed a variety of problems facing Russia, the numerous responses that had come to the editorial office in support of the letter, and the prominent people who had signed it. In an attempt to impress the audience, he named "the patriarch of Soviet literature," Leonid Leonov,* and a "member of the Presidential Council," Valentin Rasputin, repeating this title twice for significance.

---

*Leonid Leonov (born 1899) is one of the oldest Russian living writers. He authored numerous boring novels and stories with a pretension of philosophical significance. Always politically correct, he

Safonov's arguments, however, did not impress the audience, so the more sophisticated Oleg Mikhailov hastened to his aid.

"Sasha Cherny, a wonderful writer, a great favorite of mine," he said smiling, "said once that two or twenty-two phrases, torn out of context, give as poor an idea of the contents as two or twenty-two hairs, torn out of the head, do of the wealth of one's hairstyle."

This skillful Mikhailov's reply served a dual purpose, indicating not only that he and his fellow authors had been misinterpreted, but breadth and tolerance of his views: Scholars of Russian literature know that the talented Russian émigré poet Sasha Cherny, né Alexander Glikberg (1880-1932), was of Jewish origin.

When my turn to ask questions came, I suggested that those present look at a picture to get an idea of how Russia's "patriotic" press had presented the *Old Testament* that, according to Oleg Mikhailov, only a great nation could have created. I passed around a reproduction of Igor Borodin's* painting of the biblical Judith xeroxed from the journal *Molodaya Gvardia*.[18]

In the center of the picture, Holofernes sits solemnly in a magnificent armchair that resembles a throne, holding a naked woman on his lap. Her whole body—but especially her face, with a strained, vile smile—arouses a feeling of loathing and horror. The face of the mighty Holofernes is, by contrast, that of a duped simpleton. With one hand, Judith holds out a cup of wine to Holofernes, while her other hand directs a dagger at his back. The steps leading up to the throne are covered with countless severed heads. The title of the picture is *A Warning*.

Along with this "masterpiece," I exhibited a reproduction of another painting by the same artist xeroxed from the same journal. The picture, titled *The Umbrella,* showed a big, open umbrella with symbols of *glasnost* and *perestroika* on its surface; Stalin's bust; letters strung on a long rope, spelling out "the personality cult"; signs representing The Voice of America, *Liberty, Ogonyok, Moscow News, Nina Katerli*. Separate from this outward image of *perestroika,* the painting depicted a dark area beneath the umbrella where no strangers could penetrate. Here, real *perestroika* was taking place in deep shadow. Seated on the ground were small, ugly individuals, bespectacled and big-nosed. Engaged in blowing up an Orthodox temple, they were surrounded by small, crushed temples—a startling representation of the Judo-Masonic conspiracy against Russia.

---

enjoyed a reputation as one of the leading and most prestigious writers in the USSR since the 1920s. He won top Soviet awards, including Stalin and Lenin prizes and the title of the Hero of the Socialist Labor.

* See pp.52-54 (chapter3).

All this needed no comment. I only pointed out that these pictures were reproduced in full; they were not a few hairs torn out from someone's head, but the entire hairstyle that could not be misinterpreted.

Then I turned to Stanislav Kuniaev, the group's unofficial leader, with two questions. Citing his statement in *Nash Sovremennik* that "much of what had been predicted" in *The Protocols of the Elders of Zion* "has already come true in the history of the 20th century," I asked for historic facts to support this contention.

Then I redirected my attention to Kuniaev's poem *The Ether is Raging*. Written in 1975, in the period now called "stagnation," the poem railed against *glasnost,* which was barely in evidence at that time. The only independent sources of information were foreign radio stations, so they became the object of Kuniaev's attack. He was so afraid that "dead" radio-voices "with a foreign accent in every prophetic phrase" would steal his "living soul" that he applied for help to the shades of the inventors of radio—Russian engineer Alexander Popov and Italian physicist Guglielmo Marconi. These verses were published twice—in slightly different versions.

What was Popov concerned with, when Marconi did not sleep at nights— not with the **rebels** in Lisbon, not with the **fascists** in the Pentagon— but with the fates of poor sailor.[19]	What was Popov concerned with, when Marconi did not sleep at nights— not with the **villains** in Lisbon, not with the **Jews** in the Pentagon— but with the fates of poor sailors.[20]

Having read out both versions, I posed my question: "Which of the two versions was censored? You've stated that censorship strongly affects the work of Soviet writers, so I would like to know what did they make you substitute for what: *Jews* for *fascists* or *fascists* for *Jews?"*

Kuniaev had no answer to my questions, but employed a counterattack instead.

"Are you not the author of the article 'Soviet Nazi Landing in Washington?' He picked up a copy of my *Panorama* article from the table. "It is you, isn't it? It means that in reply to my 'fascists in the Pentagon,' you write 'Nazis in Washington,' don't you? Well, good."

"I call you Nazis because you are Nazis, while you call us fascists because we are Jews. Here lies the difference," I said. The liberal arm of the Soviet media had long been describing Kuniaev and his supporters as Nazis, racists, and fascists, so I only repeated what others had written before me.

Meanwhile, the pictures I passed around impressed the audience. The reaction forced Pavel Gorelov, the youngest speaker and editor-in-chief of one of the divisions of the *Molodaya Gvardia* Book Publishing House,* to take the microphone and to explain that the magazine *Molodaya Gvardia* is a separate publication. Disassociating himself from it, he heaped ample criticism on the journal and its editor-in-chief, although he never did so in the Soviet press. At home, he attacked mostly émigré "anti-patriots" like Joseph Brodsky, who—he insisted—had won a Nobel prize not for his achievements in poetry, but for his "anti-patriotism."

"I would like to add a few words to the reply to Mr. Reznik," interjected Oleg Mikhailov. "None of us sitting at this green table are contributors to the *Molodaya Gvardia* magazine."

I could not allow this comment to pass unchallenged because a good half of the permanent contributors to *Nash Sovremennik* also published their works in the *Molodaya Gvardia* and vice versa. Breaking all written and unwritten rules for academic seminars at the Kennan Institute, I interrupted the speaker.

"Excuse me, but this is a lie," I charged. "The same issue of *Molodaya Gvardia* with the reproductions of Igor Borodin's pictures carries a big article by Stanislav Kuniaev."

Since Kuniaev could not refute my allegation, he rushed to describe the message of that particular article as humane and anti-totalitarian. This was, of course, yet another blatant prevarication.

Following this Witches' Sabbath, it occurred to me that it was just a bad dream. Instead of a seminar in the leading Sovietologist institution in the center of Washington, DC, halfway between Capitol Hill and the White House, such a performance could have been staged at a *Pamyat* meeting in the Russian provinces, with brave "independent" speeches pre-approved by local party officials.

Of course, in Washington, the speakers had to improvise answers to thorny questions, but they were acting within the framework of a prepared scenario. They were united, aggressive, and ready to fight back any "Zionist provocation." Ernest Safonov even concluded his last argument with the reminder that he represented the superpower with the biggest nuclear and conventional military might in the world.

Still, I waited with special interest for Leonid Borodin to speak. A former dissident, he had spent many years in concentration camps because he had had the courage to write what he believed. This record set him apart from the horde

---

* The same company I worked for as an editor of the *Life of Remarkable People* series from 1963 to 1973 (see chapter 1).

of his colleagues who had built safe careers within the boundaries of official propaganda. For decades, they had even limited the extent of their "patriotic" vituperation of "Zionism" to a permitted degree, refraining from open antagonism with the authorities until the government had launched the policy of *glasnost*.

Although Leonid Borodin had not contradicted Kuniaev's introductory remark that the group was united, I had hoped that after listening to the litany of lies, he would divorce himself from the others. But when he spoke, Borodin confirmed their perjuries and added his own whitewash.

> "So far, not a single hair has fallen down from the head of a single Jew, while in the Caucasus people keep killing one another. I am acquainted with representatives of all Russia's major patriotic organizations. It is they, the leaders of these organizations, who are most concerned about preventing pogroms in Russia! We understand that should it happen even by wild chance, by provocation, by folly, or by design, we would pay for it with our Russia!"[21]

Thus, Russia, presumably, would be destroyed (no need to explain by whom) if at least one hair fell from a Jewish head!

At that time I had already in my possession a letter from a certain Mikhail Torbin, a resident of the settlement of Prodogishty in Moldavia (now Moldova).

> "From time immemorial, our family has traditionally celebrated all Jewish holidays. October 7, 1989, was no exception, and we were preparing for *Yom Kippur*. Our daughter and a grandson came from Kishinev to stay with us. Around 11:30 p. m., while my daughter and wife were cooking food in the kitchen, two strangers in black masks rushed into the apartment. They did not want anything from us Jews but our lives. Only God could have given my daughter the strength and wit to rebuff them. She managed to push them out and to cover her child. They relinquished my daughter only when her head was cut and covered with blood and they thought she was dead. My wife, however, fell victim to this pogrom. Trying to save us, she led them to another room where they did away with her, inflicting three fatal wounds. In our village, we were the only remaining Jewish family."[22]

While speaking in the Kennan Institute, Leonid Borodin might not have known about this particular incident in a remote settlement; but as a person "acquainted with representatives of all Russia's major patriotic organizations," he had to know of hundreds of similar acts of anti-Semitic violence. He must have been familiar with accounts of the young Jewish lawyer, asphyxiated by smoke after the door of her Moscow apartment was set on fire following numerous mail and telephone threats. Moscow TV had reported her death. One of the leading national dailies, *Trud (Labor)* verified several small pogroms in Kharkov.[23] Nor could Borodin have been unaware of the assassination of Alexander Cherny, a Jew, at a writers' recreation home near Minsk, where he was stabbed by Leningrad writer Yevgeny Nikolaev.[24] The *Literaturnaya Gazeta* ran a story about a democratic rally in the center of Moscow, where a special police detachment (OMON) had severely beaten the participants, castigating their victims with slurs like "lousy kikes" and "Zionist bastards." Writer Yuli Krelin reported the bloody incident, which had left his son injured and handicapped.[25]

It should be clearly indicated that Jewish pogroms in today's Russia could not be staged with the same panoramic scope as before the revolution, or as in places like Sumgait, Baku, and Fergana, where Armenians, Turks-Meskhetians, and other minorities were victimized. The reason lies in the elimination of the Jewish ghettos or settlements with a predominantly Jewish population. There have long been no Jewish regions, districts, or neighborhoods in former Soviet cities where raging mobs could be directed with sticks, axes, and containers of gasoline to set fires. The Jewish population is extremely dispersed now. While this poses certain technical limitations for *pogromshchiks*, it renders the Jews themselves absolutely helpless. Thus, although mini-pogroms were constantly taking place, guest speaker Leonid Borodin could steadfastly deny their existence since these relatively small events were not very much in the public eye.

When the seminar, which lasted three hours instead of the scheduled two, came to an end, Vladimir Kozlovsky, a reporter for the *Novoye Russkoye Slovo* and for the Russian service of the BBC, approached me with his microphone. "Why are you against the invitation to people with a different point of view? I believe that the pluralism that everyone champions here means precisely that you have to listen to the opinions of different people, and especially to those with whom you disagree so sharply."

I was amazed by this question since I had never opposed the invitations themselves.

"The Kennan Institute for Advance Russian Studies announced in its program that these people would represent different ethnic groups and discuss problems of different nationalities of the Soviet Union," I explained, detailing my position. "Since they do not represent even the Russian people, but only one narrow trend of the Russian public thought, I am against such an inadequate representation. I consider it a serious mistake which could lead to a misunderstanding between the audience and these people, a misunderstanding of their real views. But I think we asked them the right questions here, forced them to speak out and outline their real position."[26]

Kozlovsky also interviewed Micah Naftalin, national director of the Union of Councils for Soviet Jews. A few days later, I was pleased to find out from Kozlovsky's report how close our views were.

"These people speak about Russian nationalism, about the salvation of Russian villages, expressing their concern about alcoholism," Naftalin said. "But what they do not want to speak about is that at home they publish malicious attacks on the Jews, blaming them for all the problems about which they have spoken today. They tried to distance themselves from what they write and publish at home. In this forum, they were introduced as independent scholars, publishers, editors, and writers, and they indeed are very influential people in their country. But they were not introduced as who they really are: representatives of the most malicious nationalistic movement with anti-Semitism as their dominant motivation."[27]

The major newspapers covered the seminar, but perhaps the most accurate conclusion came from Charles Krauthammer, who wrote in the *Washington Post:*

"The collapse of the Soviet system need not produce a return to Stalinism. A revanchist, xenophobic Russia could be just as dangerous. A resentful great power, stripped of empire after a long losing war, in social and economic chaos: Half a century ago in Weimar Germany that was a prescription for disaster. History need not repeat. But it can. Seventy years ago Lincoln Steffens went to Lenin's Russia and came back saying he'd seen the future.[*] To hear some of these Russian nationalists is to glimpse a future, too. It is Russia's most archaic past. One day it might make us pine for the present."[28]

The days after

---

[*] Lincoln Steffens (1866-1936), a U. S. journalist and political philosopher, wrote after visiting Petrograd in 1919, "I have been over into the future, and it works."

Hundreds of newspapers and radio and TV stations approached the Soviet guests after the seminar. With each interview, the speakers employed the same tactic: Reviewing a wide range of topics without touching on their own anti-Semitic writings and publications. But with each interview they failed. At home they were used to playing by their own rules. They could not understand why in America, which is so proud of her freedom of speech, journalists were not satisfied with their tricky deviations from the direct questions they were asked. They earnestly believed that freedom of speech meant freedom to lie.

In the scheduled cities on their tour, they were met by hundreds of protesters who expressed their feelings so overtly that the group's escorts sometimes had problems defending them from violent attacks. They tried to conceal arrival times and hotel reservations, but the demonstrators managed to appear anyway. The tour's activities were dramatically curtailed since most of the universities and organizations which had scheduled the Russian guests to speak before wide audiences canceled their invitations or restricted the meeting to short behind-closed-door sessions with the faculties of Russian studies departments.

The president of Little Big Horn College in Montana clearly outlined her position when she rescinded the school's invitation.

"Making such a decision, I took into consideration that they have the right to freely express their views; but the very existence of the college is based on a certain position about the human rights. We cannot be neutral in this regard. There are plenty of other places for dialogue."[29]

Of course, "Zionists" were to blame for all that "mistreatment," and Semyon Reznik stood at the top of the list.

In his interview to Radio Liberty, Kuniaev said that he had consulted with the U. S. Supreme Court and would bring civil charges against me to defend his "honor and dignity." In my own interview with Liberty, I said that I was ready to meet Kuniaev not only in the U. S., but in the Russian court as well, which would cost him less. Surely, he made no attempts to file suit: It was just another demagogic move on his part.

When the group of Russian writers returned to Moscow, Ernest Safonov recounted the details of his trip in his weekly. He wrote that "Zionists" had provoked all their troubles. He wrote that Reznik's article had set the tone for the journalists, who "worked according to a pre-planned scheme of casting slurs and not listening to us."[30] Thus, I was promoted to head of the "Zionist conspiracy" against Russia.

During my first (1988) trip to Russia (partly covered in chapter six), I was astonished by the degree of freedom that I, a foreigner—and, even worse, former Soviet citizen who had "betrayed" the country—could enjoy. I visited people and places that strangers would not typically know about or would not be allowed to see if they asked. I did not ask anyone. I just called, made appointments, and never noticed any shadowing. I left the country with the confidence that the authorities had not paid any attention to my visit.

But a year later, when I decided to go to Russia again with a group of tourists organized by the Union of Councils for Soviet Jews, I encountered unexpected resistance. A couple of days before our departure, the Soviet embassy denied my—and four others'—entrance visas without any explanation. Only after extensive negotiations and pressure from the State Department were all visas granted at the eleventh hour.

When we arrived at the Moscow International Airport, Sheremetevo, additional complications ensued. Five of the 77 members of our group were not allowed through the passport-control posts, and our passports and visas were rescinded.

More and more flights arrived from around the world. Hundreds and hundreds of passengers passed through the passport-control cubicles while we five American detainees remained seated in uncomfortable chairs in the windy passageway. All my attempts (as the only Russian-speaking member of the group) to elicit an explanation were met with one standard answer: "Your visas are being worked with."

One after another, at twenty or twenty-five minute intervals, we were let through, our passports and visas returned. My visa required the longest "work," before I, too, could join the group, which had had to wait on the other side of the sacred Soviet border for more than two hours.

Why did they play out this farce? If it were a warning, I pretended that I had not understood the hint.

During this trip, I again did not notice anyone following me, but later I got proof that they had dogged my every step. Because of the last-minute cancellation of an appointment, I unexpectedly decided to visit my old friend and colleague from the *Lives of Remarkable People* series who had become chief of the nonfiction book division of another big Publishing House.

Two minutes after I left his office, he had a telephone call from a man who introduced himself as a KGB colonel and asked who his visitor had been and how he had become acquainted with me. When he answered that we had worked together many years ago, the KGB-man said, "Well, I accept your explanation, but be careful. Reznik is a dangerous Zionist agent."[*]

There is a difference, you know, in being just an "agent" of Zionism and in managing the whole Zionist conspiracy.

In response to Ernest Safonov's article, I sent a letter to the *Literaturnaya Rossia*. "If America did not welcome the ultranationalistic group," I wrote, "its members have themselves to blame; but those who are obsessed with xenophobia never look in the mirror; they examine the roots, imagining a secret plot everywhere."

The letter was never published or answered.

---

[*] At the beginning of 1990, I planned to go to Russia again, having been invited by a newly organized private publishing company. But in March of that year (at the very same time when the last details of the Russian ultranationalist trip to the United States at the taxpayers expense were being worked out at the U. S. embassy in Moscow), my trip to Russia—at my own expense—was denied by the Soviet embassy in Washington, DC—without any explanation, of course. My visa was denied again and again, and only after the problem became public—thanks to a leading Soviet liberal magazine *Novoye Vremya (The New Time)*—could I get the visa, more than a year after I had applied.

CHAPTER 9

BLOOD LIBEL

"Ritual sacrifice"

After the Kuniaev's group left the United States, the theme of Russian Nazis and their threat to Russian democracy—as well as to world peace and security—disappeared from the papers and TV screens of this country again. The entire story was soon almost forgotten.

Meanwhile in the Soviet Union—and, after its disintegration, in Russia—the Nazi continued their activities with renewed energy. *Evreyskaya Gazeta (The Jewish Newspaper)* printed a list of 49 anti-Semitic periodicals that were in circulation in 1991.[1] Soon after that, *Russkoye Voskresenie (Russian Resurrection)* reprinted its own version of this list under the title "What Every Russian Should Subscribe to, Receive, and Read (Reprint from Evreyskaya Gazeta with our Corrections and Additions)," adding a couple dozen titles to it.[2]

Russkoye Voskresenie was one of new "patriotic" publications, whose number continued to grow. They addressed practically all segments of society—from those who are nostalgic for the Communist past to those who hate Communism and idealize the Russian monarchy, from Russian Orthodox believers to atheists, from the elderly to teenagers, from intellectuals with higher education and scientific degrees to the semi-literal mob, from the industrial workers of bankrupt state enterprises to the newly born businessmen, from military personnel to the general public.

For each target audience the editors prepare a specially tailored menu. The Russian Orthodox believers fall prey to the "belief" that Jews blew up their churches, executed their clergy, and destroyed Russian spirituality. Those who long for the job security they enjoyed under socialism are indoctrinated in the role of the Jews as instigators of reforms and the consequent "selling out" of Russia to the West. At the same time, the new breed of private entrepreneurs learns that Jews headed the "anti-Russian" Socialist revolution and eliminated private ownership in the country. Publications targeted toward the elderly, those who remember the World War II and still nurse a hatred for the German Nazism, exploit the idea of a "Zionist collaboration" with the Nazis, pointing out that Hitler himself was of Jewish origin as well as the majority of his entourage. And for the youth, which is nostalgic for strict order and military romanticism, apologetic biographies of Hitler portray him as a "true German patriot" and zealous fighter against the "world Jewish conspiracy."

The "patriotic" imagination reshuffles the entire Russian and world history, looking for Jews to blame for everything. Thus, the so-called Mongol-Tatar yoke—although cast off more than 500 years ago—left a deep imprint in the Russian national consciousness. So the "patriots" have recently "found" that the yoke would not have been as cruel if it weren't for the Jews. According to their new "discoveries," the Tatars sold thousands of Russians to Jewish merchants from the Italian city of Genoa, who resold them into slavery. The conclusion is that, without the market created by the Jews, the Tatars would have had no motivation for their frequent raids to Russian soil to take more and more slaves.[*] Other publications have developed a theory that the Tatar yoke was not that bad and that all Russian sufferings originated in Khazar Kahanat.

The Khazars was a nation on the Volga river and the North Caucasus. From the 7th to the 11th century, they had an independent state, Kahanat. While the Khazars were of Turkic origin, Judaism was the official state religion of the Kahanat. According to Vadim Kozhinov, Igor Shafarevich, the late Lev Gumilev, and other "patriotic" scholars, Judaic domination in the Kahanat caused all the trouble for the neighboring Slavic tribes.[**]

---

[*] One might recall similar "discoveries" in this country by Louis Farrakhan and other extremist leaders of the black Muslim organization *Nation of Islam*. The fundamental difference, however, is that it was immediately rebuked here, while in Russia most of anti-Semitic statements are repeated again and again and remain mostly unanswered.

[**] Objective historians know that the opposite was true. Khazar Kahanat was a relatively peaceful state, depending mostly on trade. It was constantly attacked from the East by numerous nomadic tribes and shielded Slavic tribes situated to the West. Thanks to this shield, the Slavs had a couple of peaceful centuries to develop their culture to the level of statehood. Khazar Kahanat seized to exist soon after it was defeated by Russian Grand Duke Svyatoslav in 965. After that, Khaganat begab to decline; Russia had to defend herself from nomadic invasions and finally was defeated by Mongols (Tatars).

But what has dominated the "patriotic" propaganda in the 1990s is the assertion that the Jews use Christian blood in their religious ceremonies. The civilized world rejected this absurd prejudice hundreds of years ago, but now these accusations have become a part of everyday public reflection in Russia.

One short phrase in *Russophobia* about the "ritual" murder of the Czar and his family indicated to the "patriotic" organizations that the time was ripe for the exploitation of a natural public interest in the tragic fate of the Nicholas II.

During the seventy years of the Communist regime, the public has been informed only in general terms: "The Bloody Czar Nicholas was executed by the Revolutionary People according to the resolution passed by the Executive Committee of the Ural Region Soviet of the Workers and Soldiers Deputies." All details were kept secret. In the 1970s, when more and more people started to lose their faith in communism, interest in the Czar's fate increased dramatically. It was fed by a surfeit of rumors. The public was thirsty for any pieces of information—always distorted and enriched by imagination—that penetrated from the West.

Almost every visitor to Sverdlovsk (formerly Yekaterinburg) wanted to see the "House of the Special Purpose" where the Czar and his family had been held in custody for the last few months of their lives and where they were executed. The flow of pilgrims became so great, that authorities ordered the building torn down. Thus, the Czar was symbolically executed for the second time. Of course, technically Moscow effected this political decision, but the official order came from Boris Yeltsin, then the first secretary of the Sverdlovsk Region Party Committee.* Now the "patriots" who often "accuse" Yeltsin of being Jewish are constantly reminding him of that "Zionist" act.

With *glasnost* and the lessening of restrictions, numerous publications offered a depiction of that horrible night in Yekaterinburg when the Czar, Czarina, their son and four daughters, their doctor, and three servants were shot by local Bolshevik butchers. But in most cases, facts mingled with anti-Semitic lies that ranged from "exposing" all real and mythical participants in the crime as Jews to displaying such impressive details as "cabalistic signs" and phrases in Yiddish allegedly found on the site of the execution. Some authors describe how the Jewish executioners (Yakov Yurovsky or "Shaya" Goloshchekin) had separated the Czar's head from his body and delivered it to Moscow in a container of alcohol and how in the Kremlin, leading Bolsheviks

---

* Exactly as in 1918, when Alexander Beloborodov, the head of the Ural Soviet, authorized shooting the Czar and his family after he received secret instructions from Moscow.

organized a Jewish religious ceremony around the head to celebrate their satanic triumph over Holy Russia."³

Simultaneously, a more traditional version of "Jewish ritual murders" began to occupy more and more space in the "patriotic" press.

In 1990, one of the most extreme Monarchist organizations started the weekly *Zemshchina*. It mostly reprints materials from the pre-Revolutionary *Zemshchina*, a newspaper of the ultranationalistic *Union of the Russian People*. The new *Zemshchina* frequently reprints articles that "prove" that Jews are killing Christian children on a regular basis to obtain their blood for religious rites.

Other "patriotic" publications do not restrict themselves to reprints. In 1991, for example, a newly organized newspaper *Istoki (the Sources)* released an extensive article "What Endangers Our Children."[4] The author, O. Kobrina, claims that *every year* before Passover, up to 1,500 Russian children become victims of the Jewish religious practice.

Connection of times

The concept of ritual murder is rooted in the ancient past. At the beginning of the Christian era, the Romans brought such charges against the Christians. After Christianity had become a dominant religion in Europe, the accusations lay dormant—only to resurface in the twelfth century—with the Jews as their target. The libel moved from country to country, giving vent to the aggressive energy of the mob and leaving bloody footprints of tortures, cruel executions, and pogroms.

Enlightened people, often supported by their governments and church authorities, fought against this unfounded prejudice; and little by little, the public consciousness released its misconceptions and aversions—but not in Russia, where the government deliberately cultivated a hatred for the Jews.

Gavriil Derzhavin, a great Russian poet and high-level statesman of the late eighteenth and early nineteenth century, championed discriminatory anti-Jewish legislation. He insisted that the Jewish people would have to cleanse themselves of the accusations of the ritual consumption of Christian blood before the question of granting them equal rights might even be considered.

In 1817, Alexander I, who had the reputation of an enlightened monarch, issued a special resolution forbidding bringing ritual murder charges against

---

* The authors borrow these exotic "facts" from the anti-Semitic "research" of Robert Wilton, M. K. Diterikhs, and Nikolai Sokolov (see chapter 7) and enrich and embellish them to their own satisfaction.

the Jews. But several years later, just before his death, he personally authorized an investigation in the small town of Velizh, Vitebskaya Province, which turned into one of the biggest ritual trials in Russian history.

The law enforcement agencies of the empire were preoccupied with this case for about twelve years, from 1823 to 1835. Duke Khovansky, the general-governor of the province, and the new Czar Nicholas I, who personally monitored the investigation, pushed for a verdict of "guilty," so the investigators enthusiastically sought evidence against the more than forty arrested Jews, forcing confessions through psychological and physical torture.

A hundred years later, similar methods of "investigation" worked perfectly during Stalin's purges, when his secret police could force almost anyone to confess to almost anything. But at the time of Nicholas I, the investigators had more motivation than skill and consequently were not able to beat false confessions out of the arrested Jews. All accusations were based on the testimonies of three Russian women who "confessed" that they had been secretly converted to Judaism and had then participated in a number of ritual murders. But even those three witnesses were inconsistent, contradicting each other and themselves. In spite of that, the verdict authorized by the general-governor was "guilty."

The legal procedures of that time did not require a court hearing. All the files were sent to St. Petersburg for final approval. They ended up in the State Council, the highest authority after the Czar. A member of the council, Count Nikolai Mordvinov, reexamined the materials and refuted all accusations as absurd and inconsistent with the circumstances of the case. Mordvinov was the most enlightened and independent-minded Russian statesman of that time. His logic was so convincing that the State Council unanimously voted for a non-guilty verdict and for punishing only the three Russian women—with the whip and exile to Siberia—for their false testimony.

According to the law, even the Czar could not overrule a unanimous decision of the State Council (it was the only restriction to his absolute authority), so Nicholas I had to approve it. He was disappointed, however. He wrote in his resolution that the Velizh prisoners should be released from custody since the investigation had not proved their guilt. But the problem of ritual murders remained unsolved. After all, he contended, a secret Jewish sect practicing ritual murders might exist. If there were savagely cruel sects among Christians, why could there not be some among the Jews?*

---

* In 1979, I completed a historical novel based on these materials and entitled *Chaim-and-Maria*, but all my attempts to publish it in the Soviet Union failed. The book was published in Russian in the United States (Washington, D.C., 1986) and in a Hungarian translation (Budapest, 1990).

Delighted with this new tack, the Czar resolved to end the problem of Jewish ritual murder once and for all; and new work began.

After a nine-year study, an extensive report was prepared by *tainy sovetnik*⁂ Skripitsin, director of the spiritual affairs and foreign religious beliefs department of the Ministry of Internal Affairs. Skripitsin did not "solve the problem," however, but just compiled materials about ritual murder trials in different times and countries without any analysis of the charges or the reliability of the sources.

Only a limited number of copies of the report were originally printed—for the Czar, his heir, the Grand Dukes, and several high officials. Thus, it was not made public. Perhaps even those to whom the copies were presented did not read the account. But the book did not disappear forever. On the contrary, as fate has willed it, Scripitsin's report went through a number of reincarnations and became immortal.

The first reincarnation took place three decades later, when Ippolit Lyutostansky obtained a copy of the book. Lyutostansky might qualify as one of the first "professional" anti-Semites in Russia: He made his living by "exposing" the Jews and Judaism.

A former Catholic priest who pretended to be a converted rabbi and a student of the Talmud, he wrote multi-volume treatises about Jewish evil-doings against Christianity. Then he approached some rich Jews, demanding big money for his promise not to publish his manuscripts. When blackmail proved unsuccessful, he did issue his writings, which brought him a regular—though not substantial—income. In a 1876 publication, he included Skripitsin's book in its entirety without mentioning his source.

Two years later, when another ongoing ritual investigation, the Kutaisi case, intrigued the country, Skripitsin's report found its way to the pages of the newspaper *Grazhdanin (Citizen)*, where it was reprinted under the real author's name.[5] (Thus, Lyotostansky's plagiarism was revealed, but without any harm to him; his heavy volumes continued to appear in new editions confirming the constant demand for such literature.)

The next reincarnation came in 1913, coinciding with the most scandalous of all blood-libel trials, the Beilis case, which took place in Kiev.

Two-and-a-half years before the trial, Andrei Yushchinsky, a boy of 13, had been killed by a gang of thieves who suspected that he had reported their criminal activities to the police. The murderers stabbed the boy's body with a

---

⁂ *Tainy Sovetnik* means literally—*secret advisor*. It was an official rank for government civil service, equivalent to the military rank of general.

stab-awl to simulate a "ritual murder" as described by "scholars" like Lyutostansky.

At the onset of the investigation, the police identified the gang and their motives, but brought charges against Mendel Beilis, a brickyard manager, because he was the only Jew who lived in the vicinity of the murder site.

Beilis' arrest and the ritual-murder charges brought against him stressed the whole country and divided her into two camps.

Supported by the Black Hundred organizations and their numerous publications, the government saw an opportunity to reverse the democratic process initiated in the wake of the 1905 Russian revolution. The authorities hoped that the verdict of "guilty" and the wave of Jewish pogroms that it would provoke would unite Russians around the throne and that nobody would dare to demand political reforms, individual freedoms, equal rights for minorities, or a parliamentary system of government.

The entire administration of the empire, from Czar Nicholas II and his ministers to hundreds of clerks and secret police informers, worked for more than two years to build the false accusation against Beilis. Before the trial started, the authorities arrested a key defense witness and exiled him to Siberia without any accusation, just to prevent his showing up in the courtroom. The secret police bribed other witnesses—and even experts, well-known scientists—to give false testimony. Even a Russian ambassador in the Vatican was drawn into the conspiracy after the key religious expert, Catholic-priest Pranaitis, claimed under oath that the Popes' bulls, which had forbidden bringing ritual-murder charges against the Jews centuries ago, had never existed in reality. The defense asked the court to send a request to the Vatican archives for attested copies of the bulls. But, at the same time, the foreign minister—following the Czar's order—instructed the ambassador to the Vatican to hold the documents as long as possible to prevent their reaching Kiev before the end of the trial.

Liberals, on the other hand, also understood that much more lay at stake in the Beilis process than the fate of one particular Jew—or even the entire Russian Jewry. They mobilized all their intellectual resources to denounce the blood libel as such and brought to light the corruption and deceit in the investigation of Andrei Yushchinsky's murder, in particular.

Hundreds of Russia's writers, scientists, and other public figures protested this medieval inquisition. The liberal press inaugurated a large-scale campaign denouncing the ancient superstition and prejudice.

Kiev-journalist Brazul-Brushkovsky launched an independent investigation with the help of private detectives, gathering evidence from the crime neighborhood. They even succeeded in infiltrating the gang and winning the trust of one of its members to the extent that eventually the murderer frankly told his new "friends" the real story. The liberal press—uncensored at that time*—extensively covered all these findings. Sensation after sensation stressed the entire country, and the unprecedented struggle lasted for more than two years until the liberals finally won and the jury acquitted Beilis. After that, most of the Jews—as well as gentiles—became convinced that the dark ages were over even in Russia.

This optimism proved unjustified.

When society is fighting against darkness and ignorance, when lies are opposed by truth, and when tolerance and humanism counterbalance blind hatred, prejudices are being squeezed out of the mainstream of public concern. Unfortunately, invisibility can produce the false impression that these prejudices have disappeared completely. But, as a rule, they survive in the dark corners of people's minds, in cultures or subcultures—if not in entire nations, then within some marginal groups, where they pass from generation to generation. And in times of political and spiritual crises, increased social tensions, and the loss of basic humanitarian values, these provincial hatreds may spread across the whole society again like a forest fire during a severe drought.

Russian proto-Nazis understood this instinctively. Within a year of the Beilis case they tried—without success—to organize a new blood libel trial in the small town of Fastovo. Later, during the Soviet era, in 1926, the disappearance of two boys in Dagestan, North Caucasus, caused a mass Jewish pogrom. Only after the boys were found, was the mob calmed down.[6]

I can provide no verified information about such events in the later Soviet Union, but the absence of documentation indicates nothing. Soviet society was not amenable to public scrutiny, and we can expect many surprises to come to light when the KGB archives become available to study.

Officially, the Soviet Union forbade the discussion of ritual-murder accusations against the Jews. The only book about the Beilis case—based on an extensive and extremely valuable archive research conducted by the author, Alexander Taher—was published in 1932. A second edition appeared a year later,[7] but after that, the Beilis case and other related litigation were never studied and publicly discussed in the USSR. Perhaps, some of the first-generation Communist leaders honestly believed that they could wipe old prejudices out of the public consciousness. But in the real world, the authorities

---

* After the 1905 revolution, the government had to give up its control over printing presses. This does not mean that censorship was completely abolished. The government still could punish editors and writers for expressing certain ideas, but a preliminary approval was not required anymore. Thus, the press obtained much more freedom than ever before in Russian history.

cannot erase prejudices cultivated for centuries. Meanwhile, total ignorance of past history renders society defenseless when the winds shift and the topic appears on the public agenda again.

The latest reincarnations

I know from personal experience that the blood libel was alive during the entire Soviet period.

When I was growing up in one of Moscow's poorest districts in the late 1940s and 1950s, the children in my neighborhood told many stories—obviously picked up from adults—about Jews sucking Christian blood allegedly needed for the Passover bread. And my wife heard similar stories in the 1970s from her fellow-employees at a prestigious scientific institute in Moscow. They could also imbibe these concepts with their mother's milk, but I cannot overlook the likelihood that Samizdat, where this propaganda proliferated, influenced them.

I was especially stricken when a friend told me about the circulation of a lengthy manuscript retyped from a 1913 edition of the book *Report on Ritual Murders* by Vladimir Dal. I failed to get a copy of it since it was not distributed in the circles where I could usually borrow Samizdat publications. However, no imagination was needed to understand the impression this work might have on its readers; the author's name spoke for itself.

Vladimir Ivanovich Dal (1801-1872) was one of the greatest figures of nineteenth-century Russian culture. He was a doctor, then became an official of the Ministry of Internal Affairs and traveled extensively around the country. His travels gave him an opportunity to study the traditional ways of life throughout Russia, and he collected rare local words and expressions and recorded stories that explained them. His genius for ferreting out words, expressions, and proverbs, resulted in the four-volume *Defining Dictionary of the Living Russian Language*, a grandiose and unique cultural work. Not just a Russian Webster's Dictionary, the book advanced the meaning and significance of its entries through mini-stories. These explanations included so many specific details about different customs, handicrafts, ways of work, and lifestyles somehow connected to the defining word that the *Dictionary* turned into an ethnographic encyclopedia of the Russian people, the essence of the Russian national character. Dal was also a talented fiction writer and, in short, an embodiment of the Russian spirit and the personification of Russian originality. Thus, readers might well perceive his book on Jewish ritual murders as written by Mother-Russia herself.

I found this news especially unpleasant for personal reasons as well.

While Vladimir Dal was famous in many circles, his name was primarily associated with the four heavy language-reference volumes on the bookshelf. The general public knew nothing about his personality until 1971, when the *Lives of Remarkable People* series published Dal's biography. I myself edited the book, and the print-run of 200,000 copies sold out immediately and received dozens of reviews in the mass media. The book, authored by Vladimir Porudominsky, portrayed Dal as a genius-scholar, an extremely hard worker, an honest and responsible person, and as a great Russian patriot despite his Danish origin.[8] The four-volume reference book turned into a human being, a lively and charming character. Thus, it happened that I, as the editor of the book, unwillingly added prestige to Dal's blood-libel assertions.

I contacted Vladimir Porudominsky. While working on Dal's biography, he had extensively researched libraries and archives, found and analyzed an enormous amount of unknown material, and knew practically everything about Vladimir Dal.

My relationship with Porudominsky went beyond business; we had been close friends for many years. I told him about the *Report on Ritual Murders* and asked for his comments; his response did not surprise me much. He said that such a work was absolutely unknown to him and that he could guarantee it was never published during Dal's lifetime—neither under his name nor under his pen name, Cossack Lugansky. He added that neither this work nor any preliminary research materials collected for it were among Dal's manuscripts available in archives; he had never seen any mention of it in Dal's letters or other documents. If he had really been involved in the project, his papers would have indicated that commitment.

So, it seemed that Vladimir Dal had never written the *Report*. But then, who was the author? I tried to locate the 1913 edition of the book, but could not find it in the catalogs of Moscow's leading libraries. Only many years later, in the Library of Congress in Washington, D. C., could I locate a microfilm of the book: V. I. Dal, *Report on Ritual Murders* (St. Petersburg: 1913).

As I read, I found an extensive introduction filled with the words "rare" and "extremely rare." The anonymous publisher stated that only ten copies of the book had been printed in 1844 and that later almost all of them disappeared. He claimed that during Dal's lifetime the journal *Russian Archive* had planned to reprint the *Report,* but one Jewish employee secretly instructed by the Jewish leaders (!) broke into the shop at night and stole part of the manuscript. Finally, the publisher wrote:

"Almost without any changes, the *Report* was printed in the same year of 1844 under the title *Information about Murders of Christian Children by the Jews for the Purpose of Collecting Blood*. Its composition was ascribed to *tainy sovetnik* Skripitsin, who fulfilled this work under the order of the Minister of Internal Affairs, Count Perovsky, for delivery to the Emperor Nicholas I, his heir, grand dukes, and the members of the State Council. (Was reprinted in *Grazhdanin*, No. 23025, pp. 546-556)."[9]

Thus, everything became clear. The publisher himself had confirmed that the book he had printed in 1913 under the name of Vladimir Dal was identical to Skripitsin's, printed in 1844 and reprinted in *Grazhdanin* in 1878.

Samizdat circulation of that book in the 1970s had to be very narrow, first of all because of its size. There is a big difference between retyping again and again a two- or three-page document and a 300-page book. But the post-Communist era has opened unlimited opportunities for ritual propaganda, and Scripitsin's book experienced one more reincarnation: It appeared in a mass-market edition, once again under the glorious name of Vladimir Dal. Now it is widely available. It serves as a powerful tool of blood-libel propaganda, convincing readers that the notion that the Jews are using Christian blood in their religious rituals is not just a myth or a popular fairy tale, but a reality thoroughly studied and proven by as outstanding a scholar as Vladimir Dal.

From pseudo-Dal to Molodaya Gvardia

Now this propaganda influences the young generation. An article printed in the *Molodaya Gvardia* monthly in the December 1991 issue and signed by the initials **L. B.** is so spectacular that I feel compelled to quote extensively from it:

"The frequent disappearance of children and finding their corpses, bloodless and with characteristic stab wounds at certain parts of their bodies, [are well known] but all these mysterious cases either remain unexplained or are attributed to the sadism of individual criminals. As a child I lived in one of the cities in Middle Asia˙. ...A passer-by suddenly grabbed me, covered my mouth [with his hand], and dragged me into a basement. ...I regained con-

---

˙ A geographical term for the area covered by four former Soviet republics (now independent states) to the east of the Caspian Sea and to the South from Kazakhstan: Uzbekistan, Turkmenistan, Tadzhikistan, and Kirgizia. The author does not identify the republic where he lived, but it was probably Uzbekistan.

sciousness in pitch darkness, feeling a dull and cutting pain in my whole body, especially in my chest and stomach. ... [After I went out], my own blood, which I could see in the daylight, frightened me. All my clothes were stained with blood. ...

"One boy about ten to twelve years old was brutally murdered. His body was covered with numerous wounds; he had been tied up with an electrical wire, a bottle deeply inserted into his throat. ... Another victim—a boy of same age—survived, but his body was covered with stab wounds. ...The investigator who handled the case was a good-natured, thoughtful, Russian guy. Soon after the incident, he committed suicide by jumping out the window of his office. ...

"Twenty years had passed when I ran into the book by Vladimir Dal. The suspicions came to my mind. The incidents had all occurred before Passover. Stab wounds had covered the bodies of all the victims, resulting in heavy losses of blood. A bottle had been used to plug the throat. In each instance—an execution of the culprit followed with shocking immediacy. And finally, there was the mysterious death of the investigator. Perhaps they were ritual murders. Maybe the accused criminals were not the actual killers, but had only helped someone else kidnap future victims. ... Indeed, at the trial of one of them, [under a nickname] Belomor, the suspect suddenly said that he had been hired for that job by Bukharian Jews.[**] On the same day, the Uzbeks organized a Jewish pogrom. But the next day, Belomor's defense lawyer, Jewish himself, claimed that he had instructed his client to say that to convince the court that he was insane and soften his punishment."

After sharing this blood-freezing information, **L. B.** generalized:

"It is widely known that world public opinion is manipulated [by the Jews]. They succeeded in creating a moral climate in which similar crimes are considered as just customary sadistic acts. It all started with the case of Andrei Yushchinsky's murder in Kiev in the spring of 1911. ... A false opinion dominated the public that the court had not only found Beilis not-guilty for lack of evidence, but had also fully refuted the 'blood libel,' though, in actuality, no mention had been made of it."[10]

[**] After the name of Bukhara, a city in Uzbekistan where Jews have lived since ancient times. They differ from both the East European Jews (Ashkenazim) and the Spanish Jews (Sephardim).

The article, adorned with the photo of Andrei Yushchinsky's punctured head reprinted from the Beilis case materials, ends with a classical call for a pogrom, imitating the style of the Black-Hundred's leaflets.

"Russian people! It's time to stop being afraid of thinking and speaking our minds! Let us cover ourselves with the sign of the cross, overcoming the fears imposed on us! ... Any concealing or hushing up of the actual ritual crime-related facts is tantamount to direct involvement in these crimes and complicity with the tormentors of children. You can overcome this treacherous fear and open exposure by joining the martyrs. God and the Holy Virgin save all!"[11]

Molodaya Gvardia was one of the first national periodicals to start a "patriotic" crusade in the 1960s. Up to the late 1980s, it was an official publication of *Komsomol* (The Young Communist league). Its circulation varied over the years from 400, 000 to 750,000 copies.* After the magazine became "independent," it dramatically increased its advance against Jewish-Masonic fortresses and blood libel became one of the regular topics covered on its pages.

Satanic symbol—666

Such was the spiritual landscape when the tragedy in *Optina Pustyn*, one of the best-known Russian Orthodox monasteries, occurred on April 18, 1993, the first day of the Orthodox Easter. Early in the morning, a bearded man dressed in a military coat secreted himself in the bell tower. When two monks arrived to ring the bell, he stabbed them in the back. As he fled, the murderer collided with a priest on his way to the church and killed him as well.

Many witnesses saw the murderer, so the police captured him soon and he readily confessed. He was identified as Nikolai Averin, 32, a resident of Volkonsk Village, a former soldier in Afghanistan. He had spent some time in a mental hospital and received a disability pension because of his mental conditions.

Nikolai Averin had graduated from a vocational school as a musician and had been scheduled to serve his obligatory military term in a musical unit. But when he was offered the opportunity to volunteer go to Afghanistan, he agreed without hesitation. He did not want to become a target of jokes back in his vil-

---

* Later, circulation of all leading publications, both liberal and "patriotic," dropped significantly due to increased prices and distribution problems.

lage about a guy who had just blown horn the entire two years of his military service.

He returned from Afghanistan physically unscathed but emotionally fragile. He became a religious fanatic. All night long he read the Bible; he kept all fasts and never started to eat without a prayer. He expected immediate rewards from above, but God was in no hurry; Averin's enormous love for God transformed into hatred. He became suicidal and cut his veins three times, but survived. He attempted to rape a little girl, and he seriously prepared himself for his death, detailing his burial in his will. And then he killed the monks, acting—as he told the interrogator—on Satan's instruction. On his blade, the tool of the murder, the number 666 was engraved, a symbol of Satan according to some traditional beliefs.

It would seem that there is no way to interpret the tragedy as a Jewish ritual murder. First, no uncovered secrets are connected to the case. Second, the murderer had no ties with the Jews. Third, it is impossible to associate these killings with the intention to extract blood. But "there are no fortresses that Bolsheviks could not take," Joseph Stalin stated. *Pravda*, the leading Bolshevik daily, decided to take the lead in the blood-libel accusations.

For decades, *Pravda* was the number-one paper in the Soviet Union; every word printed on its pages was regarded as an instruction to act. After the Communist totalitarian state disintegrated, the authority of *Pravda* was significantly undermined, but it still retained considerable prestige and influence. In the May 5, 1993 issue, an article by Dmitry Gerasimov examined "The Satan Tribe. Who Is Behind the Murderer of the Monks?"

> "A little bit more than a year ago," the author proudly informed his readers, "writing for *Sovetskaya Rossia* [another leading Communist daily] about the attempts of the Lubavitch Hasidic sect to seize the manuscripts of Shneerson,[*] I referred to the description of the ritual murders in those manuscripts. And immediately I was severely punished; I was beaten in the literal sense of this word.
>
> "Later I had the opportunity to speak with a scholar, Doctor of Philology V. Goldenberg, who is now a citizen of Israel, and—while avoiding any

---

[*] Rabbi Joseph I. Shneerson (1880-1950) was the sixth Lubavicher Rebbe. In the 1920s, the Soviet Secret police arrested and sentenced him to death for his refusal to cooperate with the Bolsheviks. Due to international pressure, he was "pardoned" and later allowed to leave the Soviet Union, but his library filled with books and manuscripts that he and his predecessors had collected was confiscated and disappeared. Just a few years ago, it was discovered in the Moscow Lenin Library, and since that time, the Lubavitch Hasidim have been fighting for the return of their sacred possession.

Blood Libel 175

comments about the content of the manuscripts—he told me a story about Levites who, with the support of their rabbis, killed representatives of other religions *(goyim)* and sacrificed them to God. I don't want to overwhelm the reader with sadistic details, but one aspect, I believe, is interesting. According to the Levites, a symbol of the national and religious might that indicated their special relationship with God was the ritual sacrifice of a gentile—if done on the day of his holy celebration. And the better the sacrificed person was in terms of his morality, the higher God's reward would be—which explains why the children and the monks were chosen. ... According to many scholars who studied this question, these ritual murders have survived until now, for example, among the Hasidim.

"It does not matter whose hands those fanatics use—whether the hands of a teenager under a heavy dose of drugs or a madman. What is really important is the fact that religious, occult organizations are multiplying in Russia every day. According to data of the super-secret 13th department of the NKVD[*] and a similar department of the KGB, from 45 to 50 people die every year in Russia from unknown causes with signs of ritual torture. The number of sects and mason lodges is impossible to calculate. It is unlikely that we will ever know who instructed the mad Afghan veteran: An insane person is not responsible, and the court hearings where something could come to light are not needed. Today, the disciples of Satan feel comfortable in Russia, so we should rail loudly against him."[12]

Pravda added an editorial comment to the article.

"The sects of Lubavitch Hasidim, which have already organized their religious celebrations several times in the Russian holy site, the Orthodox Kremlin, according to information agencies, are getting ready for the celebration of their Chanukah and Passover in Russia. The new year of 1994 will be the year of a wave of unprecedented propaganda of Judaism and Zionism."[13]

The U. S. State Department sent a note to the Russian Embassy in Washington, DC, and to the Russian Ministry of Foreign Affairs in Moscow. The note indicated that the article in *Pravda* represented an attempt to organize a pogrom and undermine the spirit of religious tolerance in Russia. The U. S.

---

[*] Abbreviation of the name of the People Commissariat of Internal Affairs, the designation of the KGB during most of the Stalin era.

government expressed special concern that the article had established a false connection between the murder of the Orthodox monks and the demand to return the 12-thousand religious books and manuscripts of the Shneerson's library to their legitimate owner—the Lubavitch Hasidic Community. The U. S. government reaffirmed that it would continue to support this demand.

Russians replied that *Pravda* is not an official publication and does not represent the point of view of the government. However, the Russian government and its law-enforcement agencies ignored—not for the first or last time—the fact that *Pravda* acted against Russian law, which forbids "inflammation of ethnic enmity."

PART THREE

AT THE HIGHEST LEVEL

CHAPTER 10

NAZIFICATION UNDER GORBACHEV

Alexander Sukharev—Gorbachev's appointee

In the summer of 1985, the *Yuridicheskaya literatura* (Legal Literature) Publishing Company issued 200,000 copies of *The White Book: New Facts, Testimonies, Documents.* It was apparently a joint venture of two organizations, the *Anti-Zionist Committee of the Soviet Public* and the *Association of Soviet Lawyers.*

Like other related publications, *The White Book* portrayed the United States and Israel as societies of violence, crime, and genocide. Ruled by Zionists, the publications claimed, these two countries were seeking to destroy socialism from the inside, using the Soviet Jews as their instrument. *The White Book* stood out from the row because the compilers supported their message with hundreds of thoroughly selected photographs, letters, quotations, and testimonies to produce an impression of indictment or even a sentence—a kind of "Nuremberg trial over Zionism." The involvement of the Association of Soviet Lawyers lent an additional credibility to the book, giving it the aura of a legal document.

Colonel-General David Dragunsky, chairman of the Anti-Zionist Committee of the Soviet Public, and Alexander Sukharev, first vice-president of the Association of Soviet Lawyers, co-authored the introduction, which set the tone for the entire book.

"The history of international Zionism—its ideology and political experience—testify: Zionism is a frantic reaction, militant anti-communism and anti-Sovietism. ... The Soviet people have always treated and continue to treat Zionism as an ideology that concentrates in itself an apology for ethnic exclusiveness for the 'chosen people' and, thus, as an ideology both chauvinistic and racial. ... Today the struggle against Zionism—its ideology and political practice—is at the top of the agenda. That's why the Soviet people are prepared to give an adequate rebuff to Zionist provocateurs."[1]

The *White Book* was signed for printing three months after Mikhail Gorbachev became the General Secretary of the Communist Party. Soon, he appointed Alexander Sukharev, one of the quoted co-authors, to the office of the Attorney General of the USSR. In other words, at the beginning of the era of *glasnost* and *perestroika*, Gorbachev delegated control over the entire law-enforcement system to an outspoken anti-Semite.

Gorbachev's "statistics"

During his first visit to France after becoming the General Secretary, Gorbachev had to answer a question about the persecution of the Jews in the Soviet Union. He replied that the Jews enjoyed more freedom and privileges in his country than anywhere else in the world. Gorbachev supported his statement with statistics. While the Jews comprised only .69 percent of the Soviet population, he said, they occupied from 10 to 20 percent of the most prestigious top-management positions.

Unfortunately, nobody asked him about the methods used to calculate these figures.

According to available data, in the 1970s, the Jews constituted 4.1 percent of the Soviet people with higher education.[2] Later the proportion dropped due to the mass Jewish emigration and increased restrictions on their admission into colleges and universities. Normally, after completing their education, Jews, like all graduates, were given entry-level professional jobs and their obligation was to accept them for at least three years. But the most prestigious institutions or enterprises were not for the Jews. They were the last to get promotions in the companies they worked for, while transferring to another company was even more difficult for them. A popular joke about the difference between the Jews and Zionists claimed: "Jews are the Jews who work for us, while Zionists are the Jews who apply to work for us."

However, all sophisticated discriminatory techniques could not be effectively applied to all Soviet Jews, but only to the "Jews according to the fifth entry." Every Soviet citizen after 16 received an internal passport in which the fifth entry indicated his "nationality" (after last, first, and patronymic names and date of birth). The nationality of the parents determined the nationality of their child. Severe discrimination forced many Jews to alter their "fifth entry." Children of mixed marriages, for example, could choose the nationality of either parent, and almost unanimously they opted for a non-Jewish lineage. Others succeeded in "losing" their passports and acquiring a duplicate with a "good" nationality (for a bribe). Consequently, nobody can say for sure anymore what percentage of the Soviet population is Jewish and how many Jews occupy top positions. "Statistics" could be nothing more than speculation.*

But if Gorbachev had in mind the "fifth entry" Jews—they really constituted about 0.69 percent of the population—they would find it almost impossible to reach top positions. The rare exceptions required outstanding talents or an absolute lack of conscience.** In the most prestigious, according to Soviet standards, spheres of life—such as within the Communist Party apparatus, the KGB, diplomacy, and military command—there were no Jews at all. Jewish intellectuals had to concentrate on science, art, literature, journalism, medicine, and other professions where the maintenance of strict control over ethnic purity was not an easy task or where personal skills were so essential for achieving positive results that they could outweigh the "fifth entry." But even in the intellectual professions, a lot of volunteers appeared to dog the Jews.

Academician Ivan Vinogradov, director of the Institute of Mathematics of the Academy of Sciences of the USSR, fired all Jews from his institute. He was so powerful in his field that he could act with relative independence. In his anti-Semitic enthusiasm, he went much further than the authorities required. But when party bosses were determined to fire Igor Shafarevich for his dissident activities, Vinogradov answered, "I personally verified—he is not a Jew. So, I see no reason to fire him." When the statement was countered with the argument that the name "Shafarevich" sounds very Jewish, Vinogradov answered, "In my institute, I make the decision who is Jewish and who is not."[3]

---

* For example, Israeli sources estimate the current Jewish population of the former Soviet republics at about 1.5 million, while Russian "patriots" like Vladimir Soloukhin claim that in the Russian Federation alone there are about 15 million Jews.

** The Anti-Zionist Committee of the Soviet Public, for instance, was formed by the KGB from a group of prominent Jews to execute the most cynical and abusive anti-Semitic actions with their hands. Only the most outstanding villains, like David Dragunsky, could conduct these dirty activities in exchange for the benefits associated with them.

Vinogradov protected Shafarevich for many years so that he could conduct his dissident activities in relative security.

Another prominent mathematician, academician Lev Pontryagin, a blind genius who lost his vision at age of fourteen, was even more zealous in "liberating" the Soviet math from "Zionists." As the editor-in-chief of a leading mathematical journal, he did everything possible to "free" its pages from Jewish names. He provoked an international scandal after Grigory Margulis, a Soviet scientist of Jewish origin, won the Fields Prize, the most prestigious international award for mathematicians. Pontryagin mailed a letter of protest against the "Zionist provocation" to the jury and to hundreds of prominent foreign mathematicians. In 1978, in connection with his seventieth birthday, he printed an article about his own achievements in math. He outlined that his most significant service to the science and to the country was the fight against "Zionists" in Soviet mathematics.[*]

Vinogradov and Pontryagin were the two most influential mathematicians in the USSR. They inculcated their people into most of the key positions in Soviet mathematics, including the Highest Certifying Commission. For many years, not a single Jew could get an approval of his doctoral dissertation in math.

Gorbachev might not have been familiar with specific details, but the general picture should have been well-known to him when he alluded to a paradise for the Jews in the USSR.

The West quickly forgot his extravagant "statistic" after he left France, but at home the numbers were caught up and widely exploited. In his countless presentations, *Pamyat* leader Dmitry Vasiliev referred to Gorbachev's "statistics" and went further.

> "Why are you talking about the Jewish question in the Soviet Union? It simply does not exist and cannot exist. ... This is what the General Secretary said, and he is responsible for his words. ... If we analyze the proportions of Jewish representation in the Creative Unions,[**] in medicine, press, art, and science, we will find the rate not 10 to 20 percent, but 50 to 70 percent. I have nothing against it, this is all right, but under one condition: that the basic law, the Soviet constitution, is not violated." And after quoting the Constitutional propaganda statement of equality of the nationalities, he

---

[*] One of the most visible results of this "service" is the fact that the former Soviet mathematicians of Jewish origin form now the largest and the most successful group of émigré scientists at U. S. universities.

[**] Creative Unions are the prestigious Union of Soviet Writers, Union of Soviet Composers, etc.

concluded: "The basic law of the Soviet Constitution is quite clear, and there is nothing to talk about—except why? Why do representatives of the Jewish nationality—I respect these people very much—why do they break the Soviet law [by occupying too many prestigious positions]? Is it not written for them?"[4]

When *Pamyat* went out into the streets of Moscow and other cities, one of the most impressive placards read, "Down with the dictatorship of .69!" A newly formed organization, *For the Proportional Ethnic Representation*, demanded the reduction of the number of the Jews in any field to .69 percent.

General Secretary Gorbachev, whose "statistics" initiated these activities, did not pronounce a single word of condemnation regarding this propaganda.

Gorbachev's flirting with "patriotic" writers

Soon after the scandal caused by the publication of the anti-Georgian story by Victor Astafiev and his anti-Semitic letter to Nathan Eidelman, Gorbachev announced that he had had a personal meeting and long conversation with Astafiev. He characterized the writer as one of the most honest contemporary authors, who had deep concerns about the destiny of the country.

Later on, Gorbachev added another fiction writer, Vasily Belov, to the list of 100 non-alternative Communist Party nominees for the Congress of People's Deputies. This nomination especially puzzled Gorbachev's liberal supporters because at that time, the liberal press sharply criticized Belov's latest novel *All is Ahead*[5] for its poor artistic quality and an irreconcilable hatred toward Jews. The "patriots," on the other hand, extolled the novel to the skies.

"Of special notice is Brish," right-wing critic Nikolai Fed wrote, commenting on the novel's main Jewish character. "[He is] a typical carrier of evil, corrupt and the source of corruption. His principal objectives are money and his personal well-being, and he is seeking them by any means, at any cost. At the same time, Brish is devoid of any feeling of kinship with his home country. He is a guest here or, to be more exact, a night thief crushing what he cannot take away. He is a cosmopolitan in his essence, in his feeling and conviction."[6]

Belov's name on the "list of one hundred" ("the list of Black Hundred," according to a witticism circulated in Moscow) was a signal that Gorbachev sent to the "patriots" to indicate that his "liberalism" is compatible with their activities.

When the newly elected Congress of the People's Deputies formed the Supreme Soviet, Gorbachev re-nominated Alexander Sukharev to the position of Attorney General. Some deputies opposed this nomination—not because of Sukharev's anti-Zionist agenda, but because he was an elderly man with poor health. But Gorbachev lobbied hard and won a small majority of the votes for his protégé.

In 1989, 200 liberal members of the Congress of People's Deputies—alarmed by *Pamyat* activities and the connivance of the authorities—submitted an inquiry to the Presidium, demanding that the issue of rising anti-Semitism be placed on the Congress agenda. However, the request was ignored. And even more: Anatoly Lukianov, the chairman of the Supreme Soviet and then Gorbachev's closest associate, listed all inquiries received by the Presidium in his concluding speech, but omitted this one.

I myself joined with group of Russian émigré intellectuals to compose an "open letter" to Mikhail Gorbachev in support of the 200 deputies. Besides me, the letter was signed by Lyudmila Alexeeva, Raissa Berg, Lev Goldfarb, Yuri Druzhnikov, Aron Katzenelinboigen, Vladimir Matlin, Ilya Suslov, Armen Khachaturyan, and Svetlana Khachaturyan. The authors were university professors, scientists, writers, journalists, and historians; and almost all were well-known former dissidents or *refuseniks*. Two leading Russian émigré newspapers, the *Novoye Russkoe Slovo* and *Panorama*, published the letter.[7] We submitted the letter to the Soviet Embassy in Washington, DC, for delivery to the addressee, but received no answer, no measures were taken.

In March 1990, Gorbachev, who had just become the president of the USSR, formed the Presidential Council, a new ruling body to replace the Politburo. Among the non-party members of this inner cabinet, he appointed a well-known writer Valentin Rasputin, as it was mentioned in the chapter eight. (Perhaps, this was the reason why Rasputin could not come to the United States with the Kuniaev's group.)

Rasputin was one of the most talented "village prose" authors. His novels and short stories of the 1960s and 1970s had a positive response from both critics and readers. The underlying mood of his works denied the Bolshevik ideology and rule, and readers understood his Aesopian language well.

However, in the years of *glasnost*, Rasputin did not write prose. He began his political activities by leading a group of environmentalists concerned with the fate of Lake Baikal, the greatest natural reservoir of fresh and clean water on Earth with unique fauna and flora. But very soon it became evident that

Rasputin and his organization were less concerned with saving Baikal from industrial pollution than from "Masons and Zionists." Then, Rasputin expanded his activities, speaking out in numerous articles and interviews against the market economy, Western and other foreign cultural influence, and investments in the national republics' economies "at the expense of the Russian people." He was against everything and everyone but the *Pamyat* Society. In an interview with Bill Keller printed in the *New York Times Magazine,* Rasputin said:

> "I think today the Jews here should feel responsible for the sin of having carried out the Revolution, and for the shape it took. They should feel responsible for the terror. For the terror that existed during the Revolution and especially after the Revolution. They played a large role, and their guilt is great. Both for the killing of God, and of that."[8]

Mikhail Gorbachev did not see anything wrong in having a person with such views in his inner cabinet. At the 1990 Congress of Komsomol (the Young Communist League), forced by a question from the audience about the steps the authorities intended to take against anti-Semitic activities, Gorbachev said:

> "I believe that we must not allow the raging of nationalism, chauvinism, anti-Semitism, or any other 'ism.' We must proceed along the road of harmonization of inter-ethnic relations, creating legal, economic, and social conditions for people of all nationalities to feel confident wherever they happen to be. I see no other way."[9]

This was the first and the last time when the former Soviet leader, while in office, publicly pronounced the very word "anti-Semitism." Those who were accustomed to the uncommitted manner of his speech understood that he intended to do nothing about it at all.

Yakovlev

The only high-level official who tried to oppose the rising Russian chauvinism and anti-Semitism was Alexander Yakovlev, "the architect of glasnost." As we know, he had recognized the danger of ultranationlism back in the early 70s and was fired from the Central Committee for his attempts to curb it. Not

186   *Chapter 10*

until he had become a chief party ideologist did the liberal newspapers and magazines start to criticize *Pamyat* for anti-Semitic and chauvinistic activities.

Yakovlev personally characterized *Pamyat* as an anti-Semitic and pseudo-patriotic organization as well, and *Pamyat,* in return, sharply attacked him as the "agent of Zionism" within the party leadership. Dmitry Vasiliev even sent his investigators to Yakovlev's native village to research his alleged Jewish roots.

The party hard-liners considered Yakovlev their most dangerous rival and used any opportunity to sap his position directly or indirectly. The most remarkable of those attempts took place in March, 1988, when *Sovetskaya Rossia* printed a full-page letter, "I Cannot Give Up My Principles," by Nina Andreeva, a Leningrad Technological Institute teacher. The author stood for the "principles" of hard-line Communism (e. i., Stalinism) being undermined by "cosmopolitan liberals" and "reactionary nationalities" (the Jews).[10]

Yegor Ligachev, the second-in-command in the party hierarchy, inspired the article when both Gorbachev and Yakovlev were abroad. At Ligachev's direction, dozens of local party publications reprinted the article. Moscow liberals so feared this sign of a return of Stalinism that nobody dared to oppose Nina Andreeva. But three weeks later, a *Pravda* editorial sharply denounced her "principles" as a "manifesto of anti-*perestroika* forces." Alexander Yakovlev inspired the editorial after his return to Moscow, and he persuaded Gorbachev that it should be printed in the most authoritative Communist publication. For Yegor Ligachev, *Pravda's* upbraiding marked a serious defeat.

As a party official responsible for undermining *perestroika*—the policy adopted by the Communist Party Congress—Ligachev should have resigned or at least get a reprimand. But Gorbachev did not want to go that far. Neither Yegor Ligachev nor Valentin Chikin, the editor-in-chief of *Sovetskaya Rossia*, lost their positions or influence.

Since Yakovlev was the only high-ranking party official who had some understanding of what should be done in the country, Gorbachev needed him badly and encouraged him to move *glasnost* and *perestroika* forward. But, at the same time, he did not want to antagonize the hard-liners. He constantly distanced himself from Yakovlev and never defended him publicly against accusations of "anti-patriotism" and "Zionism."

In 1990, answering the question, "why had nobody been prosecuted under the Article [74 of the Russian Criminal Code] for inciting ethnic enmity?", Alexander Yakovlev said:

"I also asked this question, and more than once; and I asked the Attorney General, too. But, apparently, even the Attorney General does not dare to bring these cases to court. There is some powerful pressure which makes it impossible to apply the law. Maybe it is because there are always people who say about themselves, 'I am an internationalist, but Jews have to be beaten.'"[11]

Two points should be emphasized here. First, the Attorney General was under "powerful pressure" from his own anti-Semitic consciousness as well as from the outside. And second, which is even more important, Gorbachev never could have asked the Attorney General this question. If he had asked, Sukharev would have no other choice but to put the Article 74 into effect.

Sabotage of the Article 74

However controversial it might sound in the United States, where the freedom of expression of *any* ideas is guaranteed by the Constitution, in Russia, with her long tradition of totalitarian control over thoughts, unlimited freedoms would be extremely dangerous.

When *perestroika* began, a number of articles of the Russian Criminal Code forbade the articulation and distribution of certain views and ideas. Articles 70 and 190 provided legal ground for the arrest and sentencing of dissidents to many years of imprisonment for "anti-Soviet propaganda" or for "slander against the Soviet government and political system." The abolition of these two articles was one of the greatest achievements of the *glasnost* era.

Article 74 of the Russian Criminal Code forbids the "inflammation of ethnic tensions, insulting ethnic feelings," or articulating and distributing ideas of inequality based on race and ethnic origin. It is obvious that this article put some limitation on freedom of expression as well. But, unlike the "anti-Soviet" articles, it had not been enforced since mid-1930s, when Stalin had announced that all nationalities' problems in the USSR had been solved forever. Everybody knew that it was untrue. During the *glasnost* era, the hate crimes became so shocking, that nobody dared to demand a removal of the Article 74 from the Criminal Code even for the sake of freedom of expression. But law-enforcement agencies continued to ignore it despite numerous public requests to take legal action against *Pamyat* and its most active supporters. The liberal weekly *Nedelya* even announced a search for a scoundrel who had been interviewed on the street on TV and had disappeared after saying:

"There are 18 million Jews in this country, 18 million party members, 18 million engaged in management. All the Jews are party members; all the Jews are in management. The rest remains for everyone to understand the best he can. How shall we combat it? I know how to combat it. For myself, I am fighting. If everyone eliminates one Jew, we shall have no problems tomorrow. The means are sufficient."[12]

Challenging the authorities, the paper reproduced the picture of the speaker and appealed to its readers to identify him.

"Since the law-enforcement bodies responsible for defending the Soviet Constitution and acting according to the Criminal Code have failed to fulfill their mission, *Nedelya* has decided to assist the authorities in this case and, with the help of its readers, seek out the speaker in order to bring him to justice."[13]

This effort proved useless—as had many others before and have since—although it did not mean that the KGB and police had no skills or resources to fulfill their duties.

In 1989, a Leningrad resident, Arkady Norinsky, captured Soviet headlines. Norinsky, who identified himself as a Christian of Jewish origin, attended several *Pamyat* rallies. The malicious speeches and slogans horrified him as well as the impudent smiles of the uniformed policemen, who explained their non-interference with the simple statement, "We are Russians, too". Norinsky decided to alert the authorities. Not knowing how to go about it, he mailed threatening letters in the name of *Pamyat* to several celebrities of Jewish origin. One of the addressees took the letter seriously and printed it in *Ogonyok* magazine with his comments. The KGB needed two days to identify the anonymous author and to arrest him. Norinsky was tried and convicted for his "provocation" to a year-and-a-half of probation.

But neither the KGB nor the police have ever found those who spread rumors about Jewish pogroms, organized Nazi rallies and demonstrations, or published inciting newspapers, magazines, and books, although most of the "patriots" never hid their names and addresses.

The only exception was the case of Konstantin Smirnov-Ostashvili, a leader of one of the branches of *Pamyat* that sprang up from Vasiliev's national-patriotic front.

Smirnov-Ostashvili, with three-dozen supporters, came to the Moscow Central House of Writers, where normally only the members of the Writers

Union were admitted after showing their membership cards. But somebody let Smirnov and his group in. Breaking into the hall where the liberal writers' group *April* held its meeting, they shouted threats and anti-Semitic slogans through a megaphone. Overthrowing chairs and attacking the writers, they tried to provoke fistfights. Several writers were beaten. The brawl lasted about an hour before the police arrived. Before they left the House, the invaders cried out, "This time we have come with a megaphone, but the next time we will come with machine guns."

No one was arrested on the site, but leading *April* writers organized such a massive campaign in the liberal press that the authorities had to react. First, they charged Smirnov-Ostashvili (but not other members of the group) with hooliganism. After additional public pressure, they agreed to try him under Article 74.

After a month-long, extensively publicized hearing, the court sentenced Smirnov-Ostashvili to two years in a labor camp. The case kindled the hope that Article 74 had set a precedent for the restraint of "patriotic" activities, but the case remained the only one that came to trial. Smirnov-Ostashvili himself was to be out in about eight months for "good behavior." But a couple weeks prior to his release, he was found hanged. The officials announced that he had committed suicide; but since no details were enumerated, nobody believed it. According to the "patriots," it was, of course, the work of the Jews, while the liberal public believed that the KGB had gotten rid of him because he had already fulfilled his mission and had become a liability.

The KGB, which had initiated the struggle against the "Zionist-Masonic conspiracy," continued to actively exploit this doctrine during the *perestroika* and *glasnost* years as well. Georgian dissident Tengiz Gudava, who in 1987 had still been under arrest and investigation, later testified:

> "During the investigation at the KGB, they kept feeding anti-Semitic ravings into my ears. It appeared that it was not my native Georgian Moscow-run KGB that had put me behind bars, but the Jews who had. The dissident movement is, in the eyes of the Communists, only a branch of Zionism."[14]

Thus, it seemed only logical to assume that the KGB protected all champions of anti-Jewish and "anti-Zionist" propaganda. In 1990, Vladimir Kryuchkov, the KGB chairman himself, confirmed that the secret police supported the "patriots." Pavel Gutiontov, a columnist for *Izvestia,* commented with irony on

Kryuchkov's TV interview when he had to answer a viewer's questions about *Pamyat:*

> "*Pamyat* can be of different types; sometimes it can be very useful, genuinely patriotic, the activities of which he welcomes. There were, certainly, other types, too; but being short of time, Comrade Kryuchkov spoke about them in lesser detail. When will it be possible to at last disclose this most progressive wing of the *Pamyat* Society? Who are these remarkable people? Why are they hiding themselves? Where are the signs of their patriotic activities so highly praised by the chairman of the KGB?"[15]

Centrifugal forces

At one of his meetings with the U. S. president George Bush, Mikhail Gorbachev told him privately, "I have to weigh denouncing anti-Semitism against the danger of provoking Russian nationalism."[16]

In reality, however, he himself had contributed to the rise of Russian ultranationalism by directly and indirectly encouraging of their leaders and ideologists.

By opening his arms to them again and again, Gorbachev demonstrated his fundamental misjudgment of the processes that he had unleashed in his country.

The Jewish problem in Russia had never been just a problem of the Jews. Traditionally, it represented the nationalities' problem at large, only in the most extreme and visible form. Before the revolution, the Russian Empire had been called "the prison of nations." Under Communist rule, life in this prison became even more miserable. It was only natural that with the first signs of liberalization, inmates would begin to rebel—first, to make the regime less cruel, and then to completely destroy the prison itself.

To change the prison mentality of 130 different nationalities in a short period of time was the most serious challenge of *perestroika*. Minorities felt that Moscow had severely abused and persecuted them. Since the central government was mostly Russian and Russians dominated most of the local bureaucracies, it was not easy to convince the minorities that the Russian people were inmates of the same prison and not its warders. Even if Gorbachev had concentrated all his efforts on this problem, it would have been extremely difficult to effect a change.

But Gorbachev failed to realize the very existence of this problem. From his first day in office, his priority had been to reorganize the economy in order to produce more food and other consumer goods. He had not expected that *glasnost* would put the nationality problems ahead of all others; and even after it had already happened, he tried to ignore them.

In 1986, Gorbachev forced Dinmuhammed Kunaev, a Politburo member and the First Secretary of the Communist Party of Kazakhstan, to resign. Kunaev had built his entire career on his personal relationship with Leonid Brezhnev. Devoted to his boss, he had never hesitated to sacrifice the interests of his republic to please Moscow; thus the Kazakhs did not object to his resignation. But when Moscow appointed Gennady Kolbin to rule Kazakhstan, a violent anti-Russian uprising burst out in Alma-Ata, the republican capital. While Kunaev was Kazakh, Kolbin was Russian; thus, the Kazakh people interpreted the replacement as a sign that the Kremlin wanted to increase its control over their republic even more. After a brutal crackdown on the uprising, Kolbin was removed. But Gorbachev did not learn from this mistake.

A few months later, Gorbachev decided to calm down the nationalistic passions in Nagorny Karabakh* by doubling the quota of meat supply to the area. When this generosity did not help, he could not understand what else these people needed. A full scale war between Armenia and Azerbaijan is the result of this blindness.

People's Fronts appeared in most of the union republics and became very influential, demanding more and more autonomy from Moscow and leading up to a complete secession.

Moscow had no legal grounds on which to reject these demands. According to the Soviet constitution, the USSR was a union of 15 equal republics that voluntarily joined each other with the right to secede from the union at any time. While the real power remained in the hands of the Communist Party, the constitution was just a propaganda document with no practical application. But with *perestroika* and *glasnost,* it could not be ignored. Even some of the autonomous republics and regions also started to demand more freedoms and rights.**

Gorbachev was confident that there was too much economic interdependency between the republics and regions for secession to be beneficial to any of them. Thus, he believed that the vast majority of people in the republics would never support the secessionists. He failed to realize that not only bread is

---

* Nagorny Karabakh, a predominantly Armenian enclave in Azerbaijan, started to demand its secession from Azerbaijan and unification with Armenia.

** There were four different statuses for ethnic groups, depending on their numbers and location inside the larger group: the union republic, the autonomous republic, the autonomous province *(oblast),* and the national district *(okrug).*

needed for a human being. Rational thought could prevail in the republics only if Moscow proved to them that the iron embrace of the "older brother" had gone forever. By tolerating and encouraging the Russian ultranationalists, Gorbachev proved the opposite. If the Jews reacted to the rise of Russian ultranationalism by intensifying their demands for free emigration, than the republics also intensified their fight—for the right to "emigrate" from the Union, but together with their land, which meant to secede.

Only very fast and irreversible democratization of the society could give them reason not to leave. But instead of being ahead of this process, Gorbachev was behind. All his concessions to the republic's demands were made halfheartedly and too late, only inspiring further demands.

Yielding to this pressure, Gorbachev agreed to give the republics more rights in solving their domestic problems and offered them the "Union Treaty," in which these rights would be outlined. But three Baltic republics and Moldova, Georgia and Armenia considered the treaty a trap that would only legalize their dependence on Moscow. They refused even to discuss such a possibility. Other republics agreed to sign the Union Treaty in principle, but were not satisfied with Gorbachev's draft. They were demanding more autonomy than Moscow was ready to grant them. Gorbachev made additional concessions; but the nationalistic passions rose very fast, and what was good for the republics yesterday became unacceptable today.

After the fall of the Berlin Wall, party and non-party hard-liners began to attack Gorbachev—and especially his foreign minister Edward Shevardnadze—for their "excessive unilateral concessions to the West." Under this pressure, Gorbachev started distancing himself from Shevardnadze, as he had earlier from Yakovlev. The influence of the hard-liners increased significantly, which only urged nationalistic passions in the republics forward, making them less and less pliable. The disintegration of the Soviet Union was becoming more and more unavoidable.

The Military

Among the "anti-Zionist" publications listed in the bibliography to Alexander Romanenko's account *On the Class Essence of Zionism*,[17] books issued by *Voenizdat*—the Ministry of Defense Publisher—appeared more often than any other book-publishing company. Romanenko referred to his own articles as well, most of which appeared in such journals as *Agitator Armii i Flota (Agitator of the Army and the Navy)*, *Voennyie Znania (Military Knowledge)*, and *Kommunist Vooruzhyonnykh Sil (Communist of the Armed Forces)*. All these publications targeted the military political educators and were used for the "political training" of soldiers and officers. In the Soviet Army, political indoctrination was always as significant as the military training, or even more.

Of course, the military only followed the line of the Communist Party. But with the advent of *perestroika,* each government branch received more freedom to fulfill its tasks according to its own initiatives.

One of the first initiatives of *Voenizdat* was to launch a three-volume edition of Ivan Shevtsov, a prose writer notorious for the scandals that had accompanied his literary career.

Within the writer's community, Shevtsov had a reputation of an ungifted artist and a KGB informer. Nobody could say for sure what kind of information he provided in his secret reports to the KGB, but even his printed works were filled with denunciation. For example, one of his novels contained a dialogue in which one character called attention to the magazine *Yunost,* proclaiming it a Zionist publication because the editors separated poems on its pages by six-point stars*. All "positive" characters in Shevtsov's novels were patriotic and vigilant, always ready to identify the "Zionist provocation" in everything liberal or Western, from music and paintings to clothes and hairstyles.

In the summer of 1986, the *Voenizdat* editor signed all three of Shevtsov's volumes, which included six "patriotic" novels, for typesetting. But, unexpectedly, the publication was stopped. Most probably, it was a result of the interference of the Communist Party Central Committee, where Alexander Yakovlev had become the chief party ideologist. In 1988, the Central Committee lost its absolute control over the publishing industry, and *Voenizdat* printed the three Shevtsov's volumes in runs of 100,000 copies each."[18]

Thus, this edition was, in essence, the manifestation of what the military publisher and the Ministry of Defense stood for.

In 1990, another Ministry of Defense publication, *Voenno-istorichesky zhurnal (The Military-Historical Journal),* which had been for years an academic periodical of professional military historians, pioneered in bringing large excerpts from Hitler's *Mine Kampf* to the readership. After sharp criticism in the liberal press, General Victor Filatov, the editor-in-chief, "explained" that his intention was to familiarize his readers with the ideas of the main Soviet

---

* *Yunost (The Youth)* is not a fictional magazine; responding to Shevtsov's denunciation, the editorial board started to use only five-point stars.

** According to established rules, all Soviet books contain indications of the number of copies printed as well as the dates of signing the manuscript for typesetting and for printing. Thus, in Volume 2 of the *Selected Works* of Ivan Shevtsov, we can see on the last page: "Signed for typesetting—06.26.86. Signed for printing—08.31.88. Circulation—100,000 copies."

enemy during World War II. Minister of Defense Marshal Yazov announced that he was "satisfied" with this explanation.

During the Gulf War, General Filatov went to Iraq and covered the war for the leading military daily, *Krasnaya Zvezda (The Red Star)*. While the Soviet Union approved all anti-Iraqi resolutions in the United Nations, joined the embargo against Iraq, and supported military action against Saddam Hussein, General Filatov exposed "American imperialism and Israeli Zionism" for their aggression against the brotherly nation of Iraq on the pages of the official newspaper of the Ministry of Defense.

Most of the People's Congress Deputies who were in the military joined the chauvinistic parliamentary faction *Soyuz* (The Union) led by Colonel Victor Alksnis. The group tried to block all liberal legislation and stood for a tough policy against the republics and against the "unilateral concessions" to the West. After dismantling of the Warsaw Pact and unification of Germany, *Soyuz* and other hard-liners formed an opposition to the government, but it was a very strange opposition. It directed most of the attacks against foreign minister Edward Shevardnadze and the architect of *glasnost* Alexander Yakovlev. Gorbachev was seldomly and cautiously criticized, while other members of the government were not criticized at all. Later, it became public that, while in opposition, *Soyuz* leaders maintained secret contacts with close associates of Gorbachev, like the chairman of the Supreme Soviet, Anatoly Lukianov.

Lukianov was instrumental in creating a Dniestr Republic on the left bank of the Dniestr River. This area of Moldova is mainly populated by Russians and Ukrainians. Officially, Moscow stood for the territorial integrity of all Soviet republics and could not recognize the separatists. But Lukianov met their leaders secretly and maintained contacts with them through his political "rivals" from *Soyuz*. Lukianov and Gorbachev used the separatists to force legitimate leaders of Moldova into signing the Union Treaty, i.e., to remain within the Soviet Union.[19] When it did not help, the Dniestr separatists, supported by the Fourteenth Soviet Army stationed in the region, took control over the Dniestr region and initiated military clashes with Moldovians—in other words, started a civil war in Moldova. Hundreds of innocent people were killed and wounded; thousands fled their homes.

Moscow pretended that the Fourteenth Army—and its commander, General Lebed—conducted all the military operations without approval, but the higher military command never took any measures to stop them. Instead, rumors circulated in Moscow about violent pogroms and demonstrations organized by Moldovian nationalists in Kishinev with the rallying, "Let us drown the

Russians in the blood of the Jews" and "Let us drown the Jews in the Dniestr River and throw the Russians behind the River."

I contacted Jewish activists in Kishinev, and they assured me that while the atmosphere in the republic was tense, there had been no demonstrations under such slogans. The KGB had deliberately spread the groundless rumors about the demonstrations to justify the military operations of the Fourteenth Army.

KGB involvement could be traced to many ethnic conflicts in different Soviet republics. All segments of the Soviet society were saturated with KGB informers. Thus, if they did not instigate the bloody pogroms of the Armenians in Sumgait and later in Baku, the massacre of Turks-Meskhetians in Uzbekistan and many other ethnic clashes, they at least had known and reported about the pre-planned events in advance. But the KGB leadership concealed the information, allowing the violent riots. The main idea behind this policy was simple: The more ethnic clashes that took place in the republics, the more excuses Moscow would have to maintain control over them. In reality, however, this policy only increased uncertainty and speeded up the disintegration of the Soviet Union.

After a bloody crackdown on a peaceful demonstration in Tbilisi, Georgia, in April 1990, Moscow pretended—as in Moldova—that the local military commander, General Rodionov, had acted independently. However, he was never reprimanded. The same is true of General Achalov, who was responsible for a bloodbath in Baku, Azerbaijan, in January 1991.

But the most cynical use of military force took place in Lithuania, where the strong movement for independence had developed in such a civilized, peaceful, and organized form that it left no room for provocation.

Lithuanian problem and coup d'etat

In the spring of 1990, the newly elected parliament of Lithuania declared its independence and adopted a new constitution that placed the republican laws over the All-Union ordinances.

Gorbachev, reacting negatively to this development, tried to talk the Lithuanian leaders into a compromise, but they stood firm. To demonstrate his decisiveness, Gorbachev instituted an economic blockade of Lithuania, cutting off gas, oil, and other supplies. He hoped that economic hardship would bring the Lithuanians to reason, but achieved the opposite effect. Latvia and Estonia joined Lithuania and won sympathy in other republics, including the Russian Federation. After Boris Yeltsin was elected chairman of the Russian Parliament, he condemned the blockade and ordered Russian enterprises to resume all supplies to the Baltics.

Actions against Lithuania severely undermined Gorbachev's popularity. He became more and more dependent on the hard-liners and gave them even more authority in his government. An extreme hard-liner, Valentin Pavlov, replaced the more moderate Prime Minister Nikolai Ryzhkov. Another extreme hard-liner, Boris Pugo, became the minister of internal affairs, with General Boris Gromov, ultrapatriotic Afghan war veteran, as his first deputy. Under Gorbachev's pressure, the Congress of Peoples Deputies elected Gennady Yanaev (who would lead the coup against Gorbachev only a few months later) to the newly established office of vice-president. At the last moment, Gorbachev rejected the "500-day plan" of a radical restructuring of the economy, developed by liberal economists Stanislav Shatalin and Grigory Yavlinsky.

In December of 1990, in an emotional speech to the Congress of People's Deputies, Edward Shevardnadze warned about a forthcoming dictatorship and dramatically resigned from his office of foreign minister. Alexander Yakovlev remained the only liberal member of the Presidential Council, but lost his influence. Thus, Gorbachev surrounded himself only with the party and military "patriots."

On January 2, 1991, the *Black Berets*—special military units of the Ministry of the Interior—seized the building of the Lithuanian Communist Party Central Committee in Vilnius, and, simultaneously, the building of major publications in Riga, Latvia. Then, Moscow dispatched elite paratrooper units into the Baltic republics under the pretext of enforcing conscription into the Soviet army.[*]

On January 9, 1991, TASS, the official Soviet news agency, stated that some unnamed representatives of the Lithuanian public had allegedly demanded that "the rights of citizens and their security be protected." The next day, Gorbachev threatened to introduce "direct presidential rule" in Lithuania unless "the validity of the Soviet Constitution was fully restored." That was a signal for violent actions.

A fictional *Congress of Democratic Forces of Lithuania* immediately submitted an ultimatum to Lithuanian President Vytautas Landsbergis, demanding "consent to the Soviet President's address." But the military did not even wait for the ultimatum deadline to start their operation.

---

[*] Considering themselves citizens of independent Lithuania—not the Soviet Union—draftees refused to obey the conscription law and were supported by the Lithuanian government while Moscow regarded them as deserters.

Early in the morning on Sunday, January 13, tanks, which had surrounded the parliament, a number of government offices, and the TV Center, opened fire on an unarmed crowd, leaving 15 people killed and hundreds wounded. Vytautas Landsbergis referred to these events as Bloody Sunday[*] and said that the civil war had begun. But Moscow still tried to put a good face on the matter.

"Neither the Soviet President nor anyone from the country's central leadership gave orders to use army detachments in Vilnius. It was the initiative of the garrison commander, who complied with the request of the *Committee for National Salvation,*" commented Boris Pugo, Minister of Internal Affairs of the USSR. But immediately added, "The military actions were correct".[20]

A few days later, during a similar action in Latvia, five people were killed and dozens wounded. Estonia was next in line. The Baltic republics were to suffer the fate of Czechoslovakia in 1968.

Success of the plan would have meant the return to the strongest form of totalitarianism. But the situation in the country was quite different. The liberal public and the press already had an independent voice in Russia and came forward to defend the Baltics. Boris Yeltsin flew to Tallinn, the Estonian capital, and signed a treaty of mutual support between the Russian Federation and all three Baltic states, officially recognizing their independence. Yeltsin strongly condemned the use of force in the Baltics and warned that the Union government might repeat such actions elsewhere, including the Russian Federation.[21]

Pressed for an explanation, Gorbachev stated publicly that the troops had been used without his consent. He had to stop further military actions and accept the Baltic independence *de facto,* if not *de jure.* Thus, Gorbachev turned out to be the main loser. The remainder of his popularity among the liberals had disappeared, while the hard-liners understood that they could not rely on him either.

In a helpless attempt to prevent further disintegration and win new legitimacy for the Union Treaty, Gorbachev set up a referendum on March 17. People had to answer "yes" or "no" to the following question: Would you like to preserve the Soviet Union as a renewed federation of equal sovereign republics

---

[*] On January 9 (22), 1905, the Czar's troops in St. Petersburg opened fire against a peaceful procession of workers who marched to the Winter Palace—the Czar's residence—to present their grievances. Hundreds of people were killed that day, which is known in history as Bloody Sunday. Most historians regard it as the starting point of the 1905 Russian Revolution.

in which human rights and freedoms of all nationalities will be fully guaranteed?

The hypocrisy of this formula was shocking. What were the people casting a "yes" vote for: preservation or renovation? And was the "no" vote against keeping the republics together or against the human rights and freedoms of all nationalities?

Not surprisingly, six republics (the three Baltic republics plus Moldova, Georgia, and Armenia) refused to participate in the referendum. Russian democrats called to say "no"—not to the human rights, of course, but to Kremlin domination.

A vast majority of the voters said "yes," but six republics remained unbending. Only the Armenians changed their mind later because of their war with Azerbaidjan over the disputed territory of Nagorny Karabakh. If they insisted on their independence while their enemy remained a part of the USSR, they would find themselves at war not just with Azerbaidjan, but with the entire Soviet Union.

Finally, Gorbachev understood that he had no choice but to sign the Union Treaty with only ten (of 15) republics, granting them extensive autonomy. But such an outcome did not satisfy the hard-liners.

On Monday, June 17, 1991, Prime-Minister Valentin Pavlov unexpectedly proposed that the Supreme Soviet shift the most important executive power from the president to the prime-minister, including the right to introduce a state of emergency. Dmitry Yazov, Vladimir Kryuchkov, and Boris Pugo—the three ministers in control of the military, security, and police forces—immediately supported Pavlov. Addressing parliament, the speakers used a wide range of arguments, from Gorbachev's poor health and long working hours to his reluctance to preserve the Soviet Union from demilitarization and occupation by the Western powers. It was obvious that the hard-liners plotted to seize power by legal means, and then introduce a state of emergency.

Gorbachev was not in the Supreme Soviet that day, and he did not appear the next three days as well—as if nothing important were happening there. Only on Friday, June 21, after he had received a warning from President Bush, did he show up in the Supreme Soviet and denounce his critics. The parliament voted against Pavlov's bill, and Gorbachev turned the incident into a joke, saying to the reporters that "the coup was over."

Gorbachev's obvious indifference in defending his own authority against the "constitutional coup" produced a reasonable suspicion that he himself was involved in the conspiracy. Perhaps, he had agreed with his subordinates that a strong display of force was the only way to preserve the country from disintegration, but did not want to take personal responsibility for the actions. If so, he could agree to give the hard-liners the opportunity to do their "patriotic" work if they succeeded in convincing the Supreme Soviet to delegate them the authority. After the warning from President Bush, he might have concluded that the plan had been uncovered, and decided to back away.*

Soon after that, Alexander Yakovlev had a three-hour-long conversation with Gorbachev, trying to convince him to get rid of the "terrible people" around him, "to do something about this dirty circle." Gorbachev's answer was, "You exaggerate."[22]

Meanwhile, after the failure of the "constitutional coup," the hard-liners turned to unconstitutional means, and that coup they prepared almost publicly as well. In July 1991, *Message to the People* appeared in *Moskovskaya Pravda*, a daily controlled by hard-liners. The 12 signers of the manifesto included the "patriotic" writers (Yuri Bondarev, Valentin Rasputin, Alexander Prokhanov, and Eduard Volodin), the *Pamyat* Society (sculptor Fyodor Klykov), the most militant generals (Valentin Varennikov, responsible for the crackdown in Vilnius, and Boris Gromov), well-known Russian singer Lyudmila Zykina, parliamentary faction *Soyuz* (Yuri Blokhin), head of the newly organized Russian Communist Party (Gennady Zyuganov), The Peasants' Union (Vasily Starodubtsev, chairman), and the Association of State Enterprises (Alexander Tizyakov, president).** They demanded the replacing of liberal "traitors" in the government who "had sold out" the Soviet Union's interests to their "trans-Atlantic well-wishers" with "capable, patriotic leaders."[23]

Simultaneously, *Voenizdat* printed a brochure, *The Black Hundred and the Red Hundred* by Victor Ostretsov, in an unprecedented edition of one million copies. It sold for one ruble a copy, or next to nothing.[24] The editorial note said that the brochure "gave a true picture of *the Union of the Russian People*," a pre-Revolutionary "patriotic" organization mentioned many times in this book.

The author denounced the "Red Hundred" (the Bolsheviks) as anti-patriots and extolled the "Black Hundred" (*the Union of the Russian People*) as an organization defending Russia from revolutionaries and Jews. Ostretsov referred to the Black Hundred's terrorist activities as an invention of the "Jewish

---

* About the dramatic warning from the United States, see: Michael R. Beschloss and Strobe Talbott. *At the Highest Levels* (Boston, Toronto, London: Little, Brown, 1993) pp. 393-400.

** The Peasants' Union was an extremely conservative organization, which opposed the privatization of land ownership and private farming and demanded the preservation of the inefficient system of the collective farms; the Association of State Enterprises opposed the privatization of industry.

press."[25] Jewish pogroms, in the author's view, were staged by the Jews themselves, who aimed them against the Black Hundreders.[26]

The brochure propagated the racist ideology of the *Union of the Russian People* and insulted various ethnic groups. For example:

> "Can anyone really believe," right-wing newspapers wrote at the time, "that revolutionary Jews are dreaming of happiness for the Russian people? If they are, why don't they ask the Russian people what they want? Instead, they [revolutionary Jews] divide everyone into an 'ignorant crowd,' including all Orthodox believers and monarchists *en masse*, and 'the conscious,' with the right to exercise their authority over other people. How did it happen that the 'ignorant Russians' are always inferior while the 'conscious' Sverdlovs are superior? True, at that time, the Armenians were also accused of being inclined toward revolution. A great number of Duma members of Georgian extraction—Russophobes—leapt to the eye, too."[27]

The author's manner invited readers to follow the Black Hundred's example as articulated in the brochure.

"The programs of all the right-wing political parties promoted:
1. A demand that the State Duma, this nest of sedition, be dissolved as it presents the greatest danger to the Czarist autocracy.
2. The introduction of martial law across the country.
3. The banning of all left-wing newspapers and magazines—and the granting funds to the national-patriotic press.
4. The Jewish question and the removal of all Jews from the army and state service and the closing down of all newspapers published by Jews themselves or through figureheads.
5. The refusal of the state bank to give credits to Jewish banks. The *Union of the Russian People* maintained an opinion that it was necessary to help the Zionists create a Jewish state in Palestine and 'to promote the emigration of Jews to their kingdom.'" [28]

As we remember, Marshal Yazov, the Minister of Defense who became one of the leading figures of the coup d'etat, controlled the publishing company which had released this brochure on the eve of the coup. This was more than just symbolic. If in the quotation we substitute the Supreme Soviet for the State Duma and the party dictatorship for the Czarist autocracy, the quoted program would fully coincide with the program of the *putschists*. In the event of gaining victory, they intended to dissolve the Supreme Soviet of the USSR (as well as of the republics), to close down left-wing and Jewish (which was the same to them) newspapers, to introduce martial law, and to dismiss democratic-minded people (who, in their opinion, were all Jewish) from all prominent positions. Even the statement about the "help to Zionists" fully coincided if not with formal demands then with the actual goal of the "patriots" to drive all Jews out of the country.

This is a clear indication that while the Communist hard-liners organized the August 1991 coup, they intended to introduce not a Communist, but an ultranationalistic, "patriotic" (i. e., Nazi-like) agenda.

CHAPTER 11

NAZIFICATION UNDER YELTSIN

Yeltsin against Gorbachev. "Patriotic" aspect

On August 19, 1991, a day before the Union Treaty was to be signed, the top officials of the Gorbachev government established the State of Emergency Committee and introduced martial law. The committee included Gennady Yanaev (acting president), Valentin Pavlov, Dmitry Yazov, Vladimir Kryuchkov, Boris Pugo, Oleg Baklanov (a secretary of the Central Committee in charge of the military-industrial complex), Vasily Starodubtsev, and Alexander Tizyakov. Anatoly Lukianov, Marshal Sergei Akhrameev (Gorbachev's military adviser), General Mikhail Moiseev (the chief of the general staff), Valery Boldin (Gorbachev's chief of staff), and a number of other high-ranking officials stood behind the conspiracy as well.

The State of Emergency Committee declared Gorbachev sick and detained him in his Crimea country house. Tanks and armored personnel-carriers moved into Moscow's streets and occupied strategic locations. The Supreme Soviet of the Russian Federation (the "White House") became the center of the resistance against the coup. Tanks and special KGB units surrounded the building.

Several thousand Muscovites came to defend the White House and built barricades. Russian President Boris Yeltsin announced the coup an act of treason, called for a general strike, and demanded the troops reject the junta orders. However, this appeal did not provoke large-scale resistance. The country was mostly shocked and scared; but several thousand brave defenders of the "White

House" were ready to give their lives for democracy, and the junta did not dare to open fire. The coup failed in three days. Some leaders of the junta committed suicide; others were arrested.

Gorbachev was released from custody and re-established in the All-Union presidency, but his power was gone. Public opinion praised Yeltsin as a national hero and a true defender of democracy, while Gorbachev had to share—if not legal, then moral—responsibility for the coup.

Yeltsin used the strongest language to condemn the junta; the Communist Party apparatus, which had nursed the conspiracy; and everyone who had supported the coup. He issued a decree banning the Communist Party. (Later, the Constitutional Court reversed the ban.) He also closed for several days a few Communist and ultranationalist newspapers that had openly supported the coup—like *Pravda, Sovetskaya Rossia,* and *Den (The Day)*. He seemed eager to crush both the Red and the Brown alike since they stood in the way of the democratic process and had brought the country to the brink of civil war. Two weeks later, however, a signal came from Moscow that such was not the case.

When ABC News broadcast a joint Gorbachev-Yeltsin interview around the world, Rabbi Jack Segal from Houston, Texas, posed the question, "Do you think that anti-Semitism will become weaker in the Soviet Union now, will it remain the same, will it possibly become stronger? What about the *Pamyat* organization, which is very, very strongly anti-Semitic? What about its future?"

Boris Yeltsin answered: "I've had dealings with *Pamyat* for quite a long time, for more than one year, at least. I think it is becoming different. It is not as extreme as it was when it was started in 1987*. So it seems to me that, in general, this process will be eased. It will ease off. Intuitively, I feel this."[1]

Ironically, Yeltsin only parroted Vladimir Kryuchkov, the former chief of the KGB, one of the most extreme hard-liners and an arrested member of the junta. Thus, Yeltsin made it known that he had no intention of changing the government's approach to the "patriots." As paradoxical as it might sound, it was not totally unexpected for those who closely monitored Yeltsin.

We know that he had established relations with *Pamyat* in 1987, when he had received the Manezh Square demonstrators and promised them legal status. Later, he never condemned *Pamyat,* not even when he responded to direct questions about it. Vladimir Pozner, a Russian TV journalist, testified that in an interview with Yeltsin during his presidential campaign, he had asked him about *Pamyat* several times, but did not get a direct answer. After the interview

---

* As we know from previous chapters, *Pamyat* was founded much earlier. However, 1987 was the year when Yeltsin personally started to deal with it.

had been recorded, Yeltsin told Pozner privately that he had deliberately avoided condemning *Pamyat* in order to not antagonize "patriotic" organizations.[2]

It would seem that similar considerations guided him in the choice of his running mate. Political parties of democratic orientation recommended Galina Starovoitova, a liberal member of both the All-Union and Russian Parliaments. An ethnographer by profession, she was an expert in inter-ethnic relations. She defended the human rights of the persecuted Armenian leaders of Nagorny Karabakh. She strongly opposed Russian chauvinism and spoke out against anti-Semitism. "Patriots" often attacked her in return.

"Everyone who believes in liberal, international, and cosmopolitan ideas is a Jew in the eyes of chauvinists," Starovoitova stated later. "In the Supreme Soviet of the Russian Federation and in the Congress of the People's Deputies of Russia, I, Russian, often hear, "Go away to Israel!" There is a widespread opinion that the international Jewish Mafia supports me."[3]

Yeltsin admired Starovoitova and often employed her advice, but he did not want to be associated with a person labeled the "agent of the Jews." Although Colonel Alexander Rutskoi was little known to him, he chose this brave Afghan war hero as more acceptable to both the Red and the Brown "patriots."

Soon after the elections, President Yeltsin received Edgar Bronfman, chairman of the World Jewish Congress. During the meeting, Yeltsin strongly condemned anti-Semitism. His statement was widely publicized in the West, but never in the USSR. Perhaps Yeltsin took special measures to minimize coverage of this meeting by the Soviet media; although the elections had passed, he still avoided any confrontation with "patriotic" groups and ideologists.

In the after-the-coup euphoria, Yeltsin's (and Gorbachev's) remarks about *Pamyat* did not attract much public attention, but the "patriots" understood the message quite well. The outlawed communists hastened their conversion into the ranks of the "patriots." Soon *Novoye Vremya*, a liberal weekly, wrote:

"Boris Yeltsin gave *Pamyat* a sort of indulgence, and not one of the new political parties put forward a slogan of struggle against nationalism, chauvinism, and anti-Semitism. ... Something paradoxical is happening. August brought a blow to the conservative forces, but they became even mightier and better organized."[4]

A little bit earlier, the same magazine wrote:

"Jewish activists [in Moscow] cannot understand why Gorbachev and Yeltsin were so embarrassed when, during this TV show, a rabbi from Texas asked them about *Pamyat*. Do they feel a subconscious fear that 'the public' will suspect the two Russian presidents of involvement with the 'Jewish-Masonic conspiracy'? Nothing will help them anyway! According to *Pamyat*, every democrat is either a Jew or he is dancing to the Jewish tune."[5]

But the two victorious presidents knew why they "mumbled something incomprehensible" about *Pamyat*.[6] Their confrontation had begun in the early stage of *perestroika*. Although the coup had brought them together, both of them realized that their political struggle was about to start anew. They also realized that silent sympathizers stood behind organized ultranationalistic groups. They knew that there were a lot of patriots in all government bodies as well as among ordinary voters. Accordingly, each wanted those people on his side and not on the side of his rival.

Boris Yeltsin won this battle. In December of the same year, he met secretly with Ukrainian and Belorussian presidents in *Beloveshchinsky Pushcha* (*Beloveshchinsky* Bushes) and dissolved the Soviet Union, replacing it with the Commonwealth of Independent States. Gorbachev became the head of a nonexisting country and had to resign. Yeltsin immediately occupied Gorbachev's office in the Kremlin as well as Gorbachev's *dacha* (country house) outside Moscow. But the price he had to pay turned out to be too high.

While disintegration of the Soviet Union was already almost unavoidable, Yeltsin artificially speeded up the process. Three presidents were in such a hurry to throw Gorbachev out of office that they forgot about everything else. They did not even discuss the numerous practical questions associated with such a fundamental change, including disputed territories, a common currency, financial obligations, property rights, military command, and nuclear arsenals.

What was even more important, Yeltsin overlooked the extent of the shock experienced by the vast majority of the Russian population. The people were not ready for such a dramatic change. Overnight, more than 25 million Russian residents of non-Russian republics found themselves an unwanted and even hated minority in a number of foreign countries. Millions of others, born in mixed marriages, had identity problems. And all, together, lost the pride and dignity of belonging to a superpower.

The after-the-coup euphoria plummeted into a deep depression and disappointment. It increased from month to month as the people realized that they still would not have a more efficient economy and better living conditions in return. For most of the population, the privatization of state property started by an acting prime-minister Yegor Gaidar brought poverty, inflation, fear, and violence. Only criminal groups—the Mafia—and a small group of the new entrepreneurs (most of them also connected to the Mafia) benefited from the program. Popular feeling was that a deal had been made behind the people's backs and at their expense. Under these circumstances, they became even more receptive to ultranationalistic indoctrination. Aggressive nationalism turned into a psychological compensation for all setbacks, sufferings, and lost values.

Such a development ought to have alarmed Yeltsin and his advisers and forced them to take measures against the overt ultranationalists, as required by law. But Yeltsin continued his line of non-interference, following Gorbachev's path.

"Patriotic" press in Yeltsin's era

If in 1990, *Yevreiskaya gazeta* could list 49 anti-Semitic periodicals, then soon after the coup, it became impossible to even count them.[*] But perhaps the most characteristic sign of the new era was the dramatic change in the language of these publications.

We know how angry the *Red* and the *Brown* had become when someone called them Nazis, fascists, Black-Hundreders, anti-Semites, or even nationalists. They called themselves *patriots* and decried any other label as a "Zionist provocation." One of the most extreme "patriotic" publications, *Russkoye Voskresenie (Russian Resurrection),* stated in 1990: "Non-Russian journalists[**] have long ago turned *Pamyat* into a bugaboo and made it a synonym of such words as *fascists, chauvinists, Black-Hundreders*, etc. Now, we see how they try to stick in that list of synonyms the word *patriotism*."[7]

Two years later, however, this same paper did not want to distance itself from fascism, Nazism, or the Black Hundred anymore. The article *From the Reference Book of a Patriot-Black-Hundreder* demanded punishment for those "non-Russian" journalists who "try to stir up hostility toward such good words and notions as *patriot, Black-Hundreder*—a Russian patriot; *chauvinist*—French patriot; *pogrom*—an uprising against foreign exploiters accompanied by the destruction of their wealth amassed by robbery; *national socialism*—

---

[*] According to the latest available data, there were 158 such periodicals in mid-1994, with an estimated circulation of 3 million copies.

[**] This is intended as a reference to Jewish journalists or those whose background is allegedly Jewish.

socialism without kikes in power; *anti-Semitism*—national-liberation movement against the kikes' yoke; *Russian Orthodoxy*—the Church, in which—under normal conditions (the kikes' yoke not being a normal condition)—there is no place for the kikes."[8]

The author devoted more than half of this two-full-page article to "Adolf Aloizovich Hitler," his name framed as if in mourning.

"**HITLER WAS A MAN OF HIGH MORALITY.** Contrary to the slander promoted by the Jews, Adolf Aloizovich never indulged in lust, never stole, never lied, never consumed alcohol, never smoked, never ate meat or fish. Adolf Aloizovich was a pattern of modesty.

"**HITLER WAS A MAN OF PRINCIPLE.** For the good of the fatherland, Adolf Aloizovich did not spare himself or his friends. His foes accuse him of eliminating some of his comrades. However, it was not a reprisal, but a cleansing of the party. Executed storm troopers were the dregs of society: homosexuals and thieves (like our democratic leaders).

"**WAS HITLER SPOILED BY KIKE'S BLOOD?** No. Arthur Koestler (he had a kike's background) promoted this myth, and unfortunately many patriots picked it up (because to admit your sympathy to Hitler was dangerous).

"**WHY DID HITLER COME TO POWER?** Here we have to discuss the kikes' problem. There was not a single German professor of medicine left in Germany. ... Among significant writers, only Gerhart Hauptmann was German. All others—Manns, Brechts, Zegherses, Remarques, Feuchtvangers, and others—were *Juden* (kikes). All banks, trade, law firms—everything was in the hands of *Juden*. ... And there was a living example of Russia, ruined by the kikes. Thus, the people stood up and brought Hitler to power.

"**WHY DID GERMANY START WORLD WAR II?** 'It is not true that I or anybody else in Germany wanted to start the war in 1939. It was desired and provoked by those international political figures who were of kike origin or acted in the kikes' interests' (Adolf Hitler. *My Political Will*.)"[9]

Hitler's portrait with the German caption *"Ein Folk, Ein Reich, Ein Fuhrer"* illustrated the article, and swastikas decorated the paper's logo.

To realize how dramatic the changes in the public consciousness—which made such publications possible—could be, we have to keep in mind that nothing was as deep and widespread in Soviet society as anti-Hitler sentiments.

The Russians called World War II the Great Patriotic War, and their sacrifices and willingness to defeat Hitler had no parallels in world history. According to the latest estimates, Soviet losses in the war were about 27 million, but some historians believe that they exceeded 40 million. There was not a single family in the country that had not lost loved ones, and the survivors endured unimaginable sufferings. Hitler's troops occupied most of European Russia, and they did not spare anyone. Any sign of resistance created repercussions of enormous scale and cruelty. Thousands of villages were completely burned for "assisting the partisans." Cities and towns were destroyed as well. Germans often shot people in the streets just for fun, frequently in full view of their children or spouses. They forcibly removed to Germany millions of young men and women conscripted into *de facto* slavery. Millions of those who fled the occupied territories had no food or shelter. Since practically the entire male population was drafted into the army, women and children worked in the factories to produce weapons, ammunition, and military uniforms, often exploited for two and three shifts in a row. Women, not horses, often plowed the land. Food rations were so small that people always felt hungry. The public attributed all these tribulations to Hitler and "the German fascists," as the Nazis were called in the USSR.

Later on, Communist Party propaganda blamed the war for its failure to significantly improve the living conditions of the people to a significant degree. Official publications cultivated anti-fascist sentiments by a different means. For instance, they concealed from the public the Nazis's special treatment of Jews, gypsies, and other selected groups, but emphasized the mass extermination of the "Soviet people." Children were educated in the schools to this end. Contrary to many other areas, what they learned about the war in school was mostly in keeping with what they heard at home. Thus, it was very convincing.

Other factors contributed to the constant rekindling of war memories. Many veterans became writers, journalists, and movie producers; and they returned to the war experience again and again in their creative works. Describing the battles, the life in the trenches or in partisan detachments, they could be more truthful without serious censorship problems than when they covered the "happy, peaceful labor of the Soviet people under the wise leadership of the Communist Party." A significant percentage of all novels, poems, plays, movies, and popular songs produced in the Soviet Union for the last fifty years dealt with the war. The theme of war dominates the best of Soviet art and literature. All these works, to a greater or lesser degree, contributed to the general belief that Hitler had been the greatest evil in the history of the world and made it absolutely impossible to say something positive about him. This is one of the

210   *Chapter 11*

reasons why, on the initial stage of the *glasnost* era, Dmitry Vasiliev and other *Pamyat* leaders did not hesitate to declare Hitler Jewish.

But this mood changed dramatically after the coup and the ensuing disintegration of the USSR. Russian Nazis realized that they did not have to hide their admiration of the German Nazis and their Fuhrer anymore.

This trend spread throughout the "patriotic" publications—not just the quoted *Russkoye Voskresenie*. Surprised liberals had to admit that the open and cynical expression of Nazi sentiments had become intrinsic to public life.

> "I tried to figure out who printed *Mine Kampf* by Adolf Hitler," an author of *Novoye Vremya* wrote in January 1992. "It is not available in the bookstores. But large numbers of copies are openly sold at public presentations organized by the Yuri Bondarev's Writer's Union[*] or *Nash Sovremennik* journal or at other gatherings of Russian 'patriots.' Then the copies are warehoused till the next gathering."[10]

If at the beginning Hitler's book could be bought only at "patriotic" gatherings, soon afterward, *Mine Kampf*—as well as Hitler's apologetic biographies—began to appear everywhere, including public libraries. Publishers and booksellers no longer felt the need to hide their names. Since law-enforcement agencies did not take any legal actions to stop this encroachment, it continued to grow.

Alexander Barkashov and the Russian National Unity.

As might be expected, the political tolerance extended to Nazi publications encouraged the "patriotic" organizations to follow Hitler's lead. The traditional activities of *Pamyat*, with noisy gatherings and poor organization, became obsolete. Constant quarrels between *Pamyat's* ambitious leaders resulted only in new splits. The movement ripened to be organized on new principles and obtain a new leader.

This demand was filled by Alexander Barkashov, a black-belt karate coach with direct personal experience in combating Zionism. (He claimed that during his military service he had trained Arab terrorists and commandos on the eve of the Yom-Kippur Arab-Israeli war in 1973.)

---

[*] Formally, elderly Sergei Mikhalkov was the head of the Writer's Union of the Russian Federation as the first secretary. But actually Yuri Bondarev, the second secretary, was running the show.

Barkashov joined *Pamyat* in 1985 and became second-in-command to Dmitry Vasiliev. But in August 1990, he started his own organization, *Russkoye Natsionalnoye Edinstvo* (RNE—the Russian National Unity), a strictly disciplined paramilitary group. The goal of the RNE was similar to that of *Pamyat*: "To liberate the Russian people from communists, democrats, and Jews." Barkashov's methods, however, differed. RNE concentrated on the "military and patriotic training of youth in the spirit of Russian nationalism."[11]

"We provide general military skills, and the most important among them is obedience," a young follower of Barkashov explained. "Our ideology is based on the [three] principles of the RNE: *No* to the Jews, *yes* to the authoritarian regime, and *yes* to Great Russia. Our guardians are trained in hand-to-hand fighting, shooting, and drill; and they also attend regular political-education classes."[12]

The new organization did not go out of its way to attract media and public attention, but nevertheless its ranks grew rapidly. Full members of the RNE received the rank of *soratnik* (brother-in-arm). *Soratniks* recruited *spodvizhniks* (fellow-fighters), while *sochuvstvuyushchie* (sympathizers) formed the lowest level of membership. This structure permitted the development of a united, hierarchical, and strictly militant organization that was flexible and open to newcomers.

Barkashov did not conceal his preparation for a day when public unrest and anarchy would paralyze the police and other government bodies. In this situation, the RNE would remain the only organized force in the city and would take control of all vital services (such as food, water, and energy supplies). Then he would have the means to ascend to power and restore order.

It looked as if his time had come in August 1991, during the coup attempt. Barkashov saw that the junta's *Appeal to the People* was based on ultra-nationalistic rhetoric and was identical to his own program.

At that time, a year after launching his organization, he had several hundred stormtroopers under his command. It is not difficult to imagine what would have happened if they had appeared at the barricades and attacked the defenders of the "White House." Blood would have been spilled on both sides, and the junta would have had an excuse to "protect" her supporters. The tanks would have moved in, and the outcome of the coup might have been completely different.

But Barkashov found only high-level party officials on the list of the coup leaders. He did not trust them, so he ordered his cutthroats to abstain.

Only later, after the coup failed, did he realize that he had lost his chance. He sent a telegram of support to Gennady Yanaev, the arrested official head of the junta. It was an indirect acknowledgment of his mistake and a hint that next time he would not repeat it.

In 1992, liberal newspapers anxiously reported that entire classes of military and navy schools as well as young military officers and industrial workers were eager to join the RNE.[13]

Since Barkashov was always available to answer any questions about his ideas as well as the goals and structure of his organization, he enjoyed considerable press coverage. In one of his most extensive interviews, Barkashov explained his use of the word "Russian" in the title of his organization.

> "It is unquestionable that genetic, blood relationship is of the greatest importance. ... To say that every Orthodox believer or everyone who considers himself Russian is Russian would not be correct. A Georgian or a Jew will say, 'I am Russian because I feel so.' But perhaps he feels himself Russian to harm the Russian people."

"Could you call yourself a fascist, as Dmitry Vasiliev does,* or would this word insult you?" the journalist asked.

> "In fact, Vasiliev is not a fascist," Barkashov replied. "He just tries to capitalize on this word since it has become popular. On the contrary, he used to accuse us of having fascist views. This was the reason for our split with him. But I usually say, 'I am not a fascist; I am a Nazi.' Fascism may be associated with the current *gosudarstvenniki*.** They try to unite the people without identifying ethnic background of every particular individual. But I am a Nazi. Nazism is a national upsurge plus social justice. Our organization is based on National Socialism."

"A stylized swastika appears on the sleeve of your uniform..."

---

* Dmitry Vasiliev started to use an even more extremist rhetoric than previously but still continued to make reservations. Thus, he explained, the label "fascist" did not insult him because it meant "a bunch or bundle that unites people" and had nothing in common with "the Third Reich and national-socialism."

** *Gosudarstvenniki* (Champions of Statehood)--those "patriots," whose main concern is to reestablish a mighty, centralized Russian empire. Their most outspoken representative is Alexander Prokhanov, whom we will introduce later in this chapter.

"It is not a stylization; it is a swastika. Some people say that this symbol was discredited by World War II, but it was not. ... Swastika—in a spiritual sense—is a religious, genetic, and tribal symbol of the Russian nation."

"Specifically Russian?"

"First of all Russian, although it is a symbol of the entire white race as well. ... But in the metaphysical sense, the five-pointed star is a symbol of absolute evil, while the opposite symbol is the swastika."

"You are a Hitler sympathizer, aren't you?"

"I consider him a great hero of the German nation and all-white race. He succeeded in inspiring the entire nation to fight against degradation and the washing away of national values. Concerning his cruelty, the repressive system in the Soviet Union was on a much larger scale. Everyone keeps silence about that, but everyone says that in Germany several hundred Jews were taken to the concentration camp."

"How many members do you have in your organization?"

"I can only say *very many*. Our organization is prestigious and active. We have branches in 350 cities. Now we mostly conduct invisible work. Establishing the national authority does not mean that a group of conspirators should take the Kremlin with their rifles. First of all, we have to spread our ideology. When a significant portion of the Russian people accepts this ideology and the party based on this ideology becomes big enough in terms of quality and quantity, the national forces will seize the power. And in what way—through elections or by other means—it does not matter."

"But why are your people being trained to shoot?"

"Readiness to sacrifice ourselves for the good of our nation is the core of our ideals. That is why, in this time of current depravity and chaos, we use the methods of military-heroic education. ... We are trained to shoot, but not only to shoot."

"Is it difficult to join your organization?"

"It is very easy. We accept practically everyone. A person is assigned to a certain unit and a certain commander whose obligation is to organize the party activities and the party training. One who honestly fulfills all tasks, increases his intellectual level, and shows his dedication becomes a *soratnik*, a full and equal member of the organization. Our discipline is not just tough, it is a military discipline. The order of the commander is the law. It is the only way to build an organization which is capable of functioning."[14]

Spectrum of Nazi groups

As the liberal newspaper *Komsomolskaya Pravda* stated in 1993, RNE branches "are growing like mushrooms and they resemble each other like drops of water. In Moscow alone, there are about twenty of them. Black shirts, white-yellow-black banner, hands thrown up in a Nazi salute."[15] But the RNE was only one of many paramilitary "patriotic" organizations that emerged or dramatically increased their ranks and activities after the August 1991 coup and the concomitant disintegration of the Soviet Union.

Among others, the *Russian National Legion* headed by Sergei Maltsev was formed under the umbrella of the National Republican Party. Nikolai Lysenko, the leader of the party, is a former member of *Pamyat* as well. "The concepts of a Russian intellectual and technological superiority over the world and the struggle for the Great Russian Empire" underlined the party ideology.[16] In widely circulated leaflets (hundreds of thousands of copies), the party called for pogroms, riots and violent attacks against "people of Caucasian-Turkic origin."[17] While Barkashov trained his people only for domestic battles, Lysenko and Maltsev sent their legionnaires to different "hot spots" in former Soviet republics and Yugoslavia.

Russian émigré writer Eduard Limonov, whose pornographic novel had won some scandalous popularity in the West, also formed a neo-Nazi paramilitary group. After his return to Russia in early 1992, Limonov joined Vladimir Zhirinovsky and his Liberal-Democratic Party. He was "appointed" to the position of minister of interior in Zhirinovsky's shadow cabinet. But a secondary role did not satisfied Limonov. He found Zhirinovsky too Jewish and not enough extreme, and parted with him. Russian papers often ran pictures of him with a machine gun in the trenches of Bosnia, where he occasionally fought on the side of the "Slav-brothers"—Serbs.

Not wanting to fall behind, Dmitry Vasiliev organized a military training camp of his own. His violent invasion of the editorial office of the liberal newspaper *Moskovsky Komsomolets* attracted a great deal of publicity. The office is located in a big building that houses a number of publications and is stringently guarded. Nobody could enter without a special pass. But Vasiliev and his people had no problem (like the Smirnov-Ostashvilly group in the Writer's House two years earlier). It is worth mentioning that of the three-dozen uniformed stormtroopers, two men wore priests' cassocks.*

Although the Constitutional Court reversed Yeltsin's ban of the Communist Party of the USSR, this mighty organization had already been dead. But several new Communist parties emerged instead. The largest one, headed by Gennady Zyuganov, a former Central Committee *apparatchik*, immediately reached a membership of half a million. The party accepts "all types of property" and free market economy; thus, it does not worship Marxist-Leninist dogmas. It stands for "social justice"—free health care, free education, and job security. In all other aspects, it is strongly nationalistic. Thus, its program combines nationalism and socialism. "The renaissance of Communism is possible only with orientation on the patriotic maxims which are fashionable now," *Komsomolskaya Pravda* commented.[18]

Gennady Zyuganov is a typical Red-Brown hard-liner, but he does not want to be associated with extravagant extremists. He is an extremist of a different type—sober, balanced, and calculating. A moderate extremist.

Among eccentric Communist groups, *The Russian Communist Working Party* (RCWP), headed by Victor Anpilov, carried out numerous provocative actions. According to Eduard Limonov, Anpilov was a "Street Tribune" and he had the support of grass-root organizations throughout the country. He could organize mass demonstrations within hours.[19]

Anpilov organized mass rallies on traditional Soviet holidays like the Day of the October Revolution, the Day of the Soviet Army, and the May Workers' Day. Thousands of people unhappy with deteriorating living conditions and lost values eagerly participated. Anpilov's speeches inflamed their passions and he became very popular.

The siege of the Moscow TV Center in the Ostankino District lasted several weeks in the summer of 1992 and was especially remarkable. Anpilov and his comrades protested the "Zionist occupation" of the mass media and de-

---

* As it turned out, both of them belonged to the Russian Orthodox Church Abroad with its headquarters in the United States. Father Victor Potapov from Washington DC, who is well known and highly respected in Russia as the long-term anchor of the religious program at the Voice of America, condemned these activities and dissociated the church from Vasiliev, anti-Semitism, and any involvement in politics. But Mitropolitan Vitaly, the head of the Russian Orthodox Church Abroad as well as some other leaders of the church maintained close ties with *Pamyat* and supported its activities. The church forbade father Victor Potapov to visit Russia and threatened to defrock him if he did not obey the order.

manded access to the TV studios to publicize their ideas. Thousands of protesters from different extremist organizations—the PCWP, Working Moscow, the All-Union Communist Party of Bolsheviks, and others—attacked employees on their way in or out of the building, disturbed public order and traffic. The attackers built a tent city to keep at least a part of the crowd on site 24 hours a day.

"They don't want Yeltsin and the Jews. They want socialism," commented one liberal paper.[20] Their slogans read "Down with the occupiers in the Kremlin and Ostankino"; "Yeltsin is the shame and misfortune of Russia"; "Criminal charges against the Satanists-Zionists of Yeltsin and Co.—for the robbery of the country, for the misery of the people, for the seduction of children, for spilled innocent blood"; "The Jewish plague! Go away to the Sahara Desert, together with your AIDS."[21] Many other right-wing organizations joined the siege.

The authorities panicked and offered concessions. They suggested forming joint working committee to discuss the question of how to transfer a certain amount of broadcasting time to the "patriots" to their mutual satisfaction. "Patriotic" leaders accepted the idea and delegated to the committee two co-chairmen of the Front of National Salvation, Zyuganov and Sterligov, and two right-wing members of the Supreme Soviet, Pavlov and Isakov, but not Anpilov. According to Eduard Limonov, "patriotic" leaders—jealous of Anpilov's success—"began to squeeze him out of leadership."[22]

Anpilov was out of Moscow at that moment ("gone to agitate among military detachments"). When he returned and was informed about the deal behind his back, he became furious. He announced that he would continue his struggle regardless of the committee's decision.[23]

Finally, yielding to the pressure of the liberal press, Moscow city authorities understood that they had no choice and ordered the police to act. But Leonid Nikitin, deputy to the Chief of Moscow Police responsible for public order and a Red-Brown sympathizer, came up with a ridiculous plan. Its fulfillment required police forces of 10,000 men. This "radical" solution was deemed sabotage, and Nikitin was fired. Then fifty policemen, at night, when only a few dozen attackers remained on site, forcibly dismantled the tent city.

Next morning, Anpilov gathered his mob again and organized a march along Prospect Mira, one of Moscow's largest avenues, from Ostankino to the Rizhsky railroad station, protesting the "police's beating the people." At a large meeting on Rizhsky Square, he called for a violent attack on the "occupying government."

In spite of the criminal nature of all these activities, the authorities did not make any arrests or initiate a criminal investigation.

Two years later, President Yeltsin described the thoughts and feelings that the Ostankino riots had raised in him.

"Victor Anpilov is a former journalist who worked in Nicaragua for the Soviet State TV and Radio Company. He is a little bit crazy about revolutionary romanticism. He has chosen for himself the dangerous role of Street Fuhrer and General of Barricades. It is dangerous not only for him, but for others as well. These activities may turn into the first Russian school of organized terrorism. ...Anpilov's group is thirsty for blood ... and they are eager to get blood spilled by any means. ... It was a fascist tactic. ... It was obvious that these people were dangerous. More precisely, dangerous people acted behind these mad demonstrators. Influential government officials might secretly support provocateurs. It was impossible to create such a situation in Moscow without a mighty hand. ... It was not a spontaneous blast of emotions, but a pre-planned attempt to organize pressure on the authorities. ... I felt that they wanted to intimidate me. I felt that 'the people's riots' were artificial. It was the handwriting of the KGB."[24]

At the time of the siege, however, Yeltsin kept silence. It would seem that if the prime goal of Anpilov's and other fascist groups had been to intimidate him, they had achieved it.

All "patriotic" groups denounced Yeltsin as the head of the Jewish-Masonic conspiracy. They accused him of destroying the Russian military might, the Russian people, and the Russian spirit. They also accused him of selling out Russian national interests to the West, of being a secret Jew (claiming, for example, that his "real" Jewish name was Borukh Eltsin), and of serving American imperialism. They labeled Yeltsin's government "occupation," meaning, of course, the "Zionist occupation from inside."

Yeltsin and his government officials constantly looked the other way, pretending they did not notice.

Only once did the office of the attorney general issue a statement to declare "the activities of all political parties and public organizations of the Russian Federation targeted to inflame ethnic enmity and violence" illegal. But the statement clearly emphasized that its targets were nationalist groups in Tatar, Chechen, and other autonomous republics, i.e., minorities. Russian fascists remained inviolable.[25]

The liberal press repeatedly demanded a ban on such organizations as the Russian National Legion on the grounds that the law forbade the "creation of independent militant societies and armed formations."[26] But a high official of the Ministry of Justice argued in response that the law could not be executed because it did not specifically delineate the terms *militant societies* and *armed formations*.[27]

Yeltsin not only tolerated such officials in his administration, he set standards for them. During a public appearance in St. Petersburg, when asked how he regarded anti-Semitism in that city, he joked with a smile, "Do you really believe that anti-Semitism exists in your city?"

"I am amazed with the complacency of the government, which does not take any measures against the danger of fascism," commented Alexander Yakovlev in February, 1993.[28]

Bezverkhy case

The case of Victor Bezverkhy, tried in St. Petersburg for "inflaming ethnic enmity," was the only known exception to the rule and, as such, deserves special attention.

Victor Bezverkhy—a doctor of philosophy, a former university teacher of Marxism-Leninism, and a chairman of the political and commercial organization *Volkhv*—had a long and impressive record of fighting against the "Jewish-Masonic conspiracy." A search of his apartment turned up a note written twelve years earlier with his own blood. "I swear to devote all my life to struggle against Judaism, the deadly foe of the entire mankind,"[29] he had penned.

Bezverkhy developed a theory of *vedism** and outlined it in a number of papers and lectures. "Only the white race continues its evolution," the theory purported, "while the evolution of the yellow and black races stopped long ago. A cross between different branches of the evolutionary tree produces an inferior posterity which we call bastards. Kikes are the first large group of bastards. Hindus and gypsies comprise the second. American mulattos are the third. ... If representatives of the low races—or bastards—are present in society, social justice is impossible."[30]

Bezverkhy studied the structure of the Gestapo and compiled a card catalog of Jewish writers, artists, and composers, recording their names, addresses, and telephone numbers—allegedly for forthcoming pogroms. In 1988, even the Leningrad KGB (which never reacted to the activities of *Pamyat* or extremists

---

* From Vedas, ancient Hindu scriptures (See Chapter 5, p. 99).

like Alexander Romanenko) "issued him a warning for the inflammation of ethnic enmity, fascist propaganda, and recruitment of like-minded followers among the military."[31] But the warning had no effect.

The St. Petersburg prosecutor authorized a criminal investigation after Bezverkhy published and distributed *Mine Kampf*. During the preliminary investigation, experts found that in Bezverkhy's edition, Hitler's text had been "edited" to make it even more anti-Semitic than the original and to omit all negative judgments about Slavs. In his introduction, the publisher wrote, "*Mine Kampf*... may become a guide book for unmasking the power of the Jews over the USSR."[32]

The investigation disclosed ties between Bezverkhy and two of his students, Alexei Andreev and Yuri Belyaev, who had created and ruled the National-Social Party. Earlier, both of them had been members of *Otechestvo* (Fatherland), a group affiliated with *Pamyat;* but they had left the organization, having found it too moderate.

Guided by Bezverkhy's theory, the newspaper of the National-Social Party, *Narodnoye delo* (The People's Cause), denounced the sentence of the Nuremberg Trial. The paper stated that at the trial "the best sons of the German people had been sentenced to death only because they were devoted to peace and the progress of mankind and honestly desired good to all nations of Europe."[33] The paper also instructed the readers on how to recognize the Jews. "A Jew often has a very special configuration of his nose," it stated. "From the front, it looks like an isosceles triangle, while from the side it calls to mind the number '6.'"[34] The program of the National-Social Party said:

> "The first step in eliminating the genetic lumber should be a drastic restriction of the birthrate among the genetically worthless part of the population. ... We have to create special committees all over the country to identify the quality of the genetic material and divide the population into several categories: of no value, of low value, valuable, and super-valuable. A law of gene protection should forbid marriages between white, black, and yellow races."[35]

The party had its own stormtroopers; and from time to time, Yuri Belyaev took groups of them to Bosnia "to fight for about a month or so for fun" (on the side of the Serbs, of course).

When the hearing of the Bezverkhy case started in February 1993, there was hope that it would set a precedent for future criminal charges and trials against active fascists under the provision of the Russian Criminal Code that prohibited the inflammation of ethnic enmity. The trial, indeed, set a precedent, but of the opposite character. In spite of all the evidence presented to the court, the public prosecutor asked only for a symbolic sentence—one year of probation; but the court did not find any wrongdoing and acquitted Bezverkhy. "Patriots" immediately organized a joyful demonstration, shouting that all Jews should go to Israel before it was too late. The prosecutor did not appeal the sentence.

It is a bitter irony that this cynical profanation of law took place in the former Leningrad, the city that symbolized heroic resistance against Hitlerism. During World War II, Leningrad withstood a 900-day blockade. The city lost over a million human lives to hunger and cold, but did not let Hitler's troops in. Fifty years later, Hitler entered the city without a single shot, and the Russian court made it legitimate.

The authorities started criminal investigations against Belyaev and Andreev as well, but then quietly closed them. In Moscow, under pressure from the liberals, prosecutors authorized a criminal investigation against A. Botagov, the editor of *Russkoye Voskresenie*. But the case was closed before any charges were filed. After the December 1993 parliamentary elections, Botagov became the spokesman for Vladimir Zhirinovsky.

Attempts at Unification. Alexander Prokhanov.

In December 1992, two Russian newspaper editors—one liberal, the other patriotic—predicted the future of their country at a seminar at George Washington University.

Vitaly Tretiakov, the editor of the liberal daily *Nezavisimaya Gazeta (Independent Newspaper)*, stressed the positive achievement of the Yeltsin-Gaidar government. He cited the prevention of civil war, successful economic reforms, and the establishment of democratic institutions as proof.

The second speaker, Alexander Prokhanov, editor of the ultranationalistic newspaper *Den (the Day)*, observed with a heavy sense of irony that he must have come from a different country than his colleague. In *his* country, he said, civil war was under way—in the Caucasus and Middle Asia; the economy has almost collapsed; and the "occupation" Zionist government was selling out Russian national interests to the West.

Prokhanov drew an Apocalyptic scenario of a Russia disintegrated "up to a molecular level," meaning, of course, not just geographic, but social disintegration. However, he maintained optimism. Confident that this break-up would drive the "democrats" out of power, Prokhanov foresaw a day when the "patriots" would reestablish the Great Russian Empire as a unified, nuclear superpower dominating the world.

Conceding president Yeltsin's popularity (decreased, but still significant) Prokhanov defined the prime task of the "patriots" not in terms of overthrowing Yeltsin, but of "a puling his sting out." The sting, according to him, was Acting prime-minister Yegor Gaidar, instigator of the pro-Western government policy.

Thus, Prokhanov did not hide that in attempting to achieve their goals the "patriots" would actively help to accelerate the process of disintegration.

Alexander Prokhanov, a capable fiction and non-fiction writer with strong connections in the military establishment, has been dubbed the "Kipling of the Afghan War" and "the nightingale of the General Staff." He was the only well-known author who went to Afghanistan after the Soviet invasion and glorified "the warrior-internationalists, giving their lives for the sake of the brotherly people of Afghanistan." His newspaper *Den* was in sharp opposition to Gorbachev reforms. *Den* actively supported the August 1991 insurrection, and after the failure of the coup, the publication took an abstructionist stance against Yeltsin and his "occupation" government.

In his presentation at the seminar, Prokhanov honestly outlined the most painful problem the Russian "patriots" faced. While ambitious leaders of different groups were quick to split, accusing their former friends of Zionism, they were uneasy about merging.

There had been numerous attempts to bring them together, however. In August 1989, more than 300 representatives of different extremist organizations gathered in Moscow, founded a Unified Soviet of Russia, and adopted a joint declaration to stop "the wave of Russophobia" in the press and TV.[36] But the Unified Soviet did not show any subsequent signs of existence and became one of many stillborn babies of the "patriotic" unification. More successful was Slavyansky Sobor (Slavic Assembly), which united dozens of patriotic organizations from most regions of the country. The Sobor elected its ruling body, Duma, to coordinate activities of different "patriotic" groups and political parties. In January 1992, the third session of the Sobor gathered 700 representatives of different organizations and 100 guests in the prestigious building of the former Academy of Political Sciences in Moscow. Alexander Barkashov, a member of the Sobor's Duma, assigned 100 of his uniformed subordinates to provide security and order. Every delegate was screened and registered several times before he was allowed to participate in the gathering.

"The conference hall (with uniformed guards at the entrance once again) looked solemn. The podium was draped in red, displaying the picture of

Georgy Pobedonosets. The walls were decorated with national Slavic banners. On the presidium, leaders of the Slavic parties were seated together with Alexander Sterligov, the KGB general, who looked very impressive.

By the way, Sterligov's speech (he is an assistant to [Vice President Alexander] Rutskoi and a leader of the Officers for the Revival of Russia movement) met with the greatest of interest among the delegates. Briefly, in a military manner, he branded the current Russian government insolvent and accused Burbulis and Shakhrai* of an attempt to push aside Rutskoi, 'who eventually understood what sort of company these people were.'"[37]

Alexander Prokhanov and his newspaper deserved special credit for establishing Slavyansky Sobor since the *Den* persistently followed the line of unification of "patriotic" forces.

But the greatest achievement of Prokhanov and his newspaper was the formation of the Front of National Salvation (FNS). If Slavyansky Sobor were a semi-political and semi-cultural organization, the FNS had a strictly political agenda.

The Front was established at its first congress, on October 24, 1992.

But the unity still remained too shaky—not because of differences of opinions, but because of personal ambitions. Thus, Anpilov and his group were not accepted. Vladimir Zhirinovsky attended the Congress and was ready to sign any documents to be among the leaders. He was ignored, however, and left the session during the intermission when forty members of the organizational committee quarreled behind closed doors for the limited number of leading positions.

Without a sole recognized leader, they established and filled nine (!) co-chairmen positions. But still not all ambitions were satisfied. "Offended Sergei Baburin, who was elected only to the Political Council, talked angrily from the door with red cheeks," testified Eduard Limonov, who was left out as well.[38]

The most visible among the co-chairmen were former KGB general, Alexander Sterligov; Gennady Zyuganov (a former party functionary who became the chairman of the newly organized Russian Communist Party); Deputy of the Supreme Soviet, Ilya Konstantinov (who was elected on a democratic ticket but later proved to be an ultranationalist); another deputy, and the head of the Constitutional-Democratic Party, Mikhail Astafiev (who went through a similar evolution).

---

*   Two leading members of the Yeltsin cabinet of that time.

But the election of a horde of co-chairmen could solve only part of the problem. To get them to work together, they needed a coordinator; and in the competition for this position Konstantinov overpowered Zyuganov.

Thus, from the very beginning, the Front of National Salvation was pregnant with future splits. Still, it was a serious achievement for Alexander Prokhanov, who "had united all of them thanks to his sociable disposition and romantic imperialism."[39]

Prokhanov did not care, which "patriotic" ideology prevailed—Red, Brown, or a mixture. His idol was not an ideology, but military might based on national aspiration.

"I am not a Communist," Mr. Prokhanov proclaimed at George Washington University. "I am a Russian imperialist."

I was in the audience of the forum and could not resist reminding Prokhanov that he had built his entire career by serving the most extreme totalitarian forces of the Soviet military clique. Indeed, he glorified not only the Afghan, but other dirty wars unleashed by the Communists during the last two decades—in Ethiopia, Nicaragua, Cambodia, and other Third World countries. And, of course, he had endorsed the Cold War.

"You lost all these wars, Mr. Prokhanov," I told him. "Is that not enough? If you consider yourself a Russian patriot, then perhaps the time has come for you to surrender and join the liberals in their attempts to prevent the disintegration of Russia up to a molecular level."

Vowing that he would never surrender, Prokhanov predicted that he would eventually win.

After the seminar at George Washington University, the situation in Russia developed more in accordance with Prokhanov's—not Tretiakov's—scenario.

Yielding to the heavy pressure of the hard-liners, Yeltsin dismissed Yegor Gaidar and appointed a new prime minister, Victor Chernomyrdin, a henchman of the military-industrial complex. While Chernomyrdin could only slow down—not reverse—Gaidar's reforms, the psychological impact of this replacement was powerful. Yeltsin's readiness to "compromise" with the hard-liners only encouraged them to increase their pressure.

Stalemate

When Yeltsin was elected president of the Russian Federation in June 1991, only a narrow majority of the Supreme Soviet of the Russian Federation supported him. During the August coup, he received almost unanimous support. But after the disintegration of the USSR, the number of his supporters in the parliament went down from day to day while the opposition grew and used a more and more aggressive "patriotic" rhetoric.

The chairman (speaker) of the parliament, Ruslan Khasbulatov became Yeltsin's main rival. Having the majority of the deputies on his side, he opposed Yeltsin's nominees for the key government positions. Thus, Yegor Gaidar, whom Yeltsin had appointed to run the government, was the *acting* prime minister because the parliament refused to approve his nomination. Khasbulatov sabotaged most Yeltsin-Gaidar legislative initiatives targeting economic reform. He continually introduced constitutional amendments to reduce the president's authority and increase the power of the parliament. Capitalizing mostly on the opposition to the painful economic reforms, Khasbulatov did not hurry to associate himself with the Red-Brown extremists, but finally joined their ranks, too. As Mikhail Astafiev stated later, "Khasbulatov had been heavily influenced by Yeltsin, and we did not throw our support to him until he displayed a more radical stance. He would never have dared to change his position without our pressing him to change. Thus, we should not betray him now."[40]

Similarly, Vice President Alexander Rutskoi—being a part of the government—made anti-Yeltsin statements, accused top government officials of corruption, and gave speeches at Slavyansky Sobor congresses and to other ultranationalistic organizations. At first, such challenges to the government policy occurred only occasionally and were attributed to Rutskoi's quarrelsome character. But eventually, Rutskoi also joined the Red-Brown opposition and became its leader.

Ethnic tensions within the Russian Federation and in other former Soviet republics also helped to increase nationalistic passions.

Some autonomous republics—including Tatarstan, Sakho, and Tuva—started to demand their independence or more autonomy from Russia; the Chechen Republic unilaterally declared its independence. Territorial disputes between North Osetia and Ingushetia, two autonomous republics in the North Caucasus, culminated in bloody clashes. On another side of the Caucasian Range (the official border of the Russian Federation), South Osetia declared independence from Georgia in order to join North Osetia and become a part of the Russian Federation. Georgians moved their troops into the revolt region, escalating ethnic clashes.

Violence spread over most of the Caucasus and Middle Asia, forcing hundreds of thousands of refugees to flee to Russia. In Kuban, Rostov, and other predominantly Cossack provinces, a strong movement against letting

"Caucasian" refugees in emerged. Protests often led to violence and murders. Ultranationalism became the predominant ideology of the Cossack's public organizations. The old way of life—which included corporal punishment—achieved respectability.

Strong anti-German sentiments in Saratov Province forced Yeltsin to back away from his promise to let ethic Germans return from exile to the land of their permanent settlement in the Volga River region.*

Trying to ease tensions between Moscow and the autonomous republics, Yeltsin promised them limited self-rule, but utranationalists interpreted this step as "anti-Russian." To achieve "equality" with minorities, some provinces in Ural, Siberia, and the Far East unilaterally raised their status to the republic's level as well. Even Yeltsin's home province *(oblast),* Sverdlovsk, declared itself the Ural Autonomous Republic. Just like Gorbachev on the eve of the Union's disintegration, Yeltsin was losing control over the country.

In April 1993, in an attempt to strengthen his authority, Yeltsin conducted a referendum. The majority of voters still supported their democratically elected president, although his popularity had waned. The renewed mandate gave Yeltsin the opportunity to regain the initiative and carry out the decisive measures against fascists required by law. Right-wing deputies of the Supreme Soviet could not be arrested or tried because of their parliamentary immunity. But Yeltsin could ruin them politically by strong legal actions against Nazi organizations, paramilitary units, and their publications since among these groups, the right-wing legislators had their most active and organized supporters.

However, once again he did not make use of the weapons at his disposal, and the opposition, both inside and outside the Supreme Soviet, continued to grow—unhindered by the referendum.

Endless political clashes at the top left the country without real authority, and corruption reached unprecedented proportions. Without adequate legislation and without institutions and officials willing and capable of implementing the existing laws and regulations, privatization of the economy turned into *prikhvatization* (according to popular pun), or robbery. The newborn "wild capitalism" offered unlimited opportunities for government officials at different levels to "privatize" state enterprises directly into their personal Swiss bank accounts or multi-million-dollar real estates in California or the Bahamas. Meanwhile, most of the working men and women—not to mention the elderly and the handicapped—turned into beggars who could not afford their daily bread. Even in the military, the "private" sales of arms—including tanks, heli-

---

* See more about the Volga Germans in chapter 1, p. 27.

copters, and heavy artillery—reached mass proportion. Shootings and robberies became routine even in Moscow, one of the safest cities in the world just a few years earlier. Racketeering, bodyguards, hired killers became habitual, although Russians had never heard of these evils before. Law enforcement agencies often united with organized crime.

Perhaps the most dangerous facet of this unbearable situation was that Russian society confused this almost unlimited anarchy with democracy. On the initial stage of *perestroika,* the Russians knew that their Communist system failed, while in the West capitalism and democracy worked. So, most of the people believed in private enterprise and democracy. But the society did not realize that democracy requires a certain level of self-discipline and obedience to the law.

Without the rule of law, democracy turns into anarchy or into totalitarianism. Gorbachev did not realize this fundamental principle of democracy—and failed. Yeltsin followed his path. Just as his predecessor had, he repeatedly turned from one extreme to another, only compromising democracy in the eyes of a growing segment of the society.

Yeltsin's Pyretic victory

On September 21, 1993, Yeltsin issued decree No. 1400, dissolving the Supreme Soviet. According to the Constitution, he had no legal authority to do so, and Yeltsin himself admitted later that he had broken "the formal law."

The "White House" refused to obey the illegal decree and voted to impeach Yeltsin and replace him with Vice President Rutskoi.

For two weeks, the "White House" was surrounded by the police, cut off from media—even from electricity and hot water. (It had an independent cold water supply from artesian wells.) But every day, more and more armed extremists penetrated the building. On Sunday, October 3, a crowd of "patriots" gathered in a Moscow square, then marched to the "White House," and smashed the police cordons.

Rutskoi proclaimed that the "Second October Revolution" had begun and ordered the storming of the mayor's headquarters and the TV Center.

Armed Red-Brown groups took over Moscow's streets. The police disappeared. Yeltsin disappeared as well.

With ultimate power hanging in the balance, Alexander Barkashov and his Brown storm troopers could not remain neutral. The RNE was one of the leading armed forces in the Moscow streets. Victor Ampilov and his Red stormtroopers did not lag behind. They stormed police stations and disarmed the police officers, then assailed their warehouses to commandeer more arms and ammunition. They did not hesitate to spill the blood of those who stood in their way. The attackers fought a fierce battle for control of the mayor's office. Another major target was the "Zionized" TV Center in Ostankino.

Chaos ran rampant for about sixteen hours. And then, tanks appeared in the Moscow streets, surrounded the "White House," and opened point-blank fire. The "White House" answered with sniper fire. According to some witnesses, during the fighting, both sides labeled their rivals "kikes" and "Jews."

It was the first military fight in Moscow since October 1917. Official data say that more than 150 people were killed and about 900 wounded, but the real numbers might be much higher. The leaders of the besieged Red-Brown forces—Rutskoi, Khasbulatov, General Makashov, Ilya Konstantinov, Victor Anpilov—were arrested along with many others. Barkashov fled, but was caught after two months in hiding.

Yeltsin issued a decree banning ten publications that actively supported the Supreme Soviet, including *Den, Pravda,* and the *Sovetskaya Rossia.** Political parties and groups that had participated in the violence on the side of the "White House" were banned as well and not allowed to participate in the new parliamentary elections.

But hundreds of fascist publications—including such veterans as *Nash Sovremennik* and *Molodaya Gvardia* were not banned. The extremist political parties had not directly participated in the confrontation—and were not excluded from the early parliamentary elections. The National-Republican Party and its paramilitary *Russian National Legion* had abstained because Nikolai Lysenko understood that Rutskoi and Khasbulatov had no real chances; two months later, Lysenko became a deputy of the new parliament. Vladimir Zhirinovsky and his Liberal-Democratic Party had not participated in the battle either. The Communist Party of the Russian Federation under Gennady Zyuganov (unlike Anpilov's party) had remained uninvolved, although Zyuganov's co-chairmen of the Front of National Salvation —Konstantinov and Astafiev—had fought together with Rutskoi and Khasbulatov in the "White House."

Although the lack of unity among the "patriots" remained their weakest link, in the critical situations it had served to their advantage. The paradox of the August 1991 coup had been repeated. The Red and the Brown were defeated, but they survived and became even stronger.

---

* The ban on *Pravda* and the *Sovetskaya Rossia* was lifted in a couple weeks. Prokhanov resumed his paper under a different title, *Zavtra (Tomorrow).*

The same could not be said about the winners. The "Bloody Sunday and Monday" in Moscow destroyed Yeltsin's already-damaged reputation as a national leader in the same or even greater proportion as the "Bloody Sunday" in Vilnius in January 1991 had destroyed Gorbachev's.

Meanwhile Yeltsin himself did not realize that. As Gorbachev had two years earlier, he lost touch with reality. Setting up parliamentary elections on December 12, he was confident that his supporters, led by Yegor Gaidar, would win a vast majority of the seats. To prevent possible future conflicts between the president and the parliament, Yeltsin convened the so-called Constitutional Assembly (comprised of high officials of all provinces) and forced its members to adopt his draft of a new constitution. On the one hand, this document proclaimed basic human rights of Russian citizens; but, on the other hand, it granted the president an almost dictatorial executive power, allowing him to rule without the parliament and even against the parliament. Yeltsin justified his haste by the need to put the new constitution on the referendum on the same day, December 12.

But all Yeltsin's calculations were wrong. People were deeply disappointed with a "democracy" which had brought the country from one crisis to another and then "solved" the problems by bloodbath.

"Patriots"—both the Red and the Brown—promised something different: High living standards, public order, reduction of crime, job security, elimination of non-Russian faces from the "Zionized" TV screen, and the restoration of the Russian superpower status.

CHAPTER 12

FROM ZHIRINOVSKY TO ZYUGANOV

Nazi with a "human face"

In May 1993, half a year before the December elections, a librarian working with teenagers in a Moscow public library testified:

"This age-group used to read detective stories, science fiction, and biographies of star-singers. But now their interests are totally different. ... Books on the history of the SS, SA, and Wermacht never remain on the shelves. No less popular are books about Stalin, Beria, Dzerzhinsky, and the leaders of the Third Reich. I asked one fifteen-year-old boy when he was returning a book on Hitler published in 1992 that had already gone through dozens of hands, 'Do you like it?' 'It's super-class!' he answered. 'That was a man! A man I admire!'"[1]

The reading trend among teenagers only reflected a much broader process in the minds and hearts of adults. Right-wing politicians immediately exploited the new opportunity. In August 1993, Vladimir Zhirinovsky, feeling that his time was approaching, offered *Izvestia*, a leading and most prestigious liberal newspaper, an article in which he openly portrayed himself as a Nazi.

"National-Socialism is a combination of the most important principles of socialism with a national idea," Zhirinovsky stated. The philosophy of National-Socialism is the philosophy of an ordinary man, a Philistine, if you like, who wants to live quietly in his apartment, to have a loving wife, healthy children, and job security. He also wants to rummage a little bit in his small countryside garden on weekends and to go somewhere for vacation once a year. He does not want to bother anyone and does not want to be bothered. He is not a hero and ... does not want to lie down under a tank for the sake of principles."[2]

This harmless and peaceful Nazi Philistine needs, however, a Russia "within the borders of the beginning of this century or, at least, of 1977." (That means taking back all former Soviet republics and other neighboring countries like Poland and Finland.) This harmless Nazi needs a Russia that will have "all types of weapons"; "several new intelligence services"; and "will be able to start a military operation in any part of the globe within an hour."[3] Zhirinovsky proclaimed in the article what he later repeated publicly hundreds of times: Russian soldiers "will wash their boots in the Indian Ocean."[4]

Otto Latsis, an *Izvestia* staff columnist, stressed in his comments that editors "had no hesitation to give space for the views so different from our own." They did it because Zhirinovsky had won six million votes in the 1991 presidential elections—"an indication that too many Russians shared his views."[5]

However, during his 1991 campaign, Zhirinovsky never directly associated himself with the Nazis. He named his newly organized party Liberal-Democratic, initially confusing many people. In 1993, he did not need this camouflage anymore. On the contrary, he boasted his Nazi views, confident that they were to his advantage. And three months later, he won more than 20 million votes and his party became the largest faction in a new Russian parliament.

Zhirinovsky's mystery

Vladimir Zhirinovsky belongs to the baby-boom generation. He was born in 1946 in Alma-Ata, the capital of Kazakhstan, one of the largest but most sparsely populated and undeveloped Soviet republics. His ethnic origin—so important in Russia—is a mystery.

Vladimir's mother was a Russian woman, Alexandra Pavlovna Makarova. She acquired the last name Zhirinovsky after her marriage. With her first husband, Andrei Zhirinovsky, she had four children.

Vladimir was her fifth child. He was born 18 months after Andrei's death in 1944. The widowed Alexandra Pavlovna had an affair with Volf Edelstein, who married her to make their child legitimate. Alexandra, however, did not want a Jewish last name and so remained Zhirinovsky, but their son was registered Vladimir Volfovich Edelstein. The fifth entry in his birth certificate—and later in his passport—was "Russian" (after his mother), but his last and patronymic name betrayed his Jewish background.

Vladimir did not remember his father, who was killed in a car accident when Vladimir was a baby. But he carried the name Edelstein until he turned 18.[6] Since he planned to enter Moscow University and knew that a Jewish heritage could present an insuperable obstacle, he took his mother's name. Perhaps he wanted to change his patronymic name as well and bury his Jewish roots forever, but the law prohibited that.[*]

In deed, Zhirinovsky claims that archive documents that indicate his Jewish roots have been falsified. In his autobiographic account, *The Last Throw to the South*, as well as in his numerous interviews, he insisted once and again on the purity of his Russian blood. Although he speaks readily about his mother, and her ancestors and relatives, he avoids any details concerning his father's side of the family.

"I am Vladimir Zhirinovsky," he stated. "I have the Russian name Vladimir, but my father's name was Volf. That was how he was recorded in his birth certificate and in his passport. But my mother called him Vladimir, and it would be easier for me to be Vladimir Vladimirovich. Due to some bureaucratic regulations, I am Vladimir Volfovich. I am proud of my name because it is the name of my father, although it sounds strange to the Russian ear."[7]

That is all we can find on this sensitive subject in his book. There is not even any direct indication of his father's last name. If he were Volf Zhirinovsky, then who was Andrei Zhirinovsky?

Having become a widow again, Alexandra Zhirinovsky received no support in raising her children. Her next lover, vocational school student twelve years younger than she, had no income and she had to feed him as well. The family occupied one room in a communal apartment where they had to share the kitchen and the bathroom with neighbors. In his childhood, Vladimir never

---

[*] The law allowed changing a person's last and first name, but not the patronymic name or nationality.

had toys, children's books, or even his own bed; he always felt hungry. He did not have friends among the students of his school, perhaps because of anti-Semitic prejudices, but he, of course, does not mention that.

The high school he attended was not the best school in Alma-Ata, and he was not the best student in the school. Nevertheless, he went to Moscow and entered the Institute of Asian and African Countries, affiliated with Moscow State University.

Such institutions of higher learning were mostly accessible to the offspring of Moscow party and intellectual elite. Only money or special connections could help an average student from a remote province gain acceptance. Since his mother did not have money for a lucrative bribe, the likely alternative is that the young man had connections. Someone very powerful (the KGB?) wanted him to be in the Institute.

In the years after his graduation—he majored in Turkish—he worked for the Committee of Youth Organizations. Its goal was establishing wide-ranging relationships with youth organizations abroad. Like all institutions engaged in foreign contacts, it worked under the direct control of the KGB.

The Committee sent Zhirinovsky to Turkey to work as an interpreter. But eight months later he ran into problems with the Turkish authorities and had to leave the country. Zhirinovsky has never explained what actually happened. Most probably, he had a secret KGB assignment, but was not cautious enough.

It was a major setback. His career in the most prestigious field—diplomacy—was over. Back in Moscow, after having served his military term, he enrolled in night school, received a jurisprudence degree, and became a legal council for *Mir* publishing house. In 1983, he decided to emigrate to Israel, but later he changed his mind.

In 1988, due to *perestroika* and *glasnost*, "informal" organizations started to emerge in the Soviet Union, including the first Jewish organization, *Shalom*. Zhirinovsky became one of its most active directors, which suggests that the KGB might have sent him to monitor and manipulate *Shalom's* activities.

But Zhirinovsky's involvement with the Jewish movement did not last long. He was needed for a much more significant role.

In early 1990, the Communist authorities acknowledged publicly that the one-party system had become obsolete. They permitted other political parties. Vladimir Zhirinovsky immediately organized the first of the new parties, the Liberal-Democratic Party of Russia (LDP). Of course, he denies any involvement of his party with the KGB or other official bodies. But before the party was founded, KGB Chief Vladimir Kryuchkov received Zhirinovsky and talked with him for a couple of hours. The opening session of the party took place in the Hall of Columns of the USSR, one of Moscow's most prestigious buildings. This was a clear indication that the new party enjoyed the support of the authorities. A year later, the LDP nominated Vladimir Zhirinovsky to run for the Russian presidency.

While the official program of the Liberal-Democratic Party was indeed liberal and democratic in many aspects, Zhirinovsky's rhetoric was ultranationalistic and "patriotic" and he had financial resources to conduct his campaign.

According to Russian nationalists, a person with some portion of Jewish blood could not be a real Russian patriot. That is why Zhirinovsky is so uncomfortable with his patronymic name. Looking for a way out of the controversy, he once quipped, "My mother was Russian, and my father was a lawyer." Surprisingly, this cynical joke contributed to his popularity. (Later, however, he insisted that the media had combined his unrelated statements on two different occasions: Once he had answered a question about his mother's nationality and the second time, about his father's occupation.)

He came in third—after Boris Yeltsin and former Soviet prime-minister Nikolai Ryzhkov—amassing more than six million votes. It was an incredible success for a practically unknown politician. Nevertheless, Western observers as well as Russian "democrats" ignored that alarming signal. They considered Zhirinovsky a clown without real political force behind him.

In August 1991, he announced his support of the coup against democracy. But, after crashing the coup, Yeltsin avoided any confrontation with ultranationalists, so Zhirinovsky's position remained non-damaged. He traveled abroad and around the country, gave many interviews, founded three newspapers of ultranationalistic orientation, and established relations with some newborn "national" capitalists who financed his activities.

With his selfish and uncompromised character, he could not find common ground with other ultranationalistic groups. At Red-Brown rallies, leaders of different "patriotic" organizations distanced themselves from Zhirinovsky, so he had to build his own platform or not participate at all. In June 1992 most of Red-Brown groups joined Victor Anpilov in his siege of the Ostankino TV Center, but not the LDP. Zhirinovsky conducted other activities to attract public attention. He announced that he had formed a "shadow cabinet" and called a press conference to introduce the members and the agenda. "The hall was overcrowded, although main journalist forces were sent to Ostankino while we were surrounded by secondary reporters," testified Eduard Limonov, the shadow chief of the Bureau of Investigations.[8]

Zhirinovsky was inexhaustible, inventing different tricks to permanently warm up public interest and keep the media busy. At the same time, he avoided direct confrontation with the authorities. Limonov, who later parted with him, describes him as a coward. He ridicules his bulletproof clothes and his habit of walking out only with his bodyguard although nobody has threatened his life or safety.

When President Yeltsin issued his controversial decree No. 1400 to dissolve the Supreme Soviet dominated by hard-liners, there were no doubt, with whom Zhirinovsky sympathized. But he remembered his mistake in August 1991, and did not take sides. Because of his cowardliness, or because of his political intuition, he remained neutral.

After the crackdown on the Supreme Soviet, Yeltsin set elections of the new parliament, composed of two chambers—the State Duma (comparable to the U. S. House of Representatives) and the Council of the Federation (the Senate). The country was divided into 225 electoral districts to elect 450 deputies of the State Duma; 225 seats were reserved for representatives of different political parties and another 225 for individual representatives of the districts. To be eligible for nomination, a party had to collect 100,000 signatures in its support all over the country; individual runners needed 5000 signatures in their districts. If a party acquired more than five percent of the votes, it would get a number of seats in the Duma in proportion to the percentage of the votes.

In the upper chamber, 178 senators would represent 89 "subjects of federation," i.e., regions and autonomous republic.

This composition of new legislative bodies and sophisticated electoral rules were outlined in a draft of a new Russian constitution. But a draft is only a draft. To turn it into a legal document, Yeltsin scheduled a referendum on the same day, December 12. Thus, during the election campaign, the constitution did not exist yet, so the rules had no legal base. But this "formality" was not a problem in Russia, with her traditional neglect of the law.

Zhirinovsky's success in the elections was especially remarkable in the context of the extremely short campaign, when he had to run against people whose programs and personalities were much better known.

Among the thirteen competing parties, Zhirinovsky had at least two main rivals. One of them was the leader of the democratic intellectuals, Yegor Gaidar, with his Russian Choice Party. His political agenda had been well-known from the time when he had served as acting prime minister. The agenda of another rival, Gennady Zyuganov, with his Communist Party, did not differ much from Zhirinovsky's, but Zyuganov symbolized the stability and security of the Brezhnev era.

In comparison with them, Zhirinovsky was mostly known for his extravagant escapades. But in a specific, post-Communist, Russian climate, he was the man of the day. Since there was no time left for campaigning all over the country, TV became the main tool for all candidates.

Professor Aron Belkin, Russian psychiatrist and president of the Russian Psychoanalytical Association, points out in his book *Zhirinovsky's Era:* "Practically, Zhirinovsky appeared on the TV screens three and a half times (I consider a half the show when all candidates participated together). And nobody supported him. Not one respected politician, author, or scientist said publicly a word in his defense. Newspapers established a general ironic and disrespectful tone; people use such a tone telling jokes. ... It was just impossible to imagine more uncomfortable conditions."[9]

However, even under such conditions, Zhirinovsky succeeded in displaying his agenda and delivering his message.

- Russia for Russians—within the borders of former Soviet Union, the Czar's empire, or even more.
- Military build up, since everything could be achieved only by force, including prosperity, job security, social welfare, and public order.
- All suspects are shot on the spot to combat crime.
- No Jewish faces on the TV screens and elsewhere.
- No autonomy to minorities.

Zhirinovsky did not hesitate to promise everything the people wanted to hear—up to granting every woman a sober husband and supplying every drunkard with cheap vodka. And, of course, he promised to destroy all Russia's "Zionized" enemies, both inside and outside.

These primitive tactics proved to be smart: Zhirinovsky knew his audience better than anyone else. Exploiting people's disappointment in Yeltsin's "democracy" and pressing their most sensitive buttons, he won 20 million votes and outplayed the other 12 parties. "Contacts between such a leader and his audience capture a subconscious sphere, completely bypassing rational thinking."[10]

Presidential nominee

After the elections in Russia, former U. S. State Secretary Jim Baker suggested in a TV interview that there was bad news and good news coming from Moscow. The bad news was the "unexpected" victory of Vladimir Zhirinovsky, while the good news was the adoption of the new Russian Constitution. The constitution not only legalized new legislative bodies, but granted the president the authority to govern without the parliament and even against the parliament.

Baker's conclusion seemed logical: If you have a president you like and a parliament you dislike, extraordinary presidential power looks promising. But in the new political climate in Russia, Yeltsin simply could not execute his legal authority. His forthcoming actions underscored that inability.

One of the first legislative acts of the State Duma was declaring amnesty to all the participants of the August 1991 and October 1993 coups. Yeltsin tried to postpone the implementation of the decree, but his law-enforcement officers were so enthusiastic that they released all his rivals immediately. Rutskoi, Khasbulatov, General Makashov, Anpilov, Barkashov, co-chair and coordinator of the Front of National Salvation Ilya Konstantinov, and other Red-Brown leaders have returned to the public and political life. All charges against them were dropped, the investigations closed. The court investigation of the 1991 coup was closed as well.

Boris Yeltsin, who had been the most popular leader in Russia in 1991, two years later became a heavily wounded lame duck—just when he had succeeded in legalizing his almost-unrestricted dictatorial power. Although he planted the tree of dictatorship for himself, the fruits will be gathered by his successor.

Vladimir Zhirinovsky was the first to announce his intention to run for the presidency in 1996. In his new capacity of the leader of the largest parliamentary faction, he had to demonstrate his political "flexibility." In many interviews with foreign journalists, Zhirinovsky tried to move away from the image of himself as an unstable Fuehrer who was ready to destroy the world with nuclear bombs. He backed away from his claims to Alaska. In his book, he offered the United States and other great powers a deal. They should not prevent Russia from advancing to the south up to the Indian Ocean; and Russia, in return, would not oppose their advance to the south either. The United States would control Central and South America; Western Europe would re-colonize Africa; Japan and China would spread their authority over all Far Eastern territories to the south—up to Australia. In other words, the big powers will divide their spheres of influence by moving south instead of confronting each other by moving west or east.

This openly advertised gangsterism so sharply contradicts all recognized standards of civilized behavior in the international arena that it could hardly be taken seriously. But it may produce the impression that this vicious, inexperienced politician at least says what he really means. This is not the case, however. The map of the future Russian empire on the wall of his office includes not only all former Soviet republics, but Finland, Poland, and, of course, Alaska. But even these territories are not everything he wants. To understand better both his intentions and influence on the masses, we should listen to the people indoctrinated with his rhetoric. Here is a letter that came from Russia to *America Illustrated* magazine* shortly after Zhirinovsky won the elections:

"I am an average Russian woman, and I hate all of your America. Recently, I joined the party of V. V. Zhirinovsky. Soon we Russians will show you Americans who you are. Vladimir Volfovich Zhirinovsky says that Alaska is Russian soil and you must return it to us. If you do not give it back the easy way, we will take it the hard way. Zhirinovsky's army will destroy all of you stinking Americans. As soon as V. V. Zhirinovsky becomes president of Russia, you stinking Americans will be shown your real place in the world. Your number is tenth. Your lousy rag is disgusting and American women are ugly. Al Gore's wife looks like a pig and his daughters are hideous scarecrows.** Mr. Zhirinovsky's sister, Lubov Andreevna Zhirinovsky, says that California, too, should belong to Russia. It is not American land anyway, but Mexican, and Americans stole California, Texas, and other territories from Mexico. And now all these lands should be transferred to the Russian people, and every single Russian will get his piece of land in California or Texas or elsewhere in America. And stinking Americans will work for us as slaves. God help Mr. Zhirinovsky to become president, and then we will destroy almost all of you Americans and make slaves of those who survive. And then we Russians will establish our order in the rest of the world. Lyudmila."[11]

This outcry of hatred and pain came from the button of a dark consciousness. The author is mad and naive, but she expressed the feelings of millions of Russians who seek psychological compensation for their misfortunes in blaming someone else for their sufferings—and looking for revenge. Zhirinovsky and other fascists offer them such a compensation. Here lies the source of their political strength, which is so difficult to understand in the West. "Among all our current problems, the most painful and catastrophic consequences might come from the chain reaction of ultranationalism. I meet my old friends, and often see absolutely different people in the same corporal form. ... They have

---

* The U. S. Information Agency published this monthly in Russian and Ukrainian languages for distribution in Russia and other former Soviet republics. The publication was closed in October 1994 for budget reasons.

** The Gore family was on the cover of the October 1993 issue of the magazine.

238   *Chapter 12*

become fanatics blind from hatred and thirsty for blood," Aron Belkin testifies in his psychoanalytical account on the Zhirinovsky's era.[12]

Yeltsin's "patriotic" agenda

During the September 1993 political crisis, Yeltsin proposed to set up early presidential elections on June 12, 1994. But after the October crackdown of the Supreme Soviet, he backed away from this promise. He said many times that he would not run for re-election after his term expired in 1996, but backed away from this promise as well.

After the amnesty that the new parliament extended to the leaders of the "Second October Revolution," Zhirinovsky declared that the next presidential campaign would pit him against former vice-president Alexander Rutskoi. Later, however, Zhirinovsky realized that he had signed off Boris Yeltsin prematurely.

"Boris Nikolaevich Yeltsin is an absolutely mystical person. He has been buried politically and physically dozens of times. But dozens of times he has revived. He did not drown [after he fell] in the river. He survived an emergency landing of his plane. He was not killed in a car accident. He won in two putsches. He outplayed Gorbachev. He destroyed such a party [The Communist Party of the USSR]. He is a hero from a Russian popular tale. ... He has political intuition. That's why he cannot be understood logically. Neither can I. Both of us are mystical figures. ... That's why of the candidates for the next presidency, Yeltsin is my most dangerous competitor."[13]

There were serious reasons why Zhirinovsky changed his mind about Yeltsin's chances in Russia's political future.

After the months of confusion that followed the parliamentary elections, Yeltsin offered a "National reconciliation and consent program." It meant that Yeltsin offered a consent to the Red and the Brown. Zyuganov refused to sign the "Agreement," while Zhirinovsky agreed. Since that time, Yeltsin has been moving closer to ultranationalists and distancing himself from the democrats. One of the most spectacular indications of Yeltsin's transformation was his appearance at a retrospective exhibition of the most famous nationalistic artist, Ilya Glazunov. Among other "patriotic" works, there was a gigantic painting entitled *The Great Experiment*. According to the artist's idea, which he articulated in the catalog, "the painting demonstrates that the [Russian] revolution was not a natural historic development; outsiders prepared, organized, and implemented it. Russia became an object of a social experiment."[14]

The picture is extremely impressive.

In the right upper corner, the artist painted a snow-white Russian Orthodox church with a golden dome. The bells are ringing. The Czar and Czarina are flying in the blue sky over the inscription, 'God, Czar, the Church.' All the rest of the picture displays the blood-red chaos of the Bolshevik revolution. A gigantic face of Karl Marx—with emphasized Jewish features—dominates the scene. The artist shows that this man was responsible for all bloodbaths that accompanied the *great experiment*. Marx's head is inside a red five-point star. In his catalog, Glazunov explains his idea: "The five-point star is an ancient cabalistic (!) sign, symbol of evil. Marxism is connected with Satanism."[15]

To the left of the star is a cartoon of Leon Trotsky depicted as a long-nosed devil with sharp-clawed paws climbing on the Kremlin wall. Below Trotsky, the artist situated a bearded Hasid drinking Christian blood from a cup. Another Hasid holds golden coins while stigmatizing a suffering body of Mother Russia with the Soviet symbol of hammer and sickle.

The famous picture of Stalin, Roosevelt, and Churchill at the Yalta Conference is incorporated into the painting as well. Here the three leaders of the anti-Hitler coalition are seated with the Israeli flag behind them.

We can also see an ugly Black man attempting to rape a naked white woman. Glazunov does not explain in his catalog how this couple is connected with the Russian Revolution. Instead he claims that "Jacob Shiff, an American banker [of Jewish background] and a follower of Marx, who was a *Russophobe* and an enemy of Russian Orthodoxy, financed different terrorist organizations in Russia."[16]

Commenting on the exhibition, Alexander Nevzorov, former right-wing TV star and current member of the parliament, said, "You look around with horror, you are eager to understand who is opposing these Satanic hordes. The artist created works of the greatest importance and mystical power. When I looked at them, I cried."[17]

President Yeltsin's comments on the Glazunov's paintings were less emotional, but did not differ in content. After having a tour, he embraced the artist and praised his "optimistic and patriotic art."[18]

When Gorbachev conducted his halfhearted reforms, Yeltsin offered a more radical democratic agenda—and became the winner. In 1994, after realizing that this agenda had been completely discredited, he decided to take over "patriotism." Soon Alexander Prokhanov commented ironically in his newspaper that President Yeltsin had become an even greater patriot than Prokhanov himself. In the international arena, Russia started to insist on her super-power status and tried to play an active role in Bosnia, in the Middle East, and in other sensitive areas of the globe. Russian representatives are acting as spoilers everywhere. They supported Bosnian Serbian leaders in Bosnia, which were known as war criminals, and opposed decisive actions of NATO to end the bloody civil war in this country. Russia tries to come back to the Middle East to jeopardize the peace process there. Russia especially opposes the East European countries' joining NATO, claiming that this would be against Russian interests.

Bloody ethnic conflicts continue to take thousands of lives in former Soviet republics. Russian troops deployed there conduct many operations described as peace-keeping missions. In reality, they exploit the opportunity to bring the republics back under Moscow's control. Russia declares that these regions are in her sphere of interests. At the same time, Russian diplomats demand that the U. S. and other Western countries finance these "peace-keeping" missions—the first stage of Zhirinovsky's *throw to the south.*

Thus, President Yeltsin acted more and more according to Zhirinovsky's guidelines. A question remains—how successful can he be in this role?

Abkhazia

The real mission of the Russian peace-keeping operations might be more evident if you take a closer look at one of the ethnic conflict—between the former Soviet republic of Georgia and its autonomous republic Abkhazia.

Abkhazia is a precious stone of the Caucasus, the largest resort of the former Soviet Union. With its warm sea, beautiful mountains, luxuriant subtropical vegetation, and markets overstocked with exotic fruits, it attracted millions of visitors from all over the country.

About 80 thousand Abkhazians comprised only 15 to 17 percent of the republic's population of more than half-a-million. The largest ethnic group (almost half) was Georgian. The rest were Russians, Armenians, and other minorities.

For decades Abkhazians felt persecuted and discriminated by Georgians. Abkhazian nationalists dreamed breaking their republic away from Georgia and becoming part of the Russian Federation. In the USSR, this idea sounded ridiculous. It was one totalitarian state dominated by Moscow anyway. But after the Soviet Union collapsed, the situation became quite different. Abkhazian nationalists started the "war for independence" and "liberated" most of the autonomous republic. The terrorized Georgian population had to flee their homes.

Abkhazia has never had its own armed forces. The Abkhazian population is ten times smaller than the Georgian, and in Abkhazia itself there were three times as many Georgians as Abkhazians. Thus, the rebel's military superiority over Georgia would be impossible without Russian intervention.

Indeed, Russian military stationed in Abkhazia supplied the rebels with unlimited amount of weapons, including tanks and heavy artillery. Thousands of '"volunteers" penetrated Abkhazia from Russia, and Russian border-guards made no attempt to stop them. Russian troops directly participated in the fighting on the Abkhazian side as well.

Georgian president Edward Shevardnadze repeatedly accused Russia of the bloodshed although Yeltsin and his government denied any involvement. Russian Foreign Minister Andrei Kozyrev and Defense Minister Pavel Grachev tried to convince Shevardnadze—and the rest of the world—that they were doing everything possible to stop the conflict. The United Nations, NATO, and individual Western countries did not express any interest when Shevardnadze applied for their help, so he had to accept Russian mediation. A cease-fire was signed between Georgia and the Abkhazian rebels with a Russian guaranty of its implementation. Relying on this guaranty, Shevardnadze withdrew Georgian troops from Sukhumi, the Abkhazian capital, which remained under Georgian control. Thousand of civilians who had fled the city returned to their homes. But when the Georgian troops left, the rebels started their most massive attacks. They destroyed the city, killing civilians. Shevardnadze himself—after his urgent visit to Sukhumi—found himself in a trap and barely survived. But when he reminded the Russian military commanders about the guaranty, they answered that the only thing they could provide was a helicopter to rescue him personally.

The local Russian garrison had a huge military superiority over both Abkhazian and Georgian troops, but did not interfere. The rest of Abkhazia was "liberated" from the entire Georgian population. More than three-hundred-thousand refugees, with elderly and small children, had to cross snowy passes in the mountains to survive. Many froze to death.

The Kremlin's Byzantine tactics kneeled Georgia. Driven into the corner, Shevardnadze had to declare Russia "the best friend of the Georgian people." He joined the Commonwealth of Independent States, although he had refused to do it earlier. He signed an agreement with the Russian defense minister to build a Russian military base in Georgia. In return, Russia refused to recognize Abkhazian independence, although it did not help Shevardnadze to regain control over the rebellious territory. Georgian refugees still could not return home.

Thus, Yeltsin demonstrated again that while Zhirinovsky talked about "the throw to the south," *he* was actually implementing it. But, at the same time, Yeltsin did not want to alert to much his friends in the West and among Russian democrats, who still considered him their last hope. So, he pretended that he was not in control over local military commanders and did not know what was actually going on in Abkhazia. Finally, he only outplayed himself. Since he avoided taking responsibility for the bloodshed, violence, and ethnic cleansing in Abkhazia, he could not take credit either. The "throw" did not help Yeltsin to re-establish himself as a strong patriotic leader. His popularity continued to decline.

Chechen adventure

When—under *perestroika* and *glasnost*—ethnic problems became the urgent political issues in the former Soviet Union, Andrei Sakharov, the late human rights activist, offered a solution. He suggested that every ethnic region, large or small, should be granted the unconditional right to self-rule and self-determination—regardless of its previous Soviet status. Sakharov believed that this was the only way to cool ethnic passions and to preserve the integrity of the country without abusing human rights.

Mikhail Gorbachev rejected the idea as unrealistic. And very soon he was overthrown because of his "realism." Boris Yeltsin, on the contrary, widely exploited Sakharov's idea, gaining a lot of political dividends. As we remember, when Lithuania declared independence and Gorbachev responded with an economic blockade, Yeltsin successfully sabotaged Gorbachev's order. Yeltsin decisively condemned the use of force in Georgia, Azerbaidjan, and elsewhere. Campaigning for his presidency in the Russian Federation, he suggested that all regions "take as much sovereignty as they could"—in full accordance with Sakharov's idea.

In November 1991, a month before the Soviet Union collapsed, I received a letter from my Chechen friend, a poorly educated, but articulate person. Reflecting his people's feelings and hopes invoked by Yeltsin's promises, he wrote: "Let the empire collapse soon. Let the republics receive their sovereignties soon. And let the sovereign republics agree with each other to eliminate all weapons, to open all borders, and to elect one government based on the United Nations' charter and on the cooperation of all the nations living on the Planet of Earth. We should move in this direction, or the nations will lock themselves up in their shells. This can not bring anything good, but only new forms of hostility."[19]

Most of the Chechens are not narrow-minded nationalists. They do not want to lock up in their shell. They want to be free and equal members of the international community, and they deserve that as much as any other nation. Perhaps, even more than some others, if we look into the three-hundred-year-long history of their fighting.

In 19th century, these mountain people fought against imperial Russia for almost 50 years—much longer than all other Caucasian nations. During the years of the Russian revolution and civil war (1917-1921), Chechens fought for their independence again. In 1944, Joseph Stalin exiled the entire Chechen population to Siberia, Kazakhstan, and Central Asia for alleged collaboration with the German Nazis. More than one hundred thousand of them perished during the months-long journey in sealed freight-cars, without food and medical care. It was an attempt to cleanse the mountains from unreliable elements forever. But in 1957, four years after Stalin's death, the Chechens were "rehabilitated" and allowed to return to their homeland.

Thus, it was not a coincidence that when Yeltsin offered them "as much sovereignty as they could take," Chechnya was the first autonomous republic of Russian Federation to declare independence.

Yeltsin immediately forgot his own promises. He threatened to send troops to Chechnya. Chechen president Dzhakhar Dudaev (former Soviet military general) responded with a threat to start a guerrilla war throughout the country. Under pressure from his democratic supporters, Yeltsin decided to seek a political solution.

Not strictly political, to be precise. Moscow used different means to divide Chechens and get rid of Dudaev, who became a symbol of their resistance. Speaker of the Supreme Soviet Ruslan Khasbulatov, Chechen by nationality, unleashed anti-Chechen propaganda by creating a myth of the "Chechen Mafia." This Mafia was singled out as allegedly the biggest, the most brutal and best organized crime network. Even the "democratic" press contributed a lot in publicizing this myth, sowing fear and hatred against the Chechens.

Granted amnesty by the State Duma, Khasbulatov left Moscow for Chechnya and headed the anti-Dudaev opposition. Paradoxically, he became Yeltsin's ally in Chechnya. But all attempts to divide the Chechens and overthrow Dudaev failed. Yeltsin faced a dilemma: to accept the Chechen independence or to re-conquer the rebellious republic. A few years earlier, Yeltsin-the-democrat would probably have chosen the first option. But not after he became a "patriot."

The war began December 11, at the worst time of the year for a military offensive, when the daytime is short and heavy fogs cut vision. This alone indicated that the war was poorly planned. General Pavel Grachev, the Russian defense minister, claimed earlier that he needed just two hours to take control over Chechnya. But the operation went on month after month after month, turning into a major war. Russian troops were absolutely unprepared to conduct the operation—neither militarily, nor psychologically. Some officers refused to attack civilians. Even among high-military command, the operation was sharply criticized as non-professional. Some generals preferred to resign rather than take responsibility for the Chechen operation.

Chechens, on the other hand, knew what they were fighting for. During the three years of their *de facto* independence, they acquired substantial arms and ammunition, buying them from other Caucasian countries and from demoralized Russian troops. Even after the fighting began, many Russian soldiers and officers were caught selling their machine guns to Chechens, knowing that they themselves might be killed by these very weapons in a couple of hours.

Still, the Russians had an overwhelming superiority in manpower, tanks, artillery, and in air force. Experiencing a number of shameful defeats on the ground, they could indiscriminately bomb and shell Chechen cities, villages, and settlements with impunity, day and night. They completely destroyed the Chechen capital Grozny, a city of 400,000, as well as other cities and towns. Most of their inhabitants fled.

The massive and systematic bombing and shelling of civilians became the most significant part of the operation. Otherwise, the war would be senseless in terms of achieving the political goal. If Russian troops succeeded in defeating the rebels in a few days, arresting Dzhakhar Dudaev, and establishing their temporary administration, then a referendum—repeatedly offered by Yeltsin—should determine the status of Chechnya. However, nobody could have any illusion that Chechens, who comprised two-thirds of the republic's 900,000 population, would not vote unanimously for independence. Thus, it was possible to keep Chechnya within the Russian Federation only by driving the Chechens out and radically changing the demographic situation in the republic.

Pyotr Vail, a reporter for Radio Liberty, after spending two weeks in Chechnya, described this barbaric tactic:

> "The artillery—heavy, field, and tank—is conducting a massive bombardment by concentric circles, gradually moving from the periphery to the center. ... The inhabitants are squeezed out of their home and forced to leave the city, using a corridor which is free from shelling. When the area becomes almost empty, and that means that practically all people have left

and all buildings are destroyed, then the OMON [special police forces] arrive and complete cleansing."[20]

Sergei Kovalev, democratic deputy of the State Duma and human rights commissioner, spent the two first weeks of the war in Grozny. He testified about a level of human rights violation that was close to genocide. Yegor Gaidar and other influential democrats organized anti-war demonstrations in Moscow. However, the impact of these actions was limited. Since some democratic leaders remained loyal to Yeltsin, the crisis only split and demoralized the already-weak democratic camp.

Vladimir Zhirinovsky became the only political ally of Yeltsin. He supported the war, although condemned the "indecisiveness" of the military commanders. According to him, the military should turn the entire Chechnya into a big hole. In response to this "friendly criticism," the defense minister Pavel Grachev rushed to give Zhirinovsky the military rank of lieutenant-colonel.

Behind the scene

Alexei Vedenkin has dozens of faces in any given time. Having a special talent for producing false certificates, he presents himself as a military investigator of different ranks; a KGB officer; a representative of different Russian and foreign banks, companies, and foundations; a member of foreign elite clubs; and even an Obersturmbannfuehrer-SS for an Argentinean Nazi organization. Nobody knows for sure how many of these occupations are real and how many are false. He is young, handsome, cynical, and self-confident. He represents the new generation of the Russian fascist establishment.

What is definitely known about him is the first Nazi organization he founded in 1981 in his high school, when he was 16. On the membership cards that he produced himself, the title of the organization—*The New Worker National-Socialist Party of Russia*—was accompanied by the drawing of an eagle with a swastika in its claws and by Hitler's profile.[21]

After his obligatory military service, Vedenkin became a secret police informer and probably a KGB agent. Mysterious events, adventures, and deaths have accompanied most of his activities. In 1989, he was arrested and later convicted for blackmailing and bribing, but a criminal record did not damage his career. In 1991, Alexei Vedenkin worked for the Managing Department of the Communist Party Center Committee where he headed a security division. The Department controlled all Communist Party finances. When it became evident that the Party was loosing its monopoly of power, Vedenkin's job was to channel the party money abroad and deposit it in different foreign banks. The head of the management department, Nikolai Kruchina, authorized this secret operation. In August 1991, after the failure of the coup against democracy, Kruchina committed suicide. Vedenkin was the first to come to his office and remove all secret documents from his safe. Their whereabouts is still unknown; thus, billions of dollars of the party money "disappeared."

After the coup, Vedenkin became financial manager or adviser for *Vozrozhdenie (Rebirth) Foundation*, created by Russian Vice-president Alexander Rutskoi. Vedenkin participated in other enterprises as well. He established relationships with many foreign banks and multimillionaires, having contacts in Argentina, Spain, Switzerland, Austria, Australia, Brazil, and Poland. He organized a number of foreign trips and fund-raising campaigns for Vladimir Zhirinovsky. He also became a money manager and one of the leaders of *Russkoye Natsionalnoe Edinstvo* (RNE), second-in-rank after Alexander Barkashov.

In September and October 1993, during the days of parliamentary crisis and bloody clashes between Russian military and Red-Brown defenders of the "White House," General Achalov, Rutskoi's defense minister, appointed Vedenkin his deputy and delegated him to the Far East with a secret mission.[22]

Thus, acting mostly behind the scenes, Vedenkin connected different right-wing organization with each other, with former party and KGB functionaries, and with big money.

Vedenkin came out of the shadow in February 1995, when he printed an article in *Nezavisimaya gazeta* and then gave an extensive interview to Russian TV. He claimed that 90 percent of high-ranking law enforcement and security officials are sympathizers of the Russian fascist organizations. He did not conceal that Russian fascists are marching to power and that they support such actions of current government as the war in Chechnya. Vedenkin stated that Defense Minister Pavel Grachev deserves a monument for this war while his most outspoken critics, Sergei Kovalev and Sergei Yushchenkov, are the most hated enemies. "When we come to power, I will personally shoot them in the back of the heads without trial and investigation," he said calmly. "I will feel great pleasure in that."[23]

Vedenkin explained the tactics of the financial circles he represented or pretended to represent. According to him, they support simultaneously a number of fascist groups and parties in order to see, which of them would have a better chance to win parliamentary and presidential elections. "If Barkashov becomes a front-runner, we will help Barkashov; if Zhirinovsky is ahead, we will support him," he said.[24]

After his sensational interview, Alexei Vedenkin was arrested and charged with the threat of murder. Several days later, President Yeltsin issued a decree in which he ordered law-enforcement agencies to stop conniving with fascists and to take decisive legal actions against them.

The decree, however, was just a rhetorical statement with no practical application. The celebration of the 50th anniversary of the victory over Nazi Germany was approaching. In this context, Yeltsin could not remain silent about domestic fascism after Vedenkin's provocative interview. But the real meaning of his decree was disclosed in a paragraph addressed to the Russian Academy of Sciences. This paragraph demanded the working out a "scientific definition" of the term "fascism" in two weeks.

The academy did not respond to this ridiculous request, while the law-enforcement agencies embraced an excuse to ignore the presidential decree: How could they go after the fascists if the very meaning of the word "fascism" remained unknown? Alexei Vedenkin was released from custody just a few hours after Yeltsin's decree was publicized.

This was just one of many signs of how powerful and influential the Russian Nazis became.

"Nazification in geometrical progression"

If Yeltsin hoped to benefit from the Chechen war as a strong "patriotic" leader and increase his chances for re-election in 1996, he miscalculated. The majority of the people were tired, disappointed, and indifferent. Although they did not want to let Chechnya go, they did not want Russian soldiers to die in Chechnya either. The polls indicated that Yeltsin's popularity dropped to single digits and had never been as low.

In March 1995, Yeltsin told a Russian news agency that he had not decided whether to run for re-election. His wife Naina Yeltsina added that she opposed a re-election bid for family reasons, but her heart tightened when she thought about who could replace him. Later, Yeltsin repeated the same statement again and again.

There were a lot of direct and indirect signs that Yeltsin might considering canceling the presidential elections and extending his presidency beyond his legitimate term limit. If so, the war in Chechnya might be just a small move in a sophisticated Machiavellian game to increase tension in society, providing an excuse for such an extraordinary decision.

At the same time, Yeltsin and his surroundings worked on formation of loyal political blocks with a hope to win parliamentary elections in December,

1995. He approved a formation of two such blocks, a "right-centrist" under leadership of Victor Chernomyrdin, the prime-minister, and a "left-centrist" under leadership of Ivan Rybkin, speaker of the State Duma. Chernomyrdin stressed "patriotism" and stability, while Rybkin stressed stability and "social justice." Both leaders were very unpopular since the public associated them with Yeltsin's regime. But, with their unlimited resources and wide support from both Central and Russian TV, they hoped to win substantial amount of votes and drive both the liberals and the ultranationalists out of the political mainstream. However, this thoroughly calculated strategy failed. One of these two blocks could not be organized at all, and another one, headed by Chernomyrdyn, hardly received 10 percent of the votes.

Among new political leaders with presidential ambitions I have to mention a potential "strong man" general Alexander Lebed, former commander of the 14th Russian army, which played such a significant role in the unilaterally proclaimed Dnester republic that had separated itself from Moldova. For his toughness in defending the independence of this Russian republic, Lebed became very popular all over the country. He retired from the army to join national political arena. While his political group, The Union of Russian Communities, does not enjoy wide support, he personally is one of the most popular political leaders.

General Lebed, to be sure, has not introduced any new ideas, and does not have such intentions. He is not a speaker or a thinker. But he is strong, brave, self-confident, and does not hesitate to accuse top officials in corruption. In the eyes of millions of ordinary people embarrassed and disillusioned about democracy, Lobed personifies the Russian might, stability and the Russian superiority.

"The process of infiltrating fascism into the public conscience and the public itself is now under way in Russia," said Yevgeny Proshechkin, the chairman of Moscow's Anti-Fascist Center. "This process is proceeding in geometrical progression. A few years ago, a person would have felt very uncomfortable if somebody had said to him, 'In fact, your views are close to fascism, this is fascism.' But now, millions of Russians are ready to respond, 'What is wrong with fascism? It is just respect for the national feelings.' I think a dangerous event has occurred—a sharp turn in the public conscience to the belief that fascism is something good."[25]

After Proshechkin publicized his conclusion in March 1994, this trend continued to accelerate.

Vladimir Zhirinovsky is not the only right-wing runner for the Russian presidency, and, of course, nobody can safely predict that he will win the race. However, if the public conscience does not change dramatically, only that candidate would be able to defeat Vladimir Volfovich, who will convince the voters that he is even more Zhirinovsky than Zhirinovsky himself. If Vladimir Volfovich is criticized now, it is not as much for his extremism as for being ... too liberal. There are two main messages in the book *Limonov against Zhirinovsky*. First, the author denounces Zhirinovsky as a hidden Jew. And second, he claims that Zhirinovsky is a hidden democrat and that his ultranationalistic rhetoric is just a camouflage.[26] These attacks against Zhirinovsky are symptomatic. Concluding his psychoanalysis of the Zhirinovsky Era, Professor Belkin stated:

> "As any human being, Zhirinovsky may become tired and make a serious mistake, which his rivals will successfully use against him. He may fall ill and even pass away. But it will not change anything. Another Zhirinovsky will emerge, and he will not need a lot of time and effort to establish himself. ... Zhirinovsky's ideology, his strategy, and his slogans have already produced their shoots. His 'gin' has already gone out of the bottle, and he will not go back on his own will. His gin will find a body for himself—a body of an individual, even more fatal [for the Russian future] than Zhirinovsky."[27]

It seems that such an individual is Gennady Zyuganov, the head of the Russian Communist Party. After December 1995 parliamentary elections, Zyuganov's communists and Zhirinovsky's liberal-democrats exchanged their positions in the parliament: Communists won more than 22 percent of the votes, and liberal-democrats—about 12 percent, leaving all other parties and groups behind. Now, when I am writing these lines, Gennady Zyuganov looks like the most probable next president of Russia.* He is a front-runner in the presidential campaign, ahead of Vladimir Zhirinovsky, Georgy Yavlinsky and president Boris Yeltsin, who finally announced his decision to run for reelection.

Zyuganov describes himself and his party as a left-wing opposition to Gorbachev-Yeltsin reforms, which differs from the right-wing opposition of Zhirinovsky and other ultranationalists. However, Alexander Barkashov, who openly worships the "Russian swastika" and Adolf Hitler, ordered his Russian

---

* I am writing this in May 1996; the presidential elections are scheduled for June 16, 1996.

National Unity to support Zyuganov. Twenty-five non-communist groups formed a "patriotic" block to back up Zyuganov's bid for presidency as well.

In February 1996, Alla Gerber, former deputy of the Russian State Duma from Yegor Gaidar's Russian Choice party,** testified on current Russian anti-Semitism before the House Human Rights Subcommittee in Washington, DC. She quoted the latest book by Gennady Zyuganov, where he praised Stalin for his "understanding that the new [Communist] realities in the USSR should be reevaluated in concord with the century-old Russian tradition. This understanding caused a dramatic change in the state ideology of the Soviet Union during the period from 1944 to 1953." [28]

In other words, Zyuganov refers to the last decade of Stalin's tyranny, which had started with an exile of entire ethic groups—Chechens, Kalmyks, Crimean Tatars, and a number of others—to Central Asia and Siberia and ended with an extensive anti-Semitic campaign. This campaign led to a destruction of an entire Jewish culture, execution of prominent Jewish writers and leaders of the Jewish Antifascist Committee, and culminated in the "doctor's plot." (We have discussed all these events in different parts of the book.)

The book *Behind the Horizon* by Gennady Zyuganov is spectacular in other aspects as well. This "moderate" admirer of Joseph Stalin does not use the slogans such as "kill kikes—save Russia." He does not explain that swastika is a traditional Russian symbol. He does not support his statements with quotations from the *Protocols*. He speaks about *geopolitics, human civilization,* and *global development.* As a self-declared communist and—*de facto*—red-brown "patriot," Zyuganov cannot admit that the current crisis in Russia is a result of the bankruptcy of the Soviet system of government or that Russia herself might be responsible for her troubles. Thus, he is obsessed with conspiracy theories. According to him, the United States, secretly using *russophobes* within the Russian society as their fifth column, disintegrated the USSR, and now they are disarming, colonizing, and turning Russia into a secondary power to exploit her as an unlimited resource of cheap raw materials.

Zyuganov believes that, in order to survive in the long run, Russia should return to socialist and nationalist outlook, to reestablish her military might, to reunite the former Soviet republics under her leadership, to renew "close ties" with the former socialist countries of Eastern Europe, and to challenge the United States and their allies elsewhere in the world. This is the same as Vladimir Zhirinovsky's philosophy, although Zyuganov articulates it in a more

---

** In December 1995 parliamentary election the party failed to break the five-percent barrier and has no representation in the new State Duma.

decorous form. He intends to lead the country according to his political vision, but he promises to act more effectively and intelligently than Leonid Brezhnev and his entourage. Alla Gerber stressed in her testimony that, while some Western analysts consider Zyuganov a kind of a social-democrat, he is a national-socialist.

The possibility still remains that president Yeltsin will outmaneuver Zyuganov in the elections or find a pretext to cancel or postpone them. But he himself has to pursue the policy of a gradual nazification of Russia—just to survive politically. In an attempt to counterbalance his unpopular reforms, Yeltsin's supporters praise him as a tough guy and a patriot. Nikita Mikhalkov, a celebrated movie star and producer, declared in a TV show that real Russian patriots should vote not for the person they like, but for the person most needed to the country. Such a person, according to him, is Boris Nikolayevich Yeltsin—because he is a real Russian, and not just a Russian man but a Russian *muzhik*. "Russia is a woman *(baba)*," Mikhalkov added, "and she needs a *muzhik*." An intellectual would find this "patriotic" reasoning hardly convincing; but the appeal is addressed to the most primitive instincts of ordinary people already indoctrinated with ultranationalist propaganda.

The national-patriotic "gin" has become the real ruler of the country, so his specific embodiment is a matter of secondary significance.

INSTEAD OF CONCLUSION

"THE JOB OF THE NEXT GENERATION"

May 9, 1995, two parades in Moscow marked the Fifty anniversary of the victory over Nazi Germany. Veterans of the World War II marched in Red Square, and the military marched in Victory Square in front of a new grandiose Monument of Victory. Yeltsin had promised President Clinton and other foreign guests that the units fighting in Chechnya would not participate in the parade, but he did not keep this promise.

On the same day, May 9, in the United States, National Public Radio broadcast an interview with a Muscovite, Irina Kamenkovich, whose parents had fought in World War II. Describing a meeting of veterans in her neighborhood, she said:

"When I saw this huge crowd of poor neglected people with their worn-out clothes, their worn-out shoes, I knew that it's difficult for them even to get a haircut because you have to pay a lot for that. It didn't even look the traditional Soviet show. They always made a great show of it. [But] this time there was no money even for that. [The veterans] were ushered into the hall. Of course the words of congratulation were spoken. But after that, the young man who was the municipal authority's representative said that it was a shame that they were so penniless to fail to make the proper presents for the veterans, that the order of the president to benefit the veterans was not supported by even a kopeck of money. And I was sitting there and thinking only of the huge monument [built on Victory Square] which took all the money. I was thinking about the pompous presentation when all great people of the world will come to Moscow, and the Russian authorities would show them another Potemkin village."[1]

When the young official asked veterans whether they had any requests of the municipal authorities, they were silent. Irina Kamenkovich raised her hand and said, "Well, could you provide at least a bucket of paint and a brush so that we can paint over the swastikas on the garages and some buildings in the neighborhood?"[2]

According to Irina, this thing seriously troubled the veterans. They keep talking about the swastikas, the fascists, and the fascist demonstrations, asking why the authorities do not stop them. "What's the good of being the victors if we have to watch it now going all over again," Irina said, articulating their concerns. "What kind of victory are we celebrating now if we have all the signs of the new wave of fascism?"

"I already have an example of what comes out of it," the Muscovite woman continued, "because my child was just sitting in an armchair, scribing something on her leg with a felt-tin pen, and when I looked at her leg and saw that she was drawing a swastika, I asked her why. 'Do you know what are you doing, what you are drawing?' She told me she had no idea, but it was all over the neighborhood of her school. Children are getting used to drawing this. Children are used to this sign. They don't see anything dangerous in it. It seems to be the job of the next generation to fight down the new fascists in the motherland of the people who had stopped the European fascism. Now we have to stop our own."[3]

I have only to express my hope that the next generation of Russian antifascists will succeed.

REFERENCE NOTES

INTRODUCTION

1. John Dunlop, *The Faces of Contemporary Russian Nationalism* (Princeton, NJ: Princeton University Press, 1983); see also: John Dunlop, *The New Russian Nationalism* (The Washington Papers/116: Preager Special Studies, 1985).
2. Alexander Yanov, *The Russian Idea and the Year 2000* (Oxford, England: Oxford University Press, 1987).
3. Walter Laqueur, *Black Hundred. The Rise of the Extreme Right in Russia* (New York: HarperCollins Publishers, 1993).
4. Ibid., p. 210.
5. *Izvestia,* December 18, 1993, p. 3.
6. Brym, Robert J., and Andrei Degtyarev, "Anti-Semitism in Moscow: Results of an October 1992 Survey," *Slavic Review*, Spring 1993, pp. 1-12.

CHAPTER 1

1. Alexander Yakovlev, "Protiv antiistorizma," *Literaturnaya Gazeta*, November 15, 1972.
2. Yuri Loshchits, *Goncharov,* The Lives of Remarkable People Series (Moscow: Molodaya Gvardia Publishers, 1977).
3. Mikhail Lobanov, *Alexander Ostrovsky*, The Lives of Remarkable People Series (Moscow: Molodaya Gvardia Publishers, 1979).
4. Vadim Pigalev, *Bazhenov,* The Lives of Remarkable People Series (Moscow: Molodaya Gvardia Publishers, 1980).
5. Sergei Semanov, *Brusilov,* The Lives of Remarkable People Series (Moscow: Molodaya Gvardia Publishers, 1980).
6. Mikhail Kheifets, *Tsareubiistvo v 1918 godu (murdering of the Czar in 1918)* (Jerusalem: Knigotovarishchestvo Moskva-Ierusalim, 1991), p. 142.
7. Nikolai Yakovlev, *August 1, 1914* (Moscow: Molodaya Gvardia Publishers, 1974).

8. Sergei Semanov, *Brusilov,* The Lives of Remarkable People Series (Moscow: Molodaya Gvardia Publishers, 1980), p. 205.

CHAPTER 2

1. Vladimir Begun, *Vtorzhenie bez oruzgia (Invasion without Arms)* (Moscow: Molodaya Gvardiya Publishers, 1978).
2. Ahad Ha-Am, *Izbrannye sochinenia (Collected Works),* vol. 1 (Moscow: [The publisher is not identified], 1919), p. 137.
3. Ibid., pp. 134-135.
4. Hayyim Nahman Bialik, *Pesni i poemy (Songs and Poems)* (St. Petersburg: Izdatelstvo Zaltsmana, 1914), p. 192.
5. *Mirny Trud*(Kharkov), No. 6-7, 1907, p. 95.
6. Ibid., No. 10, p. 155.
7. Quoted from: Friedrich Gorenstein, "Drezdenskiye strasti" ("The Dresden Passions"), *Slovo/Word,* No. 3-4, 1988, p. 65.
8. Sergei Gusev-Orenburgsky, *Bagrovaya kniga (The Purple Book)* (New York: Ladoga, 1983), p. 15.
9. *Mirny Trud,* No. 10, 1907.
10. Alexei Shmakov, *Rech po evreiskomy voprosu (Speech on the Jewish question)* (Moscow: Gorodskaya tipografia, 1911), pp. 31-32.
11. *Chelovek i Zakon,* No. 11, 1978.
12. A copy is in the author's archives.
13. *Sovetskaya Kultura,* June 18, 1987; *Novoye Russkoye Slovo,* January 8, 1988.
14. Ibid.
15. A copy is in the author's archives.

CHAPTER 3

1. Alexander Romanenko, *O klassovoi sushchnosti sionizma (On the Class Essence of Zionism),* (Leningrad: Lenizdat, 1986).
2. Yuri Ivanov, *Ostorozhno: sionizm! (Beware: Zionism!)* (Moscow: Politizdat, 1969; second edition, 1971); Vladimir Begun, *Polzuchaya kontrrevolyutsia (Creeping Counter-Revolution)* (Minsk: Belarus, 1973); Vladimir Begun, *Vtorzheniye bez oruzhiya (Invasion without Arms)* (Moscow: Molodaya Gvardia, 1978; second edition—1979); Yevgeny Yevseev, *Fashizm pod goluboi zvezdoi (Fascism under the Blue Star)* (Moscow: Molodaya Gvardia, 1971); Vladimir Bolshakov, *Sionizm na sluzhbe antikommunizma (Zionism in the Service of Anti-Communism)* (Moscow:

Politizdat, 1972); Lev Korneev, *Klassovaya sushchnost sionizma (The Class Essence of Zionism)* (Kiev: The Ukraine's Political Literature, 1982); L. Modzhoryan, *Mezhdunarodny sionizm na sluzhbe imperialisticheskoi reaktsii (International Zionism in the Service of Imperialist Reaction)* (Moscow: Mezhdunarodnye otnoshenia, 1984); V. Semenyuk, *Sionizm: stavka na terror (Zionism: Relying on Terror)* (Moscow: Novosti, 1984); *Ideologiya i praktika mezhdunarodnogo sionizma (Ideology and Practice of International Zionism)* (Moscow: Politizdat, 1978); *Ideologiya i praktika mezhdunarodnogo sionizma (Ideology and Practice of International Zionism)* (Kiev: Naukova Dumka, 1981), and hundreds of others.

3. Beizer, M., and S. Dyskin, R. Zelichenok, and B. Steizman, "Sionologia na konveierye—ostanovit poka ne pozdno" ("Zionology on the assembly line—it must be stopped before it is too late"), *Shalom,* No. 2, (1988): p. 16. *(Shalom* is a Moscow Samizdat journal of the Jewish Cultural Association; a copy in the author's archives).
4. Lezov, S., and S. Tishchenko, "Moskovskaya diskussia" ("The Moscow Discussion"), *22*, No. 65, 1989, pp. 111-137; speech by M. Chlenov, p. 113.
5. Alexander Romanenko, *O klassovoi sushchnosti sionizma (On the Class Essence of Zionism)* (Leningrad: Lenizdat, 1986), pp. 148-253.
6. The tape-recorded speech of Dmitry Vasiliev is in the author's archive.
7. *Sovetskaya Kultura (The Soviet Culture),* April 27, 1989.
8. V. Nasenko, *Sovetskaya Kultura*, December 10, 1988.
9. K. Korneshov, "Etot sionist *Nikon*" ("This Zionist *Nikon*"), *Sovetskaya Kultura*, April 1, 1989.
10. M. Glikman, [without a title]. A four-page manuscript; supplement: A six-page transcribed tape-recording. A copy is in the author's archives.
11. Later, reproductions of some of Igor Borodin's pictures were published in the journal *Molodaya Gvardia*, No. 1, 1990. See chapter 9.
12. M. Glikman, *op. cit.,* manuscript, p. 1.
13. Ibid., p.2.
14. Ibid.
15. Ibid., transcribed tape-recording, p. 1.
16. Ibid., manuscript, p. 4.
17. The preceding chapter dealt with one trial case; the second—in connection with V. Nosenko's article (December 10, 1988) devoted to the Alexander Kosarev commemoration meeting and to A. Romanenko's participation in it.
18. Nina Katerli, "Doroga k pamyatnikam" ("A road to Monuments"), *Leningradskaya Pravda*, October 9, 1988.
19. *A Conclusion* of experts in two pages, page 1. A copy is in the author's archives.
20. *Romanenko's Appeal* in nine pages, page 2. A copy is in the author's archives.
21. Gennady Rubinsky, "Ot lukavogo" ("From the Sly"), *Smena*, November 21, 1989; *Vestnik yevreiskoi sovetskoi kultury (VESK) (Herald of the Soviet Jewish Culture),*

January 17, 1990; a large excerpt from this article is also published in *Sovetskaya Kultura*, January 13, 1990.
22. Ibid.

CHAPTER 4

1. The work had a wide circulation in Samizdat. A copy is in the author's archives.
2. Valery Yemelianov, *Desionizatsiya (De-Zionization)* (Paris, France: 1979).
3. P. Serkis, "Gorech pomerantsa" ("Bitterness of the Wild Orange"), *Novoye Russkoe Slovo*, May 18, 1990.
4. The articles remained unpublished.
5. V. Ardamatsky, "Proisshestvie u vrat nauki" ("An Incident at the Gates of Science"), *Literaturnaya Gazeta*, February 5, 1963.
6. Yemelianov, loc. cit.
7. *Atola*, No. 13, April 2, 1990. For more details about current Russian paganism see: Yu. Vishnevskaya, "Pravoslavnye, gevalt!" ("Orthodox Believers, Gevalt!"), *Sintaksis*, No. 21, 1990, pp. 87-101.
8. *Monitor. Digest of News & Analysis from Soviet Successor States*, UCSJ. Vol. **3**, No. 31, August 7, 1992.

CHAPTER 5

1. *Leningradsky yevreiskii almanakh (Leningrad Jewish Anthology)*, No. 12, March 1987, pp. 35-40. Copy of the issue of this Samizdat publication is in the author's archives.
2. Ibid., pp. 40-41.
3. Ibid., pp. 41-42.
4. Vladimir Bondarenko, "Ocherki literaturnykh nravov" ("Sketches of Literary Customs"), *Moskva*, No. 12, 1987, p. 193.
5. Samizdat. A copy is in the author's archives.
6. Ibid.
7. Vladimir Soloukhin, "Ostavatsya samim soboi" ("Remain Oneself"), *Literaturnaya Gazeta*, April 27, 1988.
8. Vladimir Soloukhin, *Pri svete dnya (In the Daylight)*, (Moscow: [The publisher is not indicated], 1992).
9. *Pravoslavny vestnik (Orthodox Herald)*, April 1988, pp. 5-8.
10. Ibid., p. 5.

11. The letter is in the author's archives.
12. Nikolai Berdyaev, "Khristianstvo i antisemitizm" ("Christianity and anti-Semitism"), *Druzhba narodov*, No. 11, 1988, p. 206.
13. Samizdat. A copy in the author's archives.
14. Ioann, Mitropolit Sankt-Peterburgsky and Ladozhsky, *Bud veren do smerti* (Metropolitan Ioann, *Be faithful to death*) (Moscow: TOO RIP "Prosvet," AO "Novaya kniga," 1993), p. 54.

CHAPTER 6

1. Several tape-recorded speeches of Dmitry Vasiliev are in the author's archives.
2. "Programma zavoevaniya mira evreyami" ("The Program of the Conquest the World by the Jews"), *Znamya*, No. 190-200, August 28 to September 7, 1903.
3. Major works about the *Protocols of the Elders of Zion* are (in chronological order): Yuli Delevsky, *Protocoly sionskikh mudretsov: Istoria odnogo podloga (The Protocols of the Elders of Zion. History of one forgery)* (Berlin: Epokha, 1923); Vladimir Burtsev, *Protocoly sionskikh mudretsov—dokazanny podlog (The Protocols of the Elders of Zion is a Proven Forgery)* (Paris: Oreste Zeluk, Editeur, 1938); Norman Cohn, *Warrant for Genocide. The Myth of the Jewish World-Conspiracy and the Protocols of the Elders of Zion* (New York: Harper & Row, 1967); Herman Bernstein, *The Truth about "The Protocols of the Elders of Zion"* (New York: Ktav Publishing House, 1971).
4. *Vechernyaya Moskva*, February, 25, 1988.
5. I. V. Stalin, *O Velikoi otechestvennoi voinye Sovetskogo Soyuza (About the Great Patriotic War of the Soviet Union)*, the 5th edition (Moscow: Gospolitizdat, 1946), p. 173.
6. A tape-recording of the interview with Igor Sychev. The author's archives.
7. *Moskovskaya Pravda*, May 19, 1988.
8. *Ogonyok*, No. 21, 1987.
9. A tape-recording of the interview. The author's archives.
10. *Refusenik update*, UCSJ, January 1989, p. 3.
11. *Ogonyok*, No. 3, 1989.
12. A. Stepanov, *Izvestia*, January 18, 1989.
13. Yevgeny Yevtushenko, "Lzhenabat" ("False Alarm"), *Moscow News*, No. 6, 1989.
14. V. Todres, *Sovetskaya Kultura*, February 25, 1989.
15. Ibid.
16. Ibid.
17. V. Potapov, *Sovetskaya Kultura*, February 18, 1989.
18. K. Korneshov, "Etot sionist *Nikon*" ("This Zionist *Nikon*"), *Sovetskaya Kultura*, April 1, 1989.

19. *Vestnik yevreiskoi sovetskoi kultury, (Herald of Jewish Soviet Culture)* No. 8, August 2, 1989. Later this weekly publication was renamed into *Yevreiskaya gazeta (Jewish Newspaper)*.
20. Ibid.

CHAPTER 7

1. Robert Wilton, *The Last Days of the Romanovs* (London: Thornton Butterworth, 1920); M. K. Diterikhs, *Ubiystvo tsarskoi sem'i i chlenov doma Romanovykh na Urale (Murder of the Czar's Family and the Members of the Romanov's House in the Ural)* (Vladivostok: [The publisher is not identified], 1922); N. Sokolov, *Ubiistvo tsarskoi sem'i (Murder of the Czar's Family)* ([The city is not identified]: Slovo, 1925).
2. Igor Shafarevich, "Rusofobiya" ("Russophobia"), *Nash Sovremennik*, No. 6, 1989, pp. 167-192; No. 11, 1989, pp. 162-172.
3. *Oktyabr*, No. 6, 1989, p. 3.
4. Igor Shafarevich, "Svoistvo khoroshei knigi—budit mysl" ("A Good Book Awakes Thought"), *Knizhnoye Obozreniye*, No. 34, August 25, 1989.
5. Igor Shafarevich, "Rusofobiya," *Nash Sovremennik*, No. 6, 1989, p. 187.
6. Ibid., p. 188.
7. Igor Shafarevich, "Svoistvo khoroshei knigi—budit mysl," ("A Good Book Awakes Thought"), *Knizhnoye Obozrenie*, No. 34, August 25, 1989.
8. *Literaturnaya Rossia*, No. 36, September 4, 1989.
9. Ibid.
10. Ibid.
11. Ibid.
12. Ibid.
13. Ibid.
14. Ibid.
15. Igor Shafarevich, "Svoistvo khoroshei knigi—budit mysl," ("A Good Book Awakes Thought"), *Knizhnoye Obozryenie*, No. 34 ,August 25, 1989.
16. *Nedelya,* No. 47, 1989.
17. Ibid.
18. "Vse zayedino" ("Acting All Together"), *Ogonyok*, No. 48, 1989, p. 6.
19. *Novoye Russkoye Slovo*, December 1, 1989.
20. The All-Russian TV-station broadcast an interview with Victor Astafiev on February 19, 1995. A transcript is in the author's archives.

CHAPTER 8

1. A copy of the flyer is in the author's archives.
2. "Pismo pisateley Rossii" ("Letter of Russia's writers"), *Literaturnaya Rossia*, No. 9, 1990, pp. 2-4.
3. Ibid., p. 2.
4. Ibid., p. 4.
5. Ibid.
6. Ibid.
7. Ibid.
8. *Nash Sovremennik*, No. 6, 1989, pp. 161-162.
9. Valentin Rasputin, "Novgorod Address," *Veche*, May, 1989.
10. *Ogonyok*, No. 48, 1989, p. 7.
11. *The Washington Post*, March 25, 1990.
12. *The Washington Times*, March 26, 1990.
13. Semyon Reznik, "Desant sovetskikh natsistov v Vashingtonye" ("A Landing of Soviet Nazis in Washington DC"), *Panorama*, No. 470, 1990, pp. 10-11.
14. A copy of Si Frumkin Newsletter is in the author's archive.
15. *The Washington Post*, April 17, 1990.
16. Oleg Mikhailov, *Derzhavin*, The Lives of Remarkable People Series (Moscow: Molodaya Gvardia, 1977).
17. Mary McGrory, "Antisemitism, Soviet Style", *The Washington Post*, April 19, 1990.
18. *Molodaya Gvardia*, No. 1, 1990, a color loose leaf without a page number.
19. *Druzhba Narodov*, No. 9, 1976, p. 3.
20. Stanislav Kuniaev, *Rukopis (Manuscript)* (Moscow: Sovremennik, 1977) pp. 195-196.
21. Here and further, quotations from the speeches at the Kennan Institute have been collated from V. Kozlovsky's shorthand report, *Novoye Russkoye Slovo*, April 27—May 1, 1990.
22. The author's archives.
23. M. Yurchenko, "Miting v Kharkovye" ("A rally in Kharkov"), *Trud*, February 18, 1990.
24. *Problemy evreiskoi repatriatsii i kultury. Informatsionny bellyuten (Problems of the Jewish Repatriation and Culture. Information Bulletin)*, issue 20, September (Moscow: Samizdat, 1988), p.1. A copy is in the author's archives.
25. *Literaturnaya Gazeta*, April 18, 1990.
26. *Novoye Russkoye Slovo*, May 4, 1990.
27. Ibid.
28. *The Washington Post*, April 20, 1990.
29. *Novoe Russkoe Slovo*, May 4, 1990.

30. Ernest Safonov, "Russkie pisateli v SShA" ("Russian Writers in the USA"), *Literaturnaya Rossia*, No. 21, May 25,1990, p. 18.

CHAPTER 9

1. *Evreyskaya gazeta*, May 7, 1991.
2. Victor Zindulevich, *Smozhet li Shafarevich spasti svoyu reputatsiyu? Po povodu otvetov na kritiku Rusophobii (Could Shafarevich Save his Reputation? About the Answers to the Critique of Russophobia)* (Moscow: Samizdat, 1991). A copy is in author's archives.
3. See, for example: Vladimir Soloukhin. *Pri svete dnya (In the Daylight)* (Moscow: 1992).
4. O. Kobrina, "Chto ugrozhaet nashim detiam" ("What Endangers Our Children"), *Istoki*, No. 3, 1991.
5. *Grazhdanin*, No. 23-35, 1878, pp. 546-556.
6. Yu. Larin, *Yevrei i antisemitism v SSSR, (Jews and Anti-Semitism in the USSR)* (Moscow-Leningrad: Gosizdat, 1929), p. 130.
7. A. Taher, *Tsarskaya Rossia i Delo Beilisa (Czar's Russia and the Beilis Case)* (Moscow: Sovetskoye zakonodatelstvo, 1933).
8. V. Porudominsky, *Vladimir Dal*, Lives of Remarkable People series (Moscow: Molodaya Gvardia, 1971).
9. V. I. Dal, *Zapiska o ritualnykh ubiistvakh* (St. Petersburg: [The publisher is not indicated], 1913), p. XV.
10. *Molodaya Gvardia (Young Guard)*, No. 12, 1991, p. 122-126.
11. Ibid., p. 126.
12. Dmitry Gerasimov, "Sataninckoe plemya. Kto stoit za ubiystvom monakhov?" ("The Satan Tribe. Who is Behind the Murder of the Monks?") *Pravda*, May 5, 1993.
13. Ibid.

CHAPTER 10

1. Dragunsky, D. A., and A. Ya. Sukharev, "Pryedisloviye" ("Preface"), *Belaya Kniga (White Book)* (Moscow: Yuridicheskaya Literatura, 1985), pp. 7-13.
2. Nora Levin, *The Jews in the Soviet Union since 1917: Paradox of Survival,* vol. **2**, (New York: New York University Press, 1989), p. 809.

3. Victor Zindulevich, *Sumeet li Igor Shafarevich spasti svoyu reputatsiyu? (Could Igor Shafarevich Save his Reputation)* (Moscow: Samizdat, 1992). A copy is in the author's archives.
4. Tape-recorded speech of Dmitry Vasiliev in Moscow on December 8, 1985. A copy is in the author's archives.
5. Vasily Belov, "Vse vperedi" ("Everything is Ahead"), *Nash Sovremennik*, No. 7, 8, 1986.
6. Nikolai Fed, "Poslania drugu ili pisma o literature" ("Letters on Literature"), *Nash Sovremennik*, No. 4, 1989, p. 18.
7. *Novoye Russkoye Slovo*, September, 13 1989, p. 4; *Panorama*, September 22-29, 1989, p. 5.
8. Bill Keller, "Yearning for an Iron Hand," *The New York Times Magazine*, January 28, 1990, p. 48.
9. *Komsomolskaya Pravda*, April 12, 1990.
10. Nina Andreeva, "He mogu postupitsia printsipami" ("I Cannot Give up my Principles"), *Sovetskaya Rossia,* March 13, 1988.
11. *Moscow news,* July 15, 1990.
12. *Nedelya,* No. 16, 1990.
13. Ibid.
14. Tengiz Gudava, *Novoye Russkoye Slovo,* June 21, 1988.
15. Pavel Gutiontov, *Izvestia,* August 12, 1990.
16. Beschloss, Michael R., and Strobe Talbott, *At the Highest Levels. The Inside Story of the End of the Cold War* (Boston: Little, Brown, 1993), p. 226.
17. A. Romanenko, *O klassovoi sushchnosti sionizma* (Leningrad: Lenizdat, 1986), pp. 248-253.
18. Ivan Shevtsov, *Izbrannye proizvedenia (Selected Works),* vol. 2 (Moscow: Voenizdat, 1988), p. 656.
19. *Literaturnaya Gazeta,* July 1, 1992.
20. *Novoye Vremya*, 1991, No. 3, p. 6-7.
21. See: Beschloss, Michael R., and Strobe Talbott, *op. cit.*, p. 307.
22. Loory, Stuart H., and Ann Imse, *Seven days That Shook The World. The Collapse of Soviet Communism,* (Atlanta, GA: Turner, 1991), p. 26.
23. *Moskovskaya Pravda,* July 23, 1991.
24. V. Ostretsov, *Chyornaya sotnya i krasnaya sotnya (The Black Hundred and the Red Hundred)* (Moscow: Voenizdat, 1991).
25. Ibid., p.37
26. Ibid., p. 22-23
27. Ibid., p. 25
28. Ibid., p. 38.

CHAPTER 11

1. *A National Town Meeting: President Gorbachev and President Yeltsin Take Questions From Americans*, ABC News, September 5, 1991 (Transcript).
2. Erole Fox, *Freedom to Hate* (Documentary Film 1992).
3. *Novoye Russkoye Slovo*, May 7, 1993.
4. Lev Bezymensky, *Novoye Vremya*, No. 50, 1991.
5. Yakov Borovoi, "Za stolom nikto u nas ne Lifshits?" ("Nobody is Lifshits at our table?"), *Novoye Vremya*, No. 41, 1991, p. 25.
6. Ibid.
7. *Ruskoye Voskresenie (Russian Resurrection)*, No. 8 [date is not indicated, some articles suggest that it was printed in 1990 or at the beginning of 1991], p. 4.
8. Ibid., No. 7/15, p. 2.
9. Ibid., p.3.
10. Dmitry Zgersky, "Pechat Chernoi Sotni" ("The Press of the Black Hundred"), *Novoye Vremya*, N3, 1992, p.36.
11. G. Marinin, "SS raionnogo masshtaba" ("SS of the District's Scale"), *Komsomolskaya Pravda*, May 18, 1993.
12. Ibid.
13. V. Karkavtsev, "Obyknovennye fashisty" ("Ordinary Fascists"), *Komsomolskaya Pravda,* March 23, 1993.
14. A. Mitrofanov, "Ocharovatelny nazist" ("A Charming Nazi"), *Novoye Russroe Slovo,* October 19, 1993, p. 8.
15. G. Marinin, *loc. cit.*
16. Dashevsky, Victor, and Yevgeny Proshechkin, "He vystrelamy, tak vyborami" ("If not by Shooting, than by Elections"), *Novoye Vremya,* No. 46, 1993, p. 9.
17. Ibid.
18. *Komsomolskaya Pravda*, February 16, 1993.
19. Eduard Limonov, *Limonov protiv Zhirinovskogo (Limonov against Zhirinovsky)* (Moscow: Konets veka, 1994), p. 65.
20. *Megapolis Express*, June 17, 1992, p. 22.
21. *Nezavisimaya gazeta*, June 20, 1992, p.8.
22. Eduard Limonov, *op. cit.*, pp. 65-66.
23. Ibid, p. 66.
24. Boris Yeltsin, "Zapiski presidenta" ("President's Notes"), *Ogonyok,* No. 15-16, 1994, p. 19.
25. Dmitry Zgersky, *loc. cit.*
26. *Ogonyok*, No. 17, 1993, p. 7.
27. Ibid.
28. Alexander Yakovlev, *Literaturnaya Gazeta*, February 24, 1993, p. 10.

29. Yevgeny Solomenko, "Adolf Hitler v St.-Peterburge" ("Adolf Hitler in St. Petersburg"), *Izvestia,* June 10, 1993, p. 5.
30. Ibid.
31. Ibid.
32. Ibid.
33. Ibid.
34. Ibid.
35. Ibid.
36. *Russkaya mysl,* August 25, 1989.
37. *Nezavisimaya Gazeta,* January 21, 1992.
38. Eduard Limonov, *op. cit.*, p. 149.
39. Ibid.
40. *Nevskoe vremya,* October 12, 1993.

CHAPTER 12

1. *Ogonyok,* No. 19-20, 1993, p. 4.
2. V. Zhirinovsky, "Krakh chetvertogo internatsionala" ("Crash of the Fourth International"), *Izvestia,* August 28, 1993, p. 10.
3. Ibid.
4. Ibid.
5. Otto Latsis, "Prostye reshenia—primanka possiiskogo nazista" ("Simple Solutions are a Bait of a Russian Nazi"), *Izvestia,* August 28, 1993, p. 10.
6. Nike Moore, "Zhirinovsky had Jewish Name until Age 18, Records Indicate," *The Washington Times,* April 4, 1994, p.1, p.13.
7. Vladimir Zhirinovsky, *Posledny brosok na yug. (The Last Throw to the South)* (Moscow: [Publisher is not indicated], 1993) p. 5.
8. Eduard Limonov, *Limonov protiv Zhirinovskogo (Limonov against Zhirinovsky)* (Moscow: Konets veka, 1994), p. 68.
9. Aron Belkin, *Epokha Zhirinovskogo (Zhirinovsky's Era)* (Moscow: Diamant, 1994), p. 33.
10. Ibid., p. 37.
11. Copy is in the authors archive.
12. Aron Belkin, *op. cit.,* p. 175.
13. Vladimir Zhirinovsky, "O sobiratelnoi roli Rossii i molodykh volkakh" ("About the Assembling Role of Russia and about Young Wolves"), *Izvestia,* April 23, 1994, p. 4.
14. *Panorama* August 31, 1994, p. 20.
15. Ibid.
16. Ibid.

17. Ibid.
18. Natasha Zinger, "The Day Yeltsin Praised the Art of Blood Libel," *Forward*, July 29, 1994.
19. The letter is in the author's archives.
20. Pyotr Vail, "Bespokoyashchy Ogon" ("Disturbing Fire"), *Panorama*, April 12-18, 1995, p. 18.
21. Alexei Chelnokov, "Podlinnaya istoria o falshivom monstre" ("A True Story on a False Monster"), *Izvestia*, April 18, 1995, p. 5.
22. Ibid.; see also: Alexander Khinshtein, "Vozmutitel spokoistvia. Alexei Vedenkin—kto on: provocator, nazist ili agent vliyania?" ("Who is Alexei Vedenkin—A Provocateur, a Nazi or an Agent of Influence?"), *Moskovsky Komsomolets,* April 26, 1995, p. 3.
23. Russian TV, February 23, 1995. A videocassette is in the author's archives.
24. Ibid.
25. Yevgeny Proshechkin, "Interview," *Moskovsky Komsomolets*, March 1994, p. 3. (The day is not identified; clipping is in the author's archives).
26. Eduard Limonov, *op. cit*, throughout the book.
27. Aron Belkin, *op. cit.,* p. 191.
28. Gennady Zyuganov, *Za gorizontom (Behind the Horizon)* (Orel: Veshnie vody, 1995) p. 49.

CONCLUSION

1. "All Thing Considered," *National Public Radio, Morning Edition* (Washington, DC), May 9, 1995, transcript, p. 16-17.
2. Ibid., p. 17.
3. Ibid.

INDEX

—A—

Achalov, Vladislav, *195, 246*
Adamovich, Ales Mikhailovich, *127*
Ahad Ha-Am (Asher Gintsberg), *36-37*
Akhrameev, Sergei (Marshall), *203*
Alexander I, *165*
Alexander II, *92*
Alexander Nevsky (Grand Duke), *112*
Alexeeva, Lyudmila Mikhailovna, *184*
Alksnis, Victor, *194*
All-Union Communist Party of Bolsheviks, 216
Ananiev, Anatoly Andreevich, *137,140,142*
Andreev, Alexei, *219-220*
Andreeva, Nina, *145, 186*
Andropov, Yuri Vladimirovich, *45*
Anpilov, Victor, *215-217, 222, 227, 233, 236*
Anti-Semitism, 20, 23-24, 26-27, 29, 40-41, 44-47, 50-51, 53-56, 59, 64-65, 80, 93, 97, 101, 109, 125, 131, 133, 144-147, 150, 155-157, 161, 164, 166, 180-187, 189-190, 204-205, 207-208, 215, 218-2195, 231, 255, 259, 262
April (Writers Group), 189
Arafat, Yassir, *65*
Ardamatsky, Vasily, *258*

Astafiev, Mikhail, *223-224, 228*
Astafiev, Victor Petrovich, *85, 88-90, 93-962, 103, 129, 132, 142, 149, 183, 260*
Avakov, M., *43-44*
Averin, Nikolai, *173-174*

—B—

Baburin, Sergei, *222*
Bakirovs, *72-73, 79-80*
Baklanov, Oleg, *203*
Barkashov, Alexander Petrovich, *210-212, 214, 221, 227, 236, 246, 249*
Batu-Khan, *91*
Bazhenov, Vasily Ivanovich, *32*
Begun, Vladimir Yakovlevich, *35-45, 54-55, 59, 64, 71, 123, 254*
Beilis case, 167-169, 173
Beilis, Mendel, *167-169*
Beizer, M., *255*
Belkin, Aron, *235 ,237, 249, 265-266*
Beloborodov, Alexander Georgievich, *97, 132*
Belov, Vasily Ivanovich, *158, 183, 263*
Belyaev, Yuri, *219-220*
Berdyaev, Nikolai Alexandrovich, *85, 257*
Berg, Raissa Lvovna, *184*
Beria, Lavrenty Pavlovich, *229*
Bernstein, Herman, *259*

Beschloss, Michael R., *198, 263*
Bezverkhy, Victor, *218-220*
Bialik, Hayyim Nahman, *38*
Black Hundred, *11-13, 21, , 39-40, 46, 53-54, 57, 89, 131, 173, 183, 199, 207, 253, 263-264*
Blank, Alexander (Israel), *99*
Blok, Alexander Alexandrovich, *141*
Blokhin, Yuri, *179*
Blood Libel, 146, 161, 167-169, 173
B'nai-B'rith, 52
Boldin, Valery, *203*
Bolshakov, Vladimir, *256*
Bondarenko, Vladimir, *96, 256*
Bondarev, Yuri Vasilievich, *149, 199, 210*
Borodin, Igor, *56-57, 151, 153*
Borodin, Leonid, *144, 147, 154-155*
Botagov, A., *220*
Brazul-Brushkovsky, *168*
Brecht, Bertold, *208*
Brement, Marshall, *150*
Brezhnev, Leonid Illyich, *10,12, 30, 45, 54, 87, 104, 136, 147, 191, 234, 251*
Brodsky, Joseph, *153*
Bronfman, Edgar, *205*
Brusilov, Alexei Alexeevich, *32-33, 255-256*
Brym, Robert J., *251*
Builov, Anatoly, *140-141*
Bund (The Jewish Worker-Democratic Party), 50
Burbulis, Gennady, *222*
Burtsev, Vladimir Lvovich, *259*
Butmi, Gregory, *109-110*

—C—

Catherine the Great, *27*
Chaadaev, Pyotr Yakovlevich, *142*
Chekhov, Anton Pavlovich, *142*
Chelnokov, Alexei, *266*
Chenghis Khan, *91*

Chernomyrdin, Victor Stepanovich, *223, 248, 253*
Chikin, Valentin, *186*
Chivilikhin, Vladimir Alexeevich, *114*
Chlenov, Mikhail, *257*
Chukovsky, Kornei Ivanovich, *141*
Churchill, Winston, *10, 110, 239*
Clinton, William, *251*
Comte, Auguste, *85*
Cohn, Norman, *110, 259*
Communist Party Central Committee, 19, 22, 44, 46, 59, 62-63, 144, 193, 204, 245
Communist Party Leningrad City Committee, 59
Communist Party Manifesto, 28-29
Communist Party Moscow City Committee, 62
Communist Party of Kazakhstan, 191
Communist Party of Russian Federation (Russian Communist Party), 9, 126, 199, 222, 227, 234, 249, 253
Communist Pary of the USSR, 18, 20, 26, 28, 30, 42, 49, 50, 53, 62-63, 88, 104, 180-181, 183, 186-187, 191, 199, 204, 215-216, 238, 245
Cossack Lugansky, see: Dal, Vladimir Ivanovich
Czarist (Czar's) Russia (government, regime) 21, 24, 27-28, 33, 39, 41, 50, 53, 61-62, 92, 134, 165, 167,-168, 197, 200, 235, 262
Czar's family murder, 94-95, 97, 109, 126, 131,-132, 163, 260

—D—

Dal, Vladimir Ivanovich (Cossack Lugansky), *169-172, 262*
Daniel, Yuli, *87*
Decembrists' Uprising, 61-62
Degtyarev, Andrei, *255*
Delevsky, Yuli, *259*

Derzhavin, Gavriil Romanovich, *143, 147, 149, 164, 261*
Dmitry Donskoi (Grand Duke), *112, 118*
Diterikhs, M. K., *131, 260*
Dobrolyubov, Nikolai Alexandrovich, *35-36*
Dostoyevsky, Fyodor Mikhailovich, *11, 94*
Dragunsky, David, *179, 181*
Druzhnikov, Yuri Ilyich, *184*
Dubchek, Alexander, *29*
Dudaev, Dzhakhar, *243-244*
Dunlop, John, *10, 255*
Dyskin, S., *257*
Dzerzhinsky, Felix Edmundovich, *58, 107, 126, 229*

—E—

Edelstein, Vladimir Volfovich, *see:* Zhirinovsky, Vladimir Volfovich
Edelstein, Volf, *230*
Edison, Thomas, *28*
Eichmann, Karl Adolf, *109*
Eidelman, Nathan Yakovlevich, *85, 89, 93-96, 98, 98, 129, 131-132, 143, 183*
Engels, Friedrich, *18, 24-25, 50*
Erenburg, Ilya Grigorievich, *87*

—F—

Farrakhan, Louis, *162*
Fascism (Fascists), 13, 30, 37, 47, 57, 111, 127, 152-153, 207, 209, 212, 217-220, 225, 227, 237, 245-248, 252, 264
Fed, Nikolai, *183*
Feuchtvanger, Leon, *208*
Filatov, Victor, *194*
Filofey, *21*
Fonchenkov, Vasily, *102*

Front of National Salvation, 216, 221-222, 226, 236
Frumkin, Si, *148*
Frygin, G., *114, 124*

—G—

Gaidar, Yegor Timurovich, *207, 220-221, 223-224, 228, 234, 245,250, 253*
Gainov, Nikolai, 102
Gaer, Evdokia Aleksandrovna, *144, 147, 149*
Georgy Pobedonosets (Dragon Slayer), *11, 222*
Gerber, Alla, *250-251*
Glasnost, 11, 23, 30, 42, 45, 49, 55-56, 81, 85, 88-89, 93, 99-100, 104, 108, 114, 139, 147, 151-152, 154, 163, 180, 184-187, 189, 191, 194, 210, 232, 242
Glazunov, Ilya, *108, 238-239*
Glikman, M., *58, 257*
Glushkova, Tatiana, *141*
Goebbels, Joseph, *29*
Gogol, Nikolai Vasilievich, *142*
Goldfarb, Lev, *184*
Goloshchekin, Philip Isayevich, *97, 132*
Goncharov, Ivan Alexandrovich, *31*
Gerasimov, Dmitry, *174*
Goldenberg, V., *175*
Gorbachev, Mikhail Sergeevich, *8, 11, 42, 45, 49, 107, 111, 115-116, 134, 139, 179-187, 190-192, 194-199, 203-207, 221, 225-226, 228, 238-239, 242, 249, 264*
Gore, Albert, *8, 237*
Gorelov, Pavel, *144, 147, 153*
Gorenstein, Friedrich, *256*
Gorky, Maxim (Peshkov, Alexei Maximovich), *18*
Grachev, Pavel, *241, 243, 245-246*
Griboedov, Alexander Sergeevich, *107*
Gromov, Boris, *196, 199*

Grossman, Vasily Semyonovich, *133-135, 140*
Gudava, Tengiz, *189, 261*
Gumilev, Lev Nikolaevich, *162*
Gusev-Orenburgsky, Sergei, *41, 256*
Gutiontov, Pavel, *190, 263*

—H—

Hauptmann, Gerhart, *208*
Havemann, Judith, *148*
Hegel, Georg Wilhelm Friedrich, *85*
Herzen, Alexander Ivanovich, *92-93*
Highest Certifying Commission, 54, 182
Heine, Heinrich, *97*
Hillel, *42*
Hitler, Adolf, *7, 9,12,13, 27, 29, 40, 43, 46, 54, 71, 95, 109-110, 122, 133-134, 142, 145, 148, 162, 194, 208-210, 213, 219-220, 229, 245, 249, 253, 265*
Hitler, Lois, *109*
Holmes, Oliver Wendell, *150*
Holofernos, *151*
Hussein, Saddam, *194*

—I—

Imse, Ann, *261*
Ioann (Metropolitan), *104*
Isakov, *216*
Ivanov, Yuri Sergeevich, *256*

—J—

Jewish-Masonic (Zionist-Masonic, Zionist) conspiracy, 12, 42-43, 47, 49-53, 55, 57, 59, 62-64, 69-70, 72-74, 79-82, 95-98, 102-103, 105, 109, 111, 120-123, 133, 145, 148, 154-155, 157-159, 162-163, 173, 179-182, 184-185, 189-190, 192-193, 200-201, 206-207, 216-218, 220, 257, 259
Judith, *151*

—K—

Kafka, Franz, *70*
Kaganovich, Lazar Moiseevich, *55-56*
Kamenkovich, Irina, *251-252*
Kapitanchuk, Victor, *85, 101*
Karamzin, Nikolai Mikhailovich, *91, 93*
Katerli, Nina, *58-59, 152, 257*
Katzenelinboigen, Aron, *184*
Kazakov, Misha, *58*
Kedrov, Bonifaty Mikhailovich, *44*
Keller, Bill, *1851, 263*
KGB, *30, 45, 54, 63, 65-66, 68-69, 78-81, 101-104, 108, 114, 116, 127, 131, 159, 168, 175, 181, 188-190, 193, 195, 203-204, 217, 219, 222, 232, 245-246*
Khachaturyan, Armen, *184*
Khachaturyan, Svetlana, *184*
Khasbulatov, Ruslan, *224, 227-228, 236, 243*
Kheifets, Mikhail, *255*
Khinshtein, Alexander, *266*
Khomeini (Ayatollah), *103*
Khovansky (Duke), *165*
Khrushchev, Nikita Sergeevich, *18, 28-30, 87-88,112*
Klykov, Fyodor, *118-119, 199*
Kobrina, O., *164, 262*
Koestler, Arthur, *208*
Kolbin, Gennady, *191*
Korneev, Lev, *50-51, 257*
Korneshov, K., *257*
Komsomol (Yang Communist League), 33, 34, 55, 59, 115, 172, 185
Konstantinov, Ilya, *223, 227, 236*
Korotich, Vitaly Alexeevich, *124-125*
Korotkov, Yuri Nikolaevich, *18, 20, 24*

Kosarev, Alexander Vasilievich, *55, 125, 257*
Kovalev, Sergei, *245-246*
Kozhinov, Vadim, *143, 145-147, 149, 162*
Kozlovsky, Vladimir, *155-156, 261*
Kozyrev, Andrei, *241*
Krauthammer, Charles, *156*
Krelin, Yuli, *155*
Kruchina, Nikolai, *245-246*
Krushevan, Pavel Alexandrovich, *109-110*
Kryuchkov, Vladimir, *190, 198, 203-204, 212*
Kulakov, Alexander, *126*
Kulichenko, M., *45*
Kunaev, Dinmuhammed, *191*
Kuniaev, Stanislav Yurievich, *143, 146-147, 152-154*
Kutaisi case, *166*
Kutuzov, Mikhail Illarionovich, *112*
Kuzmenko, Vyacheslav Zakharovich, *44-45*

—L—

Landsbergis, Vytaustas, 196-197
Laqueur, Walter, *11,12*, 253
Larin, Yuri, *38, 260*
Latsis, Otto, *230, 263*
Lazar (Father), *104*
Lebed, Alexander, *248*
Lenin (Ulyanov), Vladimir Ilich, *18, 28, 30, 33-34, 50, 53-55, 71, 97, 99-100, 103, 110-111, 127, 131-132, 134-136, 146, 157, 174, 186, 188*
Lenin Prize, *87, 151*
Leninism, see: Marxism-Leninism
Leonov, Leonid Maximovich, *151*
Lermontov, Mikhail Yurievich, *92, 94, 141*
Levin, Alexander, *24*
Levin, Nora, *262*
Levshov, Yevgeny Mikhailovich, *117*
Lezov, Sergei, *255*

Liberal-Democratic Party, 8-9, *214, 226, 230, 232*
Ligachev, Yegor Kyzmich, *186*
Likhonosov, Victor, *149*
Limonov Eduard, *233-234, 249,*
Litvinova, Galina, *1104*
Lives of Remarkable People book series. *17-19, 23, 31, 44, 75, 143, 146, 159, 255-256, 261-262*
Lobanov, Mikhail, *31-32, 255*
Lodygin, Alexander Nikolaevich, *28*
Loory, Stuart H., *263*
Loshchits, Yuri, *31, 257*
Lukianov, Anatoly, *184, 1940, 203*
Lykoshin, Sergei, *143, 146, 149*
Lysenko, Nikolai, *214, 227*
Lyudmila, *237*
Lyutostansky, Ippolit, *166-167*

—M—

Makarova, Alexandra Pavlovna, *see:* Zhirinovsky, Alexandra Pavlovna
Makashov (General), *227, 236*
Malgin, Andrei, *142*
Maltsev, Sergei, *214*
Mann, Tomas & Heinrich, *208*
Marconi, Gulielmo, *28, 152*
Margulis, Grigory, *182*
Marshall, George, *131*
Martynov, Ivan, *54*
Marx, Karl, *18-19, 24, 50, 85, 239*
Marxism, *22, 25, 41, 47, 52, 62, 101, 103, 239*
Marxism-Leninism, *18, 30, 28, 45-47, 59, 60, 103, 136, 215, 218*
Matlin, Vladimir, *184*
McGrory, Mary, *259*
Mechnikov, Ilya Ilich, *23*
Melentyev, Yuri Nikolaevich, *24*
Men, Alexander (Father), *104*
Minin, Kuzma, *112*
Mikhailov, Oleg, *149-151, 153*
Mikhalkov, Nikita, *251*
Mikhalkov, Sergei, *210*

Modzhoryan, L., *255*
Moiseev, Mikhail (General), *203*
Moore, Nike, *265*
Mordvinov, Nikolai Semyonovich, *165*
Morits, Yunna Petrovna, *97*
Morozov, Grigory, *66*
Mozhaisky, Alexander Fyodorovich, *28*

—N—

Naftalin, Micah, *156*
Napoleon I, *115*
Napoleon III, *109, 112*
Nasenko, V., *257*
National Republican Party, 214
National-Social Party, 219
Nazism (Nazi), *7-9, 11-14, 27, 41, 43-44, 46-47, 58-59, 64, 85, 110, 123, 126, 144, 147-148, 153, 161-162, 168, 179, 188, 201, 203, 207, 209-210, 212, 214, 225, 229-230, 243, 245, 247, 251, 259, 264-266*
Nevzorov, Alexander, *239*
Nikitin, Leonid, *216*
Nikolaev, Yevgeny, *155*
Nicholas I, *21, 61, 92*
Nicholas II, *32, 95, 127, 163*
Nietzsche, Friedrich, *36-37*
Nilus, Sergei, *109-110*
Norinsky, Arkady, *188*
Novotny, Antonin, *29*

—O—

Officers for the Revival of Russia, *222*
Ostretsov, Victor, *199, 263*
Ostrovsky, Alexander Nikolaevich, *31-32, 255*
Otechestvo (Fatherland), *219*

—P—

Paganutstsi, P. N., *132*
Palamarchuk, Petr, *143, 147, 149*
Pamyat society, 101-103, 107, 110-111, 113-121, 123-127, 135, 138-140, 146-147, 153, 182-185, 187-189, 198, 204-207, 209-210, 214, 218
Parvus (Helphand) Alexander Israilevich, *98*
Pasternak, Boris Leonidovich, *87*
Patrioty, 49
Pavlov, *215*
Pavlov, Valentin, *195, 197, 203*
Pelshe, Arvid Yanovich, *68*
Perestroika, 11, 42, 49, 107-108, 115, 123, 136, 139, 147, 151, 180, 186, 189-192, 206, 225, 232, 241
Perovsky, Lev Alexeevich (count), *170*
Pestel, Pavel Ivanovich, *62*
Peter the Great, *21, 85*
Picasso, Pablo, *125*
Pigalev, Vadim Alexeevich, *31, 253*
Pinyasov, G., *140*
Polzunov, Ivan Ivanovich, *27*
Ponomareva, T., *113, 123*
Pontryagin, Lev Semyonovich, *181-182*
Popov, Alexander Stepanovich, *28, 152*
Porudominsky, Vladimir Ilich, *169, 260*
Potapov, V., *259*
Potapov, Victor (Father), *214*
Pozharsky, Dmitry Mikhailovich (duke), *112*
Pozner, Vladimir, *204-205*
Pranaitis (Catholic priest), *167*
Prokhanov, Alexander, *198, 212, 226, 239*
Proshechkin, Yevgeny, *248, 262, 264*
Protocols of the Elders of Zion, 109-110, 120, 133, 146, 152, 250, 259
Pugo, Boris, *195-197*
Purishkevich, Vladimir Mitrofanovich, *56*

Pushkin, Alexander Sergeevich, *90, 94, 96, 137-138, 140-141.*

—R—

Rappoport, *55-56*
Rasputin, Valentin Grigorievich, *143, 146-150, 184, 198, 261*
Reed, John, *7*
Remarque, Erich-Maria, *208*
Riverov, *57*
Rodionov, *195*
Romanenko, Alexander Zakharovich, *45-46, 49, 53, 53-59, 122-123, 126, 139, 192, 218, 256-257, 263*
Roosevelt, Franklin Delano, *238*
Rosenberg, Alfred, *45*
Rubinsky, Gennady, *59, 255*
Rushdie, Salman, *138*
Russian Communist Party, see: Communist Party of Russian Federation
Russian Communist Working Party (RCWP), 215
"Russian idea", 11, 253
Russian National Legion, 214, 217, 226
Russian National Unity (Russkoye Natsionalnoye Edinstvo, RNE), 210-211, 213, 225, 245, 249
Rutskoi, Alexander, *205, 221, 223, 225-226, 235, 237, 245*
Rybas, Vyacheslav, *148*
Rybkin, Ivan, *246*
Ryzhkov, Nikolai, *195, 233*

—S—

Safarov, *132*
Safonov, Ernest, *148, 150-151, 153, 157-158*
Saikin, Valery, *116*
Sakharov, Andrei Nikolaevich, *29, 241*

Saltykov-Shchedrin, Mikhail Evgrafovich, *141*
Sasha Cherny (Alexander Glikberg), *153*
Schelling, Friedrich Wilhelm Joseph, *85*
Schicklgruber, Maria Anna, *108*
Segal, Jack (Rabbi), *204*
Selivanova, Svetlana, *143, 147*
Semanov, Sergei Nikolaevich, *17, 20-22, 30-33, 43, 255-257*
Semenyuk, V., *255*
Sergius of Radonezh, *117-118*
Serkis, P., *258*
Shafarevich, Igor Rostislavovich, *129-139, 149-150, 162, 181, 260, 262-263*
Shakhrai, Sergei, *222*
Shcheglov, Vadim, *100-101*
Shatalin, Stanislav, *222*
Shevardnadze, Edward Amvrosimovich, *191, 193, 195, 240-241*
Shevtsov, Ivan Mikhailovich, *192*
Shiff, Jacob, *238*
Shmakov, Alexei Semyonovich, *42-43, 45, 256*
Shneerson, Joseph I. (Lubavicher Rebbe), *174*
Shvartsman, *55*
Sinyavsky, Andrei Donatovich, *87, 137-139*
Skripitsin, *165-166, 170*
Slavophiles, 11, 21
Slavyansky Sobor (Slavic Assembly), 220-221, 223
Smirnov-Ostashvili, Konstantin, *188, 214*
Sokolov, Nikolai Alexeevich, *131, 258*
Soloukhin, Vladimir Alexeevich, *95, 97-99, 103, 132, 149, 181, 256, 260*
Solzhenitsyn, Alexander Isaevich, *87, 88, 98, 133, 136, 138*
Stalin (Dzhugashvili), Iosif Vissarionovich, *18-20, 22, 26-30, 44, 50-51, 55, 64, 80, 86-88, 94, 99, 102, 112-113, 124, 126, 133-136,*

145-147, 149-151, 156, 165, 173-174, 185, 187, 229, 238, 242, 249-250, 259
Stalin Prize, *151*
Starodubtsev, Vasily, *198, 203*
Starovoitova, Galina Vasilievna, *204-205*
Steffens, Lincoln, *156*
Steizman, B., *255*
Stepanov, A., *260*
Sterligov, Alexander, *215, 221*
Sukharev, Alexander, *179-180, 183, 262*
Suslov, Ilya Petrovich, *184*
Suslov, Mikhail Andreevich, *68*
Suvorov, Alexander Vasilievich, *112*
Sverdlov, Yakov Mikhailovich, *111, 122-123, 127-128, 195*
Svyatoslav (Grand Duke), *162*
Svyatozarsky, A., *113*
Sychev, Igor Sergeevich, *107, 111, 113-126, 1395, 2595*

—T—

Taher, Alexander, *168, 262*
Talbott, Strobe, *198, 263*
Tishchenko, Sergei, *257*
Tizyakov, Alexander, *198, 203*
Todres, V., *259*
Tolstoi, Leo (Lev) Nikolaevich, *91-93, 96*
Torbin, Mikhail, *154*
Tretiakov, Vitaly, *219, 222*
Trotsky (Bronshtein), Leon (Lev) Davydovich, *20, 238*
Trotskyists, 20, 53
Turgenev, Ivan Sergeevich, *142*
Turkov, Andrei Mikhailovich, *141*
Tvardovsky, Alexander Trifonovich, *19*

—U—

Ulyanov, Ilya Nikolaevich, *99*
Ulyanova, Maria Alexandrovna, *99*
Union of Russian Writers (Union of the Writers of the Russian Federation), 139, 141, 149, 210, 261-262
Union of the Soviet Writers (Union of the Writers of the USSR), 27, 87-89, 94, 103, 182, 188
Uvarov, Sergei Semyonovich, *21*

—V—

Vail, Pyotr, *243, 266*
Varennikov, Valentin, *198*
Varsonafy (deacon) (Boris Khaibulin), *101*
Vasilenko, A., *113*
Vasiliev, Dmitry Dmitrievich, *79, 107-111, 114-123, 129, 182, 185, 188, 209-210, 212, 214, 257, 259, 263*
Vavilov, Nikolai Ivanovich, *19*
Vedas, Vedism, 102, 218
Vedenkin, Alexei, *244-246, 264*
Velizh case, 165
Vinogradov, Ivan Matveevich, *181*
Vishnevskaya, Yulia, *254*
Vitaly (Mitropolitan), *215*
Vodolazov, G., *134*
Voikov, Pyotr Lazarevich, *132*
Volodin, Eduard, *199*

—W—

Watt, James, *27*
Wilton, Robert, *131, 258*
Working Moscow, 215
World War I, 7, 31-32, 89, 98
World War II, 7, 18, 20, 27, 59, 64, 89, 113-114, 117, 162, 193, 208, 212, 219, 253
Wright brothers (Orville & Wilber), *27*

—X—

Xenophobia, 21, 49, 158

—Y—

Yakovlev, Alexander Nikolaevich, *21-22, 45, 110, 185-186, 191-193, 195, 198, 203, 255, 264*
Yakovlev, Nikolai Nikolaevich, *32-33, 255*
Yakunin, Gleb (Father), *101, 103*
Yanaev, Gennady, *195, 203, 211*
Yanov, Alexander, *11, 255*
Yavlinsky, Grigory, *195, 249, 253*
Yazov, Dmitry (Marshal), *193, 197, 199, 203*
Yeltsin, Boris Nikolaevich, *8, 115-117, 121, 163, 195-196, 103-207, 214-217, 219-227, 233-235, 237-247, 249-251, 264, 266*
Yeltsina, Naina Iosifovna, *229*
Yemelianov, Valery Nikolaevich, *52, 61-65, 67, 80, 256*
Yemelianova, Tamara, *68, 71-75, 77*
Yevseev, Yevgeny, *45, 54, 71, 73, 80, 256*
Yevtushenko, Yevgeny Alexandrovich, *259*
Yezhov, Nikolai Ivanovich, *94*
Yurchenko, M., *259*
Yurovsky, Yakov Mikhailovich, *94-96*
Yushchinsky, Andrei, *166-167, 172*

Yushenkov, Sergei, *245*

—Z—

Zabolotny, Daniil Kirillovich, *31*
Zeghers, Anna, *208*
Zelichenok, Roald, *257*
Zhirinovsky (Makarova) Alexandra Pavlovna, *230-231*
Zhirinovsky, Andrei, *229, 231*
Zhirinovsky, Lubov Andreevna, *237*
Zhirinovsky (Edelstein), Vladimir Volfovich, *8, 9, 12, 214, 219, 226, 229-240, 242, 245-247, 249-250, 253, 264-265*
Zhukov, Dmitry Anatolievich, *70-71, 73-74, 78*
Zindulevich, Victor, *14, 262-263*
Zinger Natasha, *266*
Zionism (Zionistists), 35-38, 40, 42-46, 49-58, 62-63, 69-74, 78-80, 94-97, 101-103, 110, 119-120, 122, 125, 133, 145, 147, 153-154, 157, 162-163, 174, 179-180, 182-185, 189, 192-193, 199-200, 207, 210, 215, 217, 220, 225, 227, 235, 256-260
Zionist-Masonic conspiracy, see: Jewish-Masonic conspiracy
Znamensky, Anatoly, *140*
Zykina, Lyudmila, *198*
Zyuganov, Gennady, *10, 198, 214-215, 221-222, 226, 234, 238, 247, 249-251, 253, 266*

ABOUT THE AUTHOR

Semyon Reznik is a Russian émigré historian, writer, and journalist. He authored eleven books and hundreds of articles printed in Russian, English, Hungarian, and other languages. He has contributed to *Commentary, The National Interest, The Washington Times, The Scientist, Society, The Present Tense, The Washington Jewish Week,* and other periodicals.

Having started his writing career in Moscow, USSR, in the early 1960s, Semyon Reznik became known as a nonconformist author of widely-read popular biographies. His book on Nikolay Vavilov, a great Soviet geneticist and a victim of Stalin's purges, was labeled *ideologically harmful* to the Soviet regime, and only the international publicity and interference of leading Soviet scientists saved the 100,000 copies from shredding. The publication of his two historical novels and dozens of essays on Russian anti-Semitism were forbidden by the Communist officials.

Forced to emigrate, Semyon Reznik came to the United States as a political refugee in 1982. He has been writing on Russian politics, history, literature, science, but mostly on Russian fascism. He is a board member of the American Association of Russian Jews (AARJ) that monitors anti-Semitism in the former Soviet Union. The ***Nazification of Russia*** is his first book available in English. It is partly based on his Russian account, *The Red and the Brown,* that enjoined extensive coverage and inspired polemics in Russia as well as in the Russian language press of Israel and the United States.